MAGNUS LINKLATER, 44, has worked as a senior editor for the *Evening Standard, The Sunday Times,* and the *Observer.* He has now been appointed Editor of the *London Daily News.* Amongst his previous books are: *Hoax: The Story of the Howard Hughes–Clifford Irving Affair; Jeremy Thorpe – A Secret Life; Massacre – The Story of Glencoe; The Falklands War; The Fourth Reich – Klaus Barbie and the Neo-Fascist Connection.* He is married with three children and lives in London.

DAVID LEIGH, 40, is chief investigative reporter of the *Observer.* He has worked on the *Guardian, The Times, The Scotsman* and the *Washington Post.* He was named Reporter of the Year and Granada TV's Investigative Journalist of the Year in 1986. Previous awards include Campaigning Journalist of the Year and a Special Award for the exposure of jury-vetting. His books include: *The Frontiers of Secrecy – Closed Government in Britain; High Time – The Life of Howard Marks; Michael Foot: a Portrait; The Thorpe Committal.* He is married, with a son and a daughter and lives in Notting Hill.

Sikorsky Black Hawk

Westland W30

The European NH90 proposal

Not With Honour

The Inside Story of the Westland Scandal

MAGNUS LINKLATER and DAVID LEIGH
with Ian Mather

SPHERE BOOKS LIMITED

First published in Great Britain by
Sphere Books Ltd 1986
27 Wright's Lane, London W8 5SW
Copyright © 1986 by Magnus Linklater and David Leigh

TRADE
MARK

Set in Times

Printed and bound in Great Britain by
Cox & Wyman Ltd, Reading

CONTENTS

	Acknowledgements	1
1	Resignation	3
2	Not One of Us	8
3	The Corporate Cripple	22
4	Exit the Fairy Godmother	39
5	The Company Doctor	49
6	The Mating Dance of the Swan	64
7	Up the Wall	80
8	'We'll take care of Heseltine'	87
9	Crisis in Cabinet	102
10	Turkey at Chequers	118
11	The Leak	133
12	Dropping the Pilot	150
13	The Fan Club	175
14	Where Power Lies	196
	Index	208

'There is no place for me with honour in such a Cabinet'

– Michael Heseltine, 9 January 1986

ACKNOWLEDGEMENTS

The Westland affair has been widely seen as a political drama, played out in the corridors of Whitehall and Westminster. But history may well record that what took place within the City of London was, in fact, of even greater significance. We would like therefore to express our gratitude to Lionel Barber of the *Financial Times*, without whose considerable assistance and professional skills many well-guarded doors would have remained closed to us.

Our political and financial sources in Britain were many, various and surprisingly generous with their information. Almost without exception, however, they have asked to remain unacknowledged. We are, nonetheless, extremely grateful to them for the time they gave us. Many senior civil servants who would have been prepared to speak more openly were instructed by their superiors not to cooperate with our researches, but we thank those who found other means of conveying the facts to us. Throughout the book we have made extensive use of verbatim quotations. These are all drawn, either from conversations repeated directly to us by one of the participants; or from testimony given to one of the three parliamentary committees set up to investigate the affair.

Among those we can thank are Signor Raffaello Teti, of Agusta in Italy; Admiral Henri Dugage of Aerospatiale in France; Bill Paul and Columbus Iselin of Sikorsky in the US. We would also like to thank for their contributions the following: Paul Webster in Paris; Dalbert Hallenstein in Rome; Bill Scobie in Los Angeles; Tony Catterall in Bonn; Julia Langdon in London.

At the *Observer*, we were given valuable assistance by Adam Raphael, Political Editor, and Anthony Howard, Deputy Editor; without the help of Jeffrey Care and members of his staff in the library, our task would have been a great deal harder; our colleagues took much of the strain caused by our absence from the paper while we were

1

writing this book; William Keegan gave us helpful advice; finally, we owe special thanks to Donald Trelford, Editor of the *Observer*, who suggested that we undertake the Westland project in the first place, and who gave us the time and encouragement to complete it.

Magnus Linklater and David Leigh
London, 1986

2

Chapter One

RESIGNATION

*'Everybody likes to win arguments. She likes to
win them rather more than many others'*

– Lord Whitelaw, May 1985

There were, it seems, only two people on Thursday 9 January 1986
who had any real sense that Michael Heseltine might resign that day.
One was his wife Anne. The other was the Prime Minister.

Their reasons for believing it were very different. In Anne
Heseltine's case it was intuition. It had come to her the previous
evening as she, her husband and some friends talked over the bitter
and public war that had been waged for almost a month between the
Secretary of State for Defence and his leader, Margaret Thatcher.

In the middle of their conversation she had said to him, 'I think you
may have to do it tomorrow – after Cabinet.'

Heseltine had disagreed. For the time being, he felt, there was a lull.
The argument between him and Mrs Thatcher over his refusal to
conform with decisions agreed by the rest of her Cabinet had settled
into something of a stalemate; neither side was willing to concede, but
neither seemed ready to force the matter towards a final crisis.
Whatever was said at the next day's Cabinet meeting, Heseltine knew
precisely where he now stood, how far he was prepared to give way,
and where he would have to stand firm.

'I think we'll get through all right,' he said.

He was not to know that Mrs Thatcher had already decided
otherwise. In the course of a meeting at Chequers the previous
weekend, attended by the Tory Chief Whip John Wakeham, and the
Deputy Prime Minister, Lord Whitelaw, she had concluded that an
ultimatum must be given to her most obstinate and belligerent
Minister.

For nearly three weeks Michael Heseltine had stood in open defiance of her request that the Cabinet should speak with one voice on the issue of Westland, Britain's only helicopter-building company. He had turned a seemingly routine political decision into a matter of burning principle. He challenged directly her authority as Prime Minister and her reputation as a leader in firm control of the affairs of state.

She was in no doubt about the likely effect of her decision. Three weeks earlier, in the course of a long and agonising discussion with her closest advisers, Mrs Thatcher had gone through a dress rehearsal of the arguments. The meeting had been convened to draft a letter to Heseltine requiring his written agreement to observe Cabinet rules and stop his public campaign on the Westland issue. It had lasted two and a half hours.

In the end she had, uncharacteristically, decided to back down. Her Press Secretary Bernard Ingham had persuaded her that if Heseltine were pushed too far he would quit. The loss of a popular and outspoken Minister would, he felt, be desperately damaging to the Government.

The letter was torn up, and the final confrontation postponed.

From that decision flowed many of the events which would present Mrs Thatcher with the gravest crisis of her political career, culminating in the resignation, not just of Michael Heseltine, but of the cleverest man in her Cabinet, the Trade Secretary Leon Brittan. It would sully her image as a straight dealer and reveal a strategy described by one elder statesman as 'conducted with all the rationality of a late-night dispute outside a pub'.

It would shed an uncomfortable light not only on the way the Government machine in Britain can be run, but how it can be used to stifle dissent and ensure that secret decisions and secret motives are protected. Above all, it would reveal a Prime Minister who has always stressed the importance of being open with the British people, presiding over an affair where concealment rather than candour was the guiding force.

Now, with her postponement of a tough decision, the Westland crisis dominated the political landscape, and Mrs Thatcher found herself forced to grasp the nettle from which she had previously shrunk.

Amongst the twenty-one Ministers who gathered that Thursday morning around the boat-shaped table in the Cabinet Room, there was little sign that the meeting would be anything but routine. Shortly after ten am, Mrs Thatcher took her usual seat in the centre with her back to the fireplace, from where she could look out over Horse

Guards Parade – or, diagonally across the table, at her rebellious Defence Secretary.

On the Prime Minister's right sat the Cabinet Secretary, Sir Robert Armstrong, and on her left Lord Whitelaw. Heseltine was flanked by Sir Keith Joseph, the Education Secretary, and the Social Services Secretary, Norman Fowler. Two down from Heseltine sat his most entrenched opponent, Leon Brittan.

The discussion was opened, as always, by the Prime Minister, who began with a roundup of forthcoming Government business in the House of Commons, including the following week's second reading debates on the Public Order Bill and the Financial Services Bill. There would also, she added, be questions about the Westland affair. The Commons were reassembling after the Christmas recess, and there would be Opposition demands for a statement about the Government's position. Questions were down for the Department of Defence on Tuesday, and for Industry on Wednesday.

Mrs Thatcher's Cabinets are not widely celebrated these days for free-ranging debate. The Prime Minister likes to keep tight control over any topic raised, to impose a strict framework, and to interrupt whenever matters stray.

Her attitude was summed up by one former Minister, Francis Pym, thus: '"This is what I want to do, this is what the country needs, and that's it." Any argument to the contrary tends to get brushed aside.'

Although all of those present were well aware of the Westland issue, few had listened to detailed argument on both sides; it had never been debated in full Cabinet. The financial crisis in the company had led to a bid for control by Sikorsky, an American company, allied with Fiat of Italy. This bid, enthusiastically recommended by the company's chairman, Sir John Cuckney, was now favoured both by the Prime Minister and the Industry Secretary, Leon Brittan, who were careful however to point out that it was a matter for the shareholders to decide.

The rival bidder was a European consortium, made up of helicopter companies from France, Germany and Italy, together with two British firms, British Aerospace and GEC. This group, brought together by Heseltine, had made up for its late arrival by the almost evangelical fervour with which he had supported it.

It was Heseltine's refusal to stand back from the argument and allow the issue to be decided by the Westland management alone that had so infuriated Mrs Thatcher.

Now, as she opened the discussion in front of her Cabinet, there was an intriguing signal, noted by just a few of those present; reaching down below the table, Mrs Thatcher drew from her case a single sheet of paper which she placed in front of her. She then made a brief opening statement.

It did not, as Heseltine recalled later, contain a great deal that was new. But it was carefully worded. Her view was that the future of Westland was a matter for the board, and the Government's attitude to the two bids was neutral and even-handed. It was therefore incumbent on all Ministers to observe collective Cabinet responsibility and refrain from any public interference in the matter. She hoped that everyone would agree to that.

Her tone was conciliatory. The time had come, she said, to forget past bitterness and concentrate on presenting an effective Government case in future. 'Let's draw a line,' she concluded.

She then invited Leon Brittan, as the 'sponsoring' Minister in charge of Westland, to speak. He took his cue from the opening statement. There was, he said, an absolute need for public reticence. He fully endorsed the Prime Minister's view.

Michael Heseltine's remarks were deceptively mild. He said he fully understood the arguments for standing back from the affair, and accepted that it was a matter for the shareholders to decide.

'But,' he added, 'I've got to answer questions of fact if they are put to my Ministry.'

There was a barely perceptible groan from a few of the assembled company. It was the third meeting in a row at which Heseltine had made his point, and by now there was a certain familiarity with the argument. He repeated an offer he had made earlier to stick to existing statements and not make any new ones.

Others now spoke up briefly, but it was soon evident that Mrs Thatcher had had enough. Stung by Heseltine's obstinacy, she proposed that all future statements should be cleared with fellow members of the Cabinet and vetted by the Cabinet Office. It was as harsh and binding a condition as she had ever imposed collectively on her Ministers.

Heseltine immediately protested. This was a fast-moving situation, he said, in which information was at a premium. Shareholders needed to know the full facts immediately if they were to reach a sensible decision. He must be able to respond rapidly if asked.

She waited impatiently as Norman Tebbit, the Party Chairman, intervened to suggest a modification of the constraint which might be acceptable to Heseltine. But the gap was too great.

Rapidly summing up the discussion, Mrs Thatcher repeated the condition for any future Ministerial statement on Westland: anything said in public must be cleared by colleagues and the Cabinet Office.

It was the end of the road. Gathering his papers together, Michael

Heseltine pushed back his chair and stood up.

'I can't accept that decision,' he announced quietly. 'I must therefore leave this Cabinet.'

He then turned and walked out, passing under the baleful stare of his former leader and out of the door behind her. It was precisely 11.10 am.

There was a moment's stunned silence. Not everyone realised immediately what had happened or appreciated its significance. 'One moment he was there, the next he was gone,' recalled one Minister. Others felt that there was a definite ambiguity in the sentence he had chosen – he had not, after all, used the word 'resign'.

But those who knew the background intimately, like Leon Brittan and the Prime Minister herself, were in little doubt that Michael Heseltine had just walked out of public office.

Mrs Thatcher despatched Sir Robert Armstrong to find out what had happened. A few minutes later he returned to whisper in her ear that her ex-Defence Secretary appeared to be outside in the street talking to the Press.

The Prime Minister, unable to hold the attention of her Ministers as they absorbed the shock of witnessing the only resignation ever to have taken place in mid-Cabinet, briskly called a coffee break.

Summoning George Younger, the Scottish Secretary, to her office, she offered him the recently vacated post of Secretary of State for Defence. The job had been free for approximately fifteen minutes.

Outside the Cabinet Room, Heseltine had retired briefly to the washroom to straighten his tie and comb his famous blond hair. He then strode out of the front door of Number Ten Downing Street.

The first recipient of official confirmation that the Defence Secretary had indeed resigned was a Press Association cameraman, David Giles. Seeing that Heseltine had emerged alone and unexpectedly early, Giles asked him what was happening.

'I've resigned from the Cabinet and I shall be making a full statement later on,' responded Heseltine.

He then walked off – as he himself recalled later – 'into the distance'.

For Anne Heseltine, the news came within half an hour when she was telephoned at home by the P.A.'s chief political correspondent, Chris Moncrieff, who asked if her husband was there.

'Come on, Chris, don't you know there's a Cabinet meeting?' she demanded.

'Haven't you heard? He's resigned,' said Moncrieff.

'Oh God!' said Mrs Heseltine.

Two minutes later her husband called and told her the news.

'I think you'd better come home for lunch today,' she said.

Chapter Two

NOT ONE OF US

*'The certainties of today are very rarely the
certainties of tomorrow'*

– Michael Heseltine, November 1983

The Carlton Club in St James's Street, London, once described by
Disraeli as 'the social citadel of Toryism', is as near to an emblem of
the British establishment as it is possible to find. For more than 150
years its membership was exclusively male. In 1982 it admitted its first
(and probably last) woman member: Margaret Thatcher.

Here, on two evenings in October and November 1985 a formidable
cross-section of the British military establishment met in private to
discuss the future direction of 'Defence and the Defence Industries'.

The gathering was not a Government affair, and it had no obvious
political status. But it certainly carried weight.

Amongst the guests was a galaxy of Generals, Admirals and Air
Chief Marshals, as well as the bosses of most of the country's major
defence suppliers. Chairing the meeting was General Sir John
Hackett, author of *The Third World War*; amongst the speakers were
Sir Raymond Lygo, Managing Director of British Aerospace, Air
Chief Marshal Sir Douglas Lowe, Chairman of Mercury Communi-
cations, General Sir Harry Tuzo, former Chairman of Marconi
Defence Systems, and the Rt. Hon. Michael Heseltine MP, Secretary
of State for Defence.

The minutes of those meetings, marked 'Private and Confidential',
reveal deep concern about Britain's ability to hold to its defence
commitments against a background of shrinking wealth.

Despite a Government committed to defence spending, demands
for tax cuts and the revenue required for other areas were beginning to
eat into the budget. At the same time there was a disturbing lack of

8

coordination in Whitehall, and bickering between Government departments about who should control resources.

But the theme of the meeting, emphasised again and again, was the need for cooperation with Europe to meet competition from the USA. Unless Britain and Europe could get together and rationalise their defence industries, urged most speakers, the future was bleak.

'A strong European defence industry is a necessary condition for making the two-way street [between Britain and America] a reality,' ran one passage.

'The magnitude of the task of achieving a satisfactory European approach can scarcely be exaggerated,' said another.

Foremost amongst the exponents of the European ideal was Michael Heseltine, and it is clear from the minutes that he dominated the occasion. One section, headed 'The Secretary of State's Commitment to a European Approach' charges that a 'lack of political resolve has impeded progress'. It requires no great imagination to hear the low growl of approval from the assembled brass echoing up to the Thomas Hooper ceilings of the Carlton Club.

There was even something reassuringly military about this tall, clean-cut figure in front of them, well on top of his brief, setting out his arguments in a firm and convincing style. The suit was immaculate, the tie sober. Only the length of the hair left something to be desired.

The fact that Heseltine went down so well is a tribute to his powers of persuasion. He would not have been so welcome three years earlier. When, in December 1982, word first spread through the services that Heseltine was likely to be Mrs Thatcher's new Defence Secretary, they were appalled. The Chief of the Defence Staff, Sir Edwin Bramall, went so far as to lobby Lord Whitelaw in an unsuccessful attempt to head off his appointment. Everything about this flamboyant and ambitious politician suggested that he was entirely unsuitable for the job.

Heseltine's reputation at the time – established during his years as Secretary for Environment – was that of a demonic cost-cutter, one of the new managerial class who liked to rip through established bureaucracies and impose their own organisation. At the DoE he was said to have abolished fifty-seven 'Quangos' (quasi-governmental organisations) in just one month. He had introduced what was claimed to be a fearsome system known as MINIS (Management Information Service), which had required all his civil servants to cost and detail their own work, and he had used that as a basis for streamlining the entire Department.

None of this sounded at all good for the MoD, where the three services guard their separate identities jealously, and where the bureaucracy (200,000 civil servants) almost outnumbers the armed forces (300,000).

But Heseltine's energy and the very flamboyance that had so worried the services stood him in good stead as he took a grip on the job. He had been chosen by Mrs Thatcher partly at least to meet the Campaign for Nuclear Disarmament head-on at a time when Cruise missiles were being brought on to the British mainland, and anti-nuclear protest was growing.

He had set about the task with enthusiasm, forming a propaganda unit in the MoD called Defence Secretariat 19 (DS19), which turned out speeches and leaflets putting the case for Cruise and Trident missiles in a series of colourful slogans, and dismissing anti-nuclear arguments as 'dangerous rubbish'.

At the same time he launched a ferocious campaign against CND's membership, accusing it of being 'led and dominated by left-wing activists ranging through the Labour Party to the Communist party', whose ultimate aim was 'to overthrow this government, the capitalist governments and the free enterprise systems of Western Europe'. He put pressure on the security service, MI5, to produce material on CND, although they were not listed at that time as a 'subversive' organisation.

Later, he turned up in person, wearing a military flak jacket, to supervise the clearing of protesters from the air force base at Molesworth in Cambridgeshire.

There is no evidence that gestures like these caused Heseltine any damage among the military or the Tory party faithful. Others, however, watching his political progress, were more doubtful about the wisdom of his high-profile style. And one or two commentators, filling in his term report, placed a question-mark in the column marked 'judgment'.

The Heseltine style can roughly be summed up as 'pitching in'. His skills, acknowledged by all who have worked closely with him, lie in seizing an issue, absorbing its salient points and pursuing it with energy until it has been dealt with to his satisfaction.

The manner in which he does so has been described as 'awesome' by one civil servant, 'formidable' by another, and 'infuriating' by a third. At the DoE senior officials, who had been told that the man who was taking over was brash, impatient and arrogant, were impressed rather by his tenacity. But to others his relentlessness looked far more like obstinacy. There were those at the DoE who talked of Heseltine's 'obsessions', his inability to recognise that some problems were susceptible to flexibility rather than unyielding force.

One such was the attempt to quantify and reorganise local government spending – a matter that has been a recurring nightmare for successive Ministers. Heseltine was convinced that the normal rules of statistical analysis and skilfully drafted legislation would solve the problem of bringing local authorities to heel.

The fury caused by his negotiations finally became counter-productive, but Heseltine refused to acknowledge that he might have been wrong to push it through: 'It was a heavyweight contest. I fell around occasionally. But in the last round I was still there,' he concluded.

Others disagreed. 'It was obvious he had to change course,' said the civil servant in charge of the programme. 'He should have said to us, "I got it wrong".'

The instances of Heseltine admitting to error are thin on the ground. His convictions date back, on his own account, to Oxford University where he achieved the double distinction of being President of the Union and setting that institution on a sound financial footing.

His background was, as he put it himself, 'South Wales commercial middle class'. As the son of a Swansea engineer whose own father had made and lost a fortune in shipping, there was never any doubt that he too would go into business. 'I *wanted* to make money,' he said later. 'I went with the grain. I did what was sensible, right, logical, natural for me.'

After a public school education at Shrewsbury, he tried but failed to get into Bristol and Reading, but was accepted by both Oxford and Cambridge.

He had always found reading and absorbing the written word difficult, but only later did he conclude that what he suffered from was a mild form of dyslexia. He devised various systems to cope with it, including relying on charts, maps and succinct notes to sum up complex problems. He still prefers being briefed to reading, but in compensation has developed a formidable memory for facts which allows him to outface many cleverer opponents.

At Oxford he joined the Conservative Association, but found it too autocratic for his taste and started a breakaway organisation called the Blue Ribbon Club. He took care, however, to remain a member of the Association. Until very recently, Heseltine has always believed in fighting his battles inside rather than outside organisations.

From early on he had certain clear ambitions – what he described later as 'priorities'. One was making money early enough to help the second, which was success in politics. Armed with a Second Class degree in Politics, Philosophy and Economics, the Presidency of the Union, and a £1,000 legacy from his grandparents, he went into the

11

property business with a friend, then into publishing with another.

A very brief stint of eight months' National Service in the Welsh Guards, which he cut short by standing, unsuccessfully, as Tory candidate for Gower, was followed by the expansion of his businesses, particularly into magazines.

In 1962 he married Anne Williams, daughter of a London solicitor. Then, shortly afterwards, came disaster when the bottom dropped out of both his property and his publishing business. For a time it seemed as if his companies were heading for bankruptcy, but thanks to his own determination to save them, and, he says, to the faith of one bank manager, he managed to pull out of trouble. It took ten years to climb back.

Later he told the journalist Susan Crosland what that period had meant to him: 'For a time there were three categories of creditors in this disastrous situation: those who sent solicitors' letters, those who had just issued writs, those whose writs were about to expire. You can guess which of the three we paid. If you do that every week – and survive – you remember the lessons.'

In 1966 he won his first seat – at Tavistock in Devon – and that year saw too the launching of his first money-spinning magazine, *Management Today*. This, together with others such as *Campaign, Accountancy Age* and *Computing*, became the backbone of Haymarket, his original publishing company, now owned 50 per cent by the Heseltine family. Haymarket's value today is estimated at something around £50 million.

Heseltine's wealth has been more methodically invested than it was made. He spent years combing the countryside for the ideal country house to add to the Belgravia town house and the Exmoor cottage. He finally found it in Oxfordshire – a perfect example of eighteenth-century architecture, with a stunning view and a large garden which he works on himself, bringing to it the same single-mindedness he bestowed on the restructuring of the DoE. He is said to have confided to a former aide that he believes he will be remembered more for the creation of the finest landscape garden in Britain this century than for any of his political achievements.

Probably the richest member of Mrs Thatcher's cabinet, Heseltine was certainly the best-dressed man. His clothes have always been impeccable and expensive, though never flashy. He chooses them with care and changes them often. There is, even sartorially, a hint of the Heseltine foible; at the height of the Westland crisis, when he was appearing on television virtually every hour on the hour, the journalist Nicholas Coleridge noted that he had changed his ties six times in the course of the day. They were, he thought, of the Jermyn Street variety, carefully chosen and knotted. He was impressed: 'For ten years the eyes of the world have been on Mr Heseltine's haircut,' he wrote, 'when all the time the big story was dangling round his neck.'

Only one other Tory Minister pays quite the same attention to sartorial detail – Margaret Thatcher. As Barbara Castle, the former Labour Minister, recalls, when Mrs Thatcher was in opposition, she used to keep her clothes in the Lady Members' Room behind the Speaker's Chair in the House of Commons. 'There would be about half a dozen garments hanging up there,' said Mrs Castle, 'and underneath them a tidy row of at least eight pairs of shoes. I can only assume that she slipped away from the Opposition front bench, nipped into this little room and did her quick change act between great parliamentary scenes.'

This, as we shall see, was not the only comparison to be made between the Secretary for Defence and his Prime Minister. But in the end it was their differences and not their similarities that would drive them to final confrontation.

Until Michael Heseltine became the darling of the Tory Conference in October 1975 with a dazzling display of populist oratory, he did not impinge greatly on the rank and file of his Party.

Until he lifted the Speaker's mace from its hallowed place in the House of Commons in May 1976, he did not impinge greatly on the country.

But his 1975 Conference speech is still remembered. It brought the party faithful to their feet as he tore into Labour's nationalisation plans and announced a moral crusade against Socialism. Since then he has given repeat performances at every annual Conference, to the mounting irritation of those colleagues who cannot match his appeal to the lady delegates, and who are even alleged to have rigged the timetable so that the television coverage is interrupted by *Play School*.

More notorious was the Episode of the Mace in May 1976 – and it is one he has found hard to live down. Accounts of it vary, but all agree that in the course of a heated debate on the Aircraft and Shipbuilding Industries Bill he lifted the ceremonial mace from its stand in front of the Speaker's Chair. Some say he waved it around his head. Others that he brandished it threateningly. He claims he merely offered it to chanting Labour MPs to demonstrate that they had broken the rules of the House.

Since that time the nickname 'Tarzan' and a certain reputation for wildness has hung persistently around him.

There was, however, nothing impetuous about the way he attempted to tackle the appalling housing conditions of Liverpool, which he visited in his capacity as 'Minister for Merseyside' at Mrs Thatcher's request after the Toxteth riots of 1981.

By all accounts, Heseltine was deeply shocked by the squalor and deprivation he encountered during a tour of the area. From then on, the Inner Cities became a Heseltine priority. He instituted a series of measures designed to lure private investment to Merseyside, and set aside one day a week at the DoE to concentrate fully on the problem, calling for 'a massive sense of common purpose' to combat inner-city decay.

It brought him little popularity. Several commentators dismissed it as a self-publicising gimmick. The people of Toxteth pelted him with eggs and tomatoes because they could not see any immediate improvement in employment or housing in their area. And amongst his cabinet colleagues it confirmed an impression that Heseltine was at root a 'Wet' – in favour of Government intervention, an opponent of Mrs Thatcher's doctrine of strict monetarism, not one of the team.

But then Heseltine was never properly speaking one of the team – either in Cabinet or the House of Commons. He is known in the Party as something of a loner, unfamiliar in the Commons tea-room, unclubbable, impatient with what he calls the 'getting-to-know-how-you-tick' syndrome of politics. He never allowed alcohol in his office at the MoD. He is not, in short, a drinking man.

More important, he never gave much time to cementing relations with his leader.

That is partly, at least, a matter of personality. One political observer who knows them both said, 'Margaret is a woman. She notices how men react to her. Michael did not find her attractive, and took no trouble with her. It was insensitivity on his part. A little flattery would have helped.'

Politically too they were never entirely compatible. It was Julian Critchley, MP for Aldershot and one of his oldest friends, who said famously, '[Mrs Thatcher] used always to say of Michael Heseltine when his name was mentioned, "Michael," she used to say, "he is not one of us."'

By that she meant that Heseltine was not part of that small group of her supporters who backed her policies instinctively – men like her former parliamentary private secretary, Ian Gow, who once said, 'The truth of the matter is that in my experience she was almost always right, and therefore there wasn't a great necessity for her to admit she was wrong.'

It is not a remark one can imagine Heseltine uttering. He had been a firm supporter of Edward Heath when he was Prime Minister and he had backed Willie Whitelaw against Mrs Thatcher to succeed him.

But following her successful campaign for the leadership he paid tribute to her resolve, and said, 'This country is longing for someone to bring an end to the bleeding.'

He had wanted to be Secretary for Industry, in charge of the very industrial policies he was later to promote, but was given Environment instead. There the question of whether he was fundamentally 'wet' or 'dry' was less important than his drive and energy. When, therefore, towards the end of 1982 – the year of the Falklands War – the Defence Secretary John Nott announced that he wished to stand down and go into business, Mrs Thatcher turned to Heseltine to take on the massive bureaucracy of the Ministry of Defence.

On 6 January 1983 Heseltine, on holiday in Tobago, received a satellite signal telling him that, at the age of forty-nine, he was to be promoted into the biggest job of his political career. He was to hold it for precisely three years and three days. It was to prove a turbulent period.

One issue on which the new Defence Secretary and his Prime Minister saw eye to eye was secrecy and the paramount need for it in Government. From the early days of her premiership, Mrs Thatcher made it clear that she did not approve of 'leaks' from her Cabinet or indeed from Whitehall. She intended, she told her Ministers, to insist on the doctrine of collective responsibility and to see to it that Government decisions were supported by the whole Cabinet. Heseltine saw no reason at the time to disagree with her.

When, later on, her administration was plagued by a series of unauthorised leaks, including one remarkably detailed account of a Cabinet discussion on the Welfare State, she instituted a series of inquiries, using Departmental investigators, MI5, the MoD police, and the Serious Crimes Squad.

Governments have always applied double standards to secrecy. Cabinet discussions are by tradition matters of the utmost confidentiality. But this has never prevented the Prime Minister's office, and sometimes other Ministers, giving journalists briefings on what has taken place. This information will tend to be selective and will normally redound to the good name of the Government.

The same applies to much broader aspects of Government policy. The anomaly has never perhaps been more brazenly spelt out than by Mrs Thatcher's Press Secretary Bernard Ingham in the course of a private speech he gave in 1981:

I must tell you that I – and I am sure my colleagues – have never regarded the Official Secrets Act as a constraint on my operations. Indeed, I regard myself as licensed to break that law as and when I judge necessary; and I suppose it is necessary to break it every other minute of every working day, though I confess the issue is so academic that I have not bothered to seek counsel's advice.

The tough budget of that year, generally recognised as the high-water mark of Thatcherism, widened the divisions between the 'dissidents' in Mrs Thatcher's Government – men like Ian Gilmour, Francis Pym, Norman St John Stevas, James Prior – and those in the 'inner Cabinet' who kept faith with monetarism – Geoffrey Howe, Norman Tebbit, Sir Keith Joseph. It further emphasised the concept of 'us and them' – what Ian Gow once characterised as the 'heroes' and the 'reptiles'.

Against this background, secrecy and a natural suspicion of those who did not share complete faith in the Thatcher doctrine tended to flourish. Civil servants began to feel the political pressure, and some reacted to it by disclosing information about the fierce debates that were taking place behind the scenes. Leaks continued, followed by inquiries to identify the leaker. After one unsuccessful search for a Whitehall 'mole', Bernard Ingham sent a warning round to every Department: 'Moles who will not face the challenge risk being reclassified as rats.'

Heseltine, as Secretary for Defence, was routinely in charge of more classified information than anyone except the Prime Minister, and he fully shared her concern about security. The propaganda unit, DS19, had been disbanded in September 1983, with its work parcelled out to another MoD unit, known in Whitehall as the 'Holocaust Desk'. But the campaign against CND continued.

He was thus infuriated when a confidential minute he had written to the Prime Minister in October 1983 about how the Government should handle the impending arrival of Cruise missiles in Britain was leaked to the *Guardian*.

Heseltine had proposed that the best way of heading off the inevitable anti-nuclear protests was for the Government to take the initiative and put the case for the missiles as publicly and vigorously as possible before CND or the Opposition had time to react to their arrival.

The minute containing his advice to the Prime Minister, and another about British troop protection of the Cruise base at Greenham Common was leaked by a Foreign Office clerk, Sarah Tisdall. She was charged under Section Two of the Official Secrets Act, and despite the prosecution's admission that there had been no threat to national security she was sentenced to six months' imprisonment.

Far more serious in security terms was the apparent leak of top secret information in 1984 from the GCHQ signals base at Ayios Nikolaos in Cyprus. Both Heseltine and Mrs Thatcher backed a rigorous inquiry by MoD investigators, and were appalled when it emerged that seven servicemen of 9 Signals Regiment might have been involved in spying, feeding top-secret information to hostile powers after being lured into a sex ring, then blackmailed.

The subsequent trial, however, revealed that the men's confessions had been forced from them by harsh interrogation methods, and all were acquitted.

In both these cases Heseltine had had the unqualified support of the Prime Minister. But the *Belgrano* affair in Spring 1984 was different. It led to serious disagreements between them about how it should be handled, and raised questions in Downing Street about his loyalty to his leader.

Throughout most of 1983 and well into 1984, the Labour MP Tam Dalyell had been pressing various ministers, including the Prime Minister, to give the House of Commons an accurate account of the sinking of the Argentine cruiser *General Belgrano* by a British submarine in May 1982, causing the loss of 368 lives.

In the immediate aftermath of the attack Heseltine's predecessor, John Nott, had given an inaccurate account of the sinking, including misleading information about the ship's route, and the time it had been detected. Ever since then, the Government, though modifying its position, had refused to publish the full facts. The affair had caused the Prime Minister personal embarrassment when she was caught out on the matter and made to look uncomfortable by a questioner during the General Election.

By March 1984 the persistence of the questions and the damage they were causing to the Government had prompted Heseltine to commission a full report on the incident from an MoD civil servant, Clive Ponting.

His reasons for doing so were straightforward. If he was to protect the Government's position, he needed to know exactly what had happened in the course of the affair, and he made sure that Number Ten was informed about what he was doing.

But the phrase he used to colleagues did not endear him to the Prime Minister. 'I want to be quite sure that there is not a Watergate in this somewhere,' he said. As one or two of those who heard it realised, finding a Watergate might easily mean identifying a Nixon. They wondered who Heseltine might have in mind.

The events coincided with a particularly sensitive period at Downing Street. An inquiry by the *Observer* had established that the Prime Minister's son, Mark Thatcher, had earned a consultancy fee following a major construction deal in Oman. The paper's reports suggested that Mrs Thatcher might have brought some influence to bear with the Sultan of Oman in order to steer the deal towards Cementation, the British company concerned. Despite outraged reactions from Number Ten, the essential facts of the inquiry were not refuted.

It was not, therefore, a good time to suggest that the Prime Minister might have been a party to deception on another matter.

Clive Ponting, newly promoted to head DS5, a division at the MoD responsible for military operations, was instructed by Heseltine to prepare an exhaustive report on the background to the *Belgrano* affair, and to draft replies for the Prime Minister to give in response to Opposition questions. He was asked to prepare two sets of replies: one based on an accurate account of what had really happened, the other to be limited statements based on earlier incorrect answers.

Ponting drew up his report – later to be known as 'the Crown Jewels' – and a series of meetings ensued at the MoD as the response was debated, with John Stanley, junior minister at the MoD and a former PPS to Mrs Thatcher, putting the case for continued concealment, and Ponting arguing for disclosure. Heseltine finally inclined to the Ponting view, and persuaded Mrs Thatcher to release more information in a long letter to Denzil Davies, Shadow Spokesman on Foreign Affairs.

But then there was an abrupt change of course. Following a lengthy meeting in Downing Street in April, Heseltine pulled back – whether as a result of Mrs Thatcher's intervention, or because he himself had changed his mind, is not known. But from a position where he appeared to have accepted that the truth should be told he switched to one of refusing any further comment. A series of questions from Dalyell, to which Ponting drafted full replies, was met with the answer, 'There is nothing that I can usefully add.'

Ponting was so disillusioned by the episode that he decided to leak an MoD minute on the affair to Dalyell to bring it into the open. He was arrested and charged under the Official Secrets Act, but was eventually acquitted after a sensational court case. Writing later about the decision to conceal rather than reveal the truth about the *Belgrano*, he commented: 'I had never come across anything so blatant in my fifteen years in the civil service. It was a deliberate attempt to conceal information which would reveal that Ministers had gravely misled Parliament for the previous two years.'

Heseltine, for his part, regarded Ponting's action as an unforgivable betrayal. He disputed his account of events, and accused him in turn of proffering inconsistent advice. But the nearest he has come to giving an explanation for his change of course was when he gave evidence in November 1984 to the Foreign Affairs Committee inquiring into the *Belgrano* affair: 'It was quite apparent to me that the more information that we provided, the more it would fuel yet more demands for more information.'

In the end Mrs Thatcher expressed public approval of her Defence Secretary's combative response, and congratulated him on the way he had hit back at Ponting's revelations.

But Heseltine himself may subsequently have had cause to ponder the moral of the story. For when, just over a year later, he clashed with the Prime Minister over the Westland affair, the issues he raised were remarkably similar.

He was to complain bitterly that undertakings had been made to him which had then been withdrawn; that information had been withheld from the public to which they had a right; that secrecy and distortion had been used at the expense of the truth.

Those were precisely the complaints that drove Clive Ponting to break the rules and speak out in public.

Towards the end of 1984, however, Heseltine was absorbed in more pressing matters.

Defence spending, over the five years of Mrs Thatcher's administration, had been deliberately allowed to rise steadily to the point where it was 23 per cent higher in real terms than it had been in 1978–79; the annual budget was nearly £18 billion, making Defence the biggest spender in the country after Social Security. And the bills coming in were staggering: the new Trident nuclear system to replace Polaris (estimated cost, £9,300 million over 20 years); the modernisation of conventional weaponry (£8,355 million); the Falklands garrison (£126 million a year); higher service pay (£3,420 million); the British Army on the Rhine (£1,899 million); the Anglo-Italian-West German Tornado fighter-bomber (£1,250 million).

Shortly, however, the shutters were due to come down as the Government's priorities shifted to other areas. No Defence Review was planned, but the Treasury had insisted that the Defence budget should fall by 0.5 per cent from the end of 1985, and drop by 0.7 per cent in 1987–8.

Heseltine had fought back, castigating their attitude as the 'Gatling gun mentality. They just sweep the arc and see what falls off the trees'.

But privately he was aware that at some point – probably sooner rather than later – there would have to be a reckoning. Attending a lunch for a select group of journalists and defence experts, Heseltine demonstrated his grasp of the realities by producing an envelope and sketching a graph on the back of it. He drew a line showing future expenditure, then another showing future revenue.

Up to a certain time, he pointed out, they could be reconciled. 'And after that,' he grinned, 'I'll be gone.' The year, he predicted, in which the lines would cross: 1986. He was nothing if not prophetic.

In the meantime, however, he plunged into the financial battle with all the enthusiasm he could muster. His first target was the Department itself. 'If you're not careful as a Minister,' he said, 'you can find yourself the titular head of the bureaucratic machine, moving relentlessly in the direction the machine wants.'

He had introduced the famous MINIS scheme that had so appalled the military when his appointment was first announced, and had centralised the administration under himself, his Permanent Under-Secretary, Clive Whitmore, and the Chief of the Defence Staff, Field-Marshal Sir Edwin Bramall. He described it at as a new 'management structure' which would greatly increase efficiency.

Soon, in his imposing office on the sixth floor of the MoD, there hung a vast and complex chart, detailing the disposition and hierarchy of his organisation.

He had also turned his attention to the commercial side of Defence, with which, as a manager, he felt instinctively familiar.

The MoD runs a vast department known as the Procurement Executive, 43,000 strong, whose role is to buy the forces' weapons and equipment. Its purchasing potential is enormous. The MoD accounts for about half the output of the aerospace industry, and one third of electronics and shipbuilding. It supports 242,000 jobs in British industry directly, and another 193,000 indirectly. At any one time ten thousand British companies are working on defence contracts.

It had not, however, always been a model of efficiency. Awful stories had emerged about its waste and mismanagement, particularly on the British torpedo programme and the rebuilding of the command centre at Northwood in Middlesex which had become known as the 'Black Hole' because of the enormous sums of money that disappeared into it.

Heseltine decided in December 1984 to break with tradition and appoint an outsider, Peter Levene, to head the Procurement Executive. There was an immediate row, not only because Levene's salary was fixed at £95,000, nearly twice as high as that of the highest-paid civil servant, but also because Levene had been head of a defence company, United Scientific Holdings, which was a major supplier to the Ministry.

Heseltine was unmoved. At the same time, he was throwing himself into the role of salesman for British arms, travelling to Jordan and

20

Egypt, and then at short notice to Saudi Arabia to argue King Fahd out of buying French Mirage 2000 bombers instead of Tornadoes, made in part by British Aerospace. This last trip was successful; in September 1985 Saudi Arabia and Great Britain signed a $4 billion contract for the supply of Tornado aircraft.

Arms sales to India also occupied much of his time. India was buying Jaguar fighter-bombers, Sea Harrier jump-jets and Sea King helicopters from Britain, and was interested in a 155-mm gun. Heseltine had plans to fly to India to nurse these deals, but in December 1984 the Indian Government suddenly cancelled his trip, accusing Britain of harbouring Sikh extremists.

His greatest effort, however, was devoted to a project for which he can claim personal credit: the European Fighter Aircraft. This was a £20 billion project for five Western European countries, Britain, France, West Germany, Italy and Spain, to pool their resources and produce around 1,000 fighters. The plane was to fly in 1995, but such are the lead times in defence procurement that the deadline for agreement among the five nations on the plane's specifications was September 1985.

By 1984, it had become apparent that the Europeans were split between the French and the other four countries. Heseltine devoted himself to trying to find a compromise to bring the French round, and though in the end he failed, he held the others together. On 2 August 1985 they announced agreement, and the EFA went ahead.

Such was his involvement in this and other projects that Heseltine did not have much time to devote to an apparently minor problem that cropped up in October 1984. That month, his Junior Minister, Adam Butler, learnt from the Chairman of Westland, Britain's only remaining helicopter company, that the firm was experiencing considerable financial difficulties.

The matter went into Heseltine's pending tray. And, for the time being, stayed there.

Chapter Three

THE CORPORATE CRIPPLE

*'The wrong helicopter, at the wrong time, for the
wrong market – and five years too late'*

– Alan Bristow, May 1985

Shelby Kirk was piloting his Westland W30 helicopter through the
blue haze above Los Angeles, heading towards John Wayne airport
with six commuters aboard, when, without warning, the control rod
on the tail rotor snapped. Immediately the machine started plunging
towards the earth.

Kirk's co-pilot, Jackson Shaw, told investigators what happened
next:

> The W30 went down in a wild, dizzying spin through a cloud
> layer. The blade was frozen at an angle. At about 500 feet the
> entire tail rotor broke loose. The passengers started screaming.
> But then we kept the plane up, and they began cheering us on. We
> plummeted down into a bunch of power-lines, bounced off and
> came down on our side. It was a miracle no one was killed.

Kirk, whose flying skills were later described as 'sensational', almost
certainly saved the lives of those on board by bringing the craft down
away from the rush-hour freeways, in Eldorado Park near Long
Beach.

But the accident that day in November 1983 demonstrated
something every helicopter pilot is familiar with; the machine he flies,
as well as being thirsty, noisy and extremely complicated, has the
aerodynamic qualities of a house-brick. If anything goes wrong, it
tends to drop out of the sky.

On this occasion, however, there were to be far-reaching

consequences. The helicopter being flown by Shelby Kirk was one of a fleet of four brand-new W30s operated by a small commuter airline called Airspur Inc. On Airspur's success rested virtually all the hopes of the Westland factory six thousand miles away in Somerset – not just for their new helicopter, but for the survival of the whole company. The crash – like so much else to do with the W30 – was a disaster.

'Our image was badly hurt,' said John Gallagher, Airspur's owner. He had obtained a cheap $40 million loan arranged by Westland from British banks, and had launched his company with the help of a grand opening party thrown by the company in Los Angeles, where girls in Union Jack outfits had dispensed free champagne.

But from the beginning there had been some uneasiness about the helicopter itself: Airspur pilots testified that they had always been unhappy with the way the plane vibrated in flight, and with what they said were minute cracks in the tail rotor mounting. When the crash occurred, the Federal Aviation Authority grounded the entire W30 fleet. The flaw probably occurred, their investigators said, when Westland's Lynx military helicopter was redesigned with a large and elegant new cabin for civilian use. This could have changed the stresses in the control gear. All the passengers in the November 1983 crash were injured, and two with broken arms sued Westland for damages.

By the following January, Westland had redesigned the tail rotor, and the helicopters were flying again. But the W30 civilian helicopter never properly recovered. For there was far more to the problem than just a safety scare. The whole idea of commuter helicopters was that they should fly people from international airports to city centre helipads, for little more than a taxi-fare. What Westland's optimists back at Yeovil had failed to take into account was that ordinary residents hated the noise.

Admiral Sir John Treacher, Westland's marketing chief, later lamented:

> When we launched the W30, we pitched it for cabin size and comfort into the commuter market which was seen by just about everybody to be on the verge of an explosion ... There was a great upsurge, in every city and every state, that the helicopter was just about in a breakthrough situation as part of the transportation system. Four years later, the FAA are bitterly disappointed ... the market simply has not developed in the way that a lot of us thought it would.

The 'environmental backlash' was impervious to a vigorous public relations campaign by the manufacturers' Helicopter Association 'to convince community residents that helicopters are an essential and economic part of the local transport system, as well as being good neighbours'. In December 1984 Airspur, near bankruptcy, sold out to a larger airline, Evergreen, and the commuter helicopters disappeared.

Westland lost more than £5 million on the operation, and with its collapse went all its hopes that the company could henceforth stand on its own feet.

It was hardly surprising that Yeovil should be out of its depth in the harsh environment of commercial buying and selling, for the company really belongs to a different world. Westland is a defence contractor, part of what President Eisenhower once called the military-industrial complex. In Britain, almost as much as in the US, vast quantities of taxpayers' money and a majority of the available research talent are soaked up by defence companies, which operate in an atmosphere completely different from any normal commercial enterprise. It is a world in which the game is to use international political and bureaucratic muscle to wrest multi-million pound contracts from governments – and to keep them flowing your way.

As far as helicopters are concerned, Westland has always been, unfortunately, a small player in a big game.

The helicopter is a relatively novel military machine; it was pioneered by Igor Sikorsky, who fled from the Bolsheviks to America in 1923. Sikorsky had been intrigued during his youth in Kiev by Leonardo da Vinci's famous drawing of a lifting spiral airscrew – the first theoretical 'rotary wing' aeroplane. Under the umbrella of a large conglomerate, United Technologies, the Sikorsky company of Stratford, Connecticut, made its first hovering flight at the outbreak of World War II; it built two observation helicopters for the US Army in 1941, and was in mass production by 1945.

At first the helicopter's unique qualities were limited to reconnaissance and rescue missions. But its possibilities in jungle warfare excited the US military. The Korean war of 1950 started the boom, as helicopters showed they could ferry in troops and equipment to patches of trackless forest and mountain, and bring casualties out again. In Vietnam in the 1960s and early 1970s, the Americans deployed thousands of helicopters, developing the 'Air Cavalry' – helicopter gunships charging into jungle battle in a style caricatured in the film *Apocalypse Now*. At sea, helicopters were used to detect and attack submarines. In Europe, where commanders wanted a quick response to the large number of Soviet tanks, the helicopter was loaded with rockets and turned into a weapon so deadly that some strategists speculated that they could make the tank itself obsolete.

24

By the late 1960s the US was turning out 8,000 helicopters a year, and other armed forces all over the world were buying them in large numbers. Sikorsky, with UT's conglomerate billions behind them, remained the biggest company, though three other US corporations also developed helicopter subsidiaries: the giant Boeing aircraft company; McDonnell Douglas (Hughes Aircraft); and Bell.

A few European countries tried to develop their own helicopter industries, although they barely sustain one company each. The French have the biggest, now a division of the state-controlled Aerospatiale plane company. Smaller companies are the Italian Agusta, and the helicopter division of Messerschmitt-Bölkow-Blohm (MBB) of West Germany. But they are all far weaker than the US companies, which set the pace with an inventiveness financed by vast domestic sales to the Pentagon. The Europeans are also less efficient; Sikorsky today produces more helicopters than all the Europeans put together, yet employs only 12,400 people against 21,000 in Europe.

It was in 1946 that Britain decided to get in on the helicopter act. A former troopship sailed from Southampton for a five-day trip to New York, with a team of Yeovil men on board headed by John Fearn, the managing director of Westland Ltd, a defence contractor with very English roots.

Set among the gentle hills on the edge of a small West Country town, the 'Westland Aircraft Works' opened in 1915 at Yeovil as a subsidiary of Petters, a farm-machinery company. It made 1,100 seaplanes for the Admiralty during World War I, and then settled down to cultivate its military links. By the 1930s Westland had been floated off into independence, in close association with John Brown Engineering. It was soon able to boast of its good contacts with the Air Ministry, which had bought its Wapiti planes and flown them over Everest, and to assert with imperial nonchalance that the Somerset works were 'immune from enemy attack'. Throughout World War II Westland churned out more than 2,000 Spitfires under sub-contract. But now the war had ended, and so had the work.

Westland had long been fascinated by helicopters. Before the war it had tried to develop a five-seater autogyro based on the ideas of a Spaniard, Juan de la Cierva. Autogyros had unpowered rotors and were pulled along by a propeller; Cierva's, however, vibrated disastrously.

This time, following the New York trip, Westland did a deal with the more successful Sikorsky, of a kind that other Europeans were to follow. It bought a license to make Sikorsky's S-51 Dragonfly helicopter, with permission to work up the design to suit its own markets. It was a good deal, followed by others. Over the next twenty years, Westland sold to its own government, and several foreign countries, a series of Sikorsky variants made at Yeovil. They included the Whirlwind and the Wessex, still in service today with the Royal Navy.

Westland grew rich. The 1957 Macmillan government encouraged the British aviation industry to meet soaring defence costs by merging into fewer, bigger groups. Westland promptly swallowed all its three helicopter rivals: Saunders-Roe (in 1959); the helicopter division of Bristol (1960) and the British aviation interests of Fairey (1960).

Westland's biggest success came when Sikorsky sold it a 1959 license for its anti-submarine craft, the S-3D. Many profitable years were spent in conjunction with the Royal Navy, using Ministry of Defence cash, to turn this into the famous Sea King helicopter. The Navy went over to the exclusive use of helicopters to lower sonars on winches beneath the thermal ocean layers which conceal Russian submarines. Westland developed the Sea King's roomy cabin so that it could be crammed full of British radar and electronics to direct the chase. (About a third of a military helicopter's price is electronics: British firms like GEC sell about £2 million of equipment to go on each modern Sea King.) Westland redesigned the machine to carry much more weight with powerful engines; fitted it with folding rotors to be stacked alongside others on a ship's deck; and made it float for emergencies.

A helicopter manufacturer with a successful basic machine can live off it for an extraordinarily long time. A helicopter lasts up to thirty years, providing lucrative orders for spares, and in 1986, Westland was in its twenty-seventh year of making new Sea Kings for sale at home and abroad.

The converse is also true, of course: when a helicopter maker flops with a new machine, it can face disaster.

But these were boom years in the helicopter business. In the 1960s both the British and French military were in the market for large numbers of the next generation of helicopters, and the Wilson government negotiated a package deal; the two countries would produce three new types – the small Gazelle, the Puma and the Lynx. France would be responsible for the first two, and Westland would have the exciting opportunity of designing its own machine for the first time – the Lynx. The actual manufacture of all three machines was to be shared out between Aerospatiale of France and Westland, strictly according to the numbers each government proposed to purchase.

The great era of Anglo-French collaboration, by no means unusually, left the English with a conviction that they had been thoroughly conned, and Westland has complained about it ever since. Such griping cuts little ice with those who have more experience of dealing with the French. Admiral Sir Raymond Lygo, for example, who, as chief executive of British Aerospace, handled many French joint deals, says:

> When you deal with the French, you have to remember the Nelsonian advice: 'Outmanoeuvre the Russian, close with the Frenchman.' It you do not, you will certainly go to the wall, but if you do close with the Frenchman he will respect you and you will have a good relationship with him, and you will have a good business. That is our experience.
>
> The French are very professional, very highly technically qualified; they are good business people, good marketeers, good salesmen; they run good companies and they are highly competitive. Aerospatiale... have endless collaborative programmes, but they are tough and competent and they know it.

His fellow-admiral, Sir John Treacher, who was to be a prominent Westland director, adopts a more mournful tone. 'You cannot expunge some things from your memory,' he reflected later.

The experience with Aerospatiale left a legacy of bitterness which was to have a critical effect when the Westland affair developed into a political battle in 1985. The French are said to have cheated, by getting 30 per cent of the production work on the Lynx, and then never buying as many of them as they had promised. The French army did not buy any at all. The French navy bought a rival Aerospatiale machine called the Dauphin instead. Altogether, instead of the promised two hundred helicopters, the French bought only twenty-six. Nor was that all. Malcolm Gilham, Westland works convenor, still does not forget: 'They screwed us over the price of the rotor head which they made under the agreement. The company tried to renegotiate the agreement but they couldn't. And they never paid us our share of the development costs.'

Furthermore, it is said at Yeovil, the teams of visiting engineers who lived for months in caravans near the Aerospatiale plant outside Paris, found their new colleagues insisted on holding technical discussions in their own language. The British engineers were required to learn French...

Westland, management and workers alike, thus entered the less buoyant world of the late 1970s with a typically English set of prejudices. It also found itself with all four of its major helicopter types

27

due to expire at around the same time – the mid to late 1980s. What was to be the shape of a further generation of helicopter-building?

At the same time, the boom was becoming a slump. World oil prices had soared. The military buying surges of Korea and Vietnam were long gone, and governments around the world had largely stocked up with helicopters. The promising sales to offshore oil-rig operators withered in the world recession. As military helicopters grew more elaborate, governments could only afford a few at a time, and more of the price was taken up in expensive missiles and electronic gear which were of no benefit to airframe manufacturers like Westland. In Britain, a Labour government was once again in power, with talk of nationalisation and defence cuts.

Westland, all of whose connections were military and Conservative, was determined not to be nationalised or 'rationalised'. After a campaign by the workforce, the 1974 Labour government left Westland independent and omitted the company from its plans to create British Aerospace. It was a risky stance for a minnow; Tory backbencher Sir Cranley Onslow later remarked sarcastically, 'Westland was about the only part of the British aerospace industry which actually should have been nationalised.'

Again, a Labour Government charted a rather unsteady course towards European collaboration and defence cuts. Defence Minister Fred Mulley made few headlines when he scrawled his name on a document in 1978 beside those of the defence ministers of France, Germany and Italy, but he forged what is still – theoretically – official British helicopter policy.

The 1978 'Declaration of Principles' said that the commercial helicopter companies of Europe would sit down with their governments to develop families of Euro-helicopters which everybody could buy. To 'maintain a strong and healthy helicopter industry' it was agreed that all four nations would 'make every effort to meet their needs with helicopters developed jointly in Europe'. The final, unspoken, thought was, 'In order to keep the Americans at bay'.

The three projects which eventually emerged were aimed at the fairly distant future and were not notably Europe-wide. One was an expensive scheme for a big naval helicopter to replace the Sea King. The French and Germans refused to join. Westland of Britain and Agusta of Italy teamed up, however, to promote it with their respective governments. Called the EH101, it was going to take £500 million of mostly government funds to develop, and the fifty or sixty machines the British navy might buy were likely to cost them £1.5 billion. Getting the project through involved hard political spade-work. One senior MoD civil servant expostulated when he saw the figures, 'These are going to cost more each than the Tornado!' – and that was billed to be one of Europe's most expensive post-war defence contracts.

The second project was for an agile 'battlefield helicopter', hard to spot on radar and equipped with high technology – guided anti-tank missiles, night vision and lightweight carbon-fibre parts. Europe split into two camps, with the French and Germans working on one version, and the Italians on a rival, eventually to be joined by Westland.

The third, and haziest, scheme was for a medium-sized transport helicopter, with a very big potential market. It was called the NH90, and in eight years remained little more than talk.

What all these plans had in common was their long-term nature: even if they came to pass, it would not be until the 1990s. Westland had to fill its factory long before that. The Labour Defence Secretary Roy Mason's 1976 defence review and the world over-capacity made it clear that the traditionally generous military contracts of the past were likely to be scarce.

Faced with this prospect, the Westland Board gathered to make a strategic decision whose scope was positively breathtaking: they decided to design and build a brand new machine, alone. It was not, on the whole, a good move. In the words of helicopter tycoon Alan Bristow, it was to be 'the wrong helicopter, for the wrong market, at the wrong time'. The W30 was about to ruin the company.

The Chairman of the Board was Toby Low, Lord Aldington, whose connections in the pre-Thatcher Tory establishment were formidable. He was a close friend of the deposed Tory Prime Minister Edward Heath, and once said in public that Heath had 'planted a tree in my garden' – the sort of remark that, after Mrs Thatcher's election as party leader, branded a man as a potentially subversive element in the eyes of the new model Conservative party. He was also warden of Winchester, where he had once been head boy, and Michael Heseltine was heard to complain of him, 'Every time he comes into the MoD, he makes me feel like a schoolboy.'

Aldington's view, understandably in view of his post-war career, was that there were few problems which could not be solved by nudging the right elbow. He inherited control of Grindlay's bank, and got a safe seat at Blackpool after the war; Anthony Eden was his son's godfather and made him a junior minister at the Board of Trade; then, after he dropped politics, Harold Macmillan granted him one of the last hereditary peerages. He went on to become a familiar figure in the boardrooms of the City.

His star rose again during the Heath government, when he was made one of a 'first eleven' of businessmen appointed to run the ports. Aldington got the Port of London while another Conservative City banker got Merseyside – ironically, this was John Cuckney, later to be given the task of sorting out the mess in Aldington's own company.

Aldington's main coup at the PLA was of a kind guaranteed to set Mrs Thatcher's teeth on edge; with beer and sandwiches, he got a 'corporatist' deal with Jack Jones, the general secretary of the Transport and General Workers' Union, to parcel out new container work among the displaced dockers. 'It was a gorgeous committee,' he was to recall. 'You couldn't get on to it unless Jack Jones and I agreed.'

His deputy chairman at Westland was Lord Aberconway, a contemporary from the board of John Brown and uncle of the Tory MP Kenneth Carlisle. Both men were approaching seventy. There was also an admiral on the board. This was Sir John Treacher, who resigned in 1977 from the Navy, where it was popularly supposed that his advancement to the very top had been blocked.

Treacher was a figure who was to become steadily more powerful at Westland. Originally, his main directorship was as chief executive of National Car Parks. He was then paid an eventual total of £435,000 by the Playboy organisation to take over its UK gaming operations for what turned out to be only four months; they failed to retain their licences. He moved over full-time to Westland, hired to try and improve its sales record, and was to play a big part in the eventual ousting of Westland's traditional management.

Like all defence contractors, Westland was in the habit of offering jobs to well-connected military and government officials rather than men with experience in industry, a practice that has only recently been tightened up in the MoD. Amongst them were Sir Ronald Melville, retired Permanent Secretary in the Ministry of Aviation Supply, who was put on the board in 1974; and General John Strawson, retired Chief of Staff, UK Land Forces, who was signed up by Westland in 1976 for an 'assault on the Middle East market'. In 1982, the company succeeded, temporarily, in hiring the recently retired MoD Permanent Secretary, Sir Frank Cooper.

Westland's long-serving managing director, to whom Mrs Thatcher was persuaded to give a knighthood in 1983, was the slightly eccentric figure of Basil Blackwell, a Yorkshire engineer with a visionary streak. 'Basil could see ten years ahead, and he could see what was going to happen tomorrow,' says a senior executive. 'But he couldn't see anything in between. He had everyone writing academic papers on the future of the helicopter. He was nowhere near hard-nosed enough.'

Blackwell, who had a mathematics first at Cambridge and another in engineering from London, was both academic and humane. The unions came to think the company was worth working for, in ways which again would have cut no ice with the Thatcherites. In the 1970s, the labour record had been appalling. Blackwell responded with conciliation. 'He was a marvellous communicator,' says Malcolm Gilham, the works convenor. 'He set up all sorts of consultative processes. We discussed all aspects of the running of the company, and the trade unions knew more than the middle managers.' A Westland executive says, 'Basil gave the unions bulky documents on programmes and sales drives, invaluable to commercial rivals.' They were never leaked.

Blackwell was keen to escape from the apron-strings of the US, but impatient of the Europeans. He once addressed the Royal Aeronautical Society in the manner of Wittgenstein, calling his lecture 'Tractatus Technologico-Philosophicus'. It was an amusing attack on government attitudes to 'technological progress' and a debunking of accountants as the 'priesthood' of modern industry. In retrospect, Blackwell seems a doomed figure.

This, however, was the group of men who planned what they hoped would be Westland's new future. The company donated regular sums to the Tory party, and large amounts to military charities, saying, 'We believe these are of benefit to the company.' The row of badges covering virtually the entire rear wall at the factory entrance spoke of their comfortable links with the Royal Navy. Critics now recall the generous and lengthy lunches to which they were entertained in the directors' dining room, known as the Directors' Mess. Among the thatched cottages and the flocks of sheep of Yeovil, everything must have seemed easier than it really was.

What the board now rashly decided to attempt – in an industry where virtually every project was a patchwork of collaboration – was to make from scratch Britain's very first purely civilian helicopter. They believed the market research (some carried out by the Department of Trade and Industry) which said that the world civil market was going to grow. A big passenger cabin was designed to go with the rotor of the old Lynx, already developed at MoD expense, and it was launched at the 1980 Farnborough Air Show. Westland may even have started to believe its own publicity:

SUCCESS BUILT ON SUCCESS: WESTLAND 30... For over 30 years, Westland have been the European leaders in helicopter design and manufacture... W30 precision engineering has been tried and tested in the most extreme conditions... unique wide-

31

bodied fuselage ideal for airline feeder services, offshore support and executive transport.

British Airways was persuaded to operate two of the new machines on the Penzance-Scilly Isles run, and Westland quoted its helicopter manager: 'Captain J. Cameron says, "The W30 is a winner."... Maybe that's why we're confident it's going to be a big success.'

In fact, it was a flop. Westland thought it would sell at least 100, at more than £3 million each. There were few takers. The Los Angeles experiment collapsed following the 1983 crash: 'Airspur became a sink down which we were pouring vast amounts of money,' one Westland executive now says.

Alan Bristow, Westland's most persistent critic, asserts:

I told them the W30 would be a disaster. I said it was an absolute non-starter: the payload is so limited and the speed so inferior. They totally ignored my advice. The Rolls-Royce engines were unreliable and hyper-complex. I'm red white and blue to the core, but they can never deliver on time or on price.

Bristow claims sarcastically that the only reason Westland was first in the marketplace with the concept of a 'commuter helicopter' was because all the other helicopter companies had more sense.

Aldington and Blackwell awoke to the fact that their £750 million of past military sales to the British taxpayer had been a cosy way of life no one else was prepared to pay for. Commercial customers wanted their machines not to break down. They wanted value for money, payment on delivery, and spares when they needed them.

There is, Aldington now says, 'far more intensive use of the helicopter by civil operators than in the defence forces except in fighting conditions'. There is fierce competition, and customers 'require short delivery times' of components. Treacher concedes, 'We faced that challenge without... appreciating the wholly different amount of money required, where no longer are sales made on the basis of progress payments and down-payments in advance.'

Only one answer presented itself. Westland would have to get away from the world of customers, and back into the well-tested practice of lobbying government departments. There were two aspects to the plan. The minor one was to persuade the British Government to use subsidy and political arm-twisting to sell twenty-one of the unsaleable W30s to India. The second, grander, strategy was to beef up the 'commuter helicopter' into a military machine, and sell it to the RAF.

The first task was to try and get some money out of Whitehall to improve the W30. Westland went to Patrick Jenkin, one of Mrs Thatcher's subsequently eclipsed Ministers, then heading the Department of Industry. It was Jenkin's department which officially 'sponsored' British industry. Westland told him that, with government 'launch aid', the W30 could be turned into an even better civil proposition. With more power and range it could be sold to North Sea oilrig operators. In a remarkably soft-headed decision, Jenkin's officials accepted this, and in February 1983 they signed up to lend Westland £40 million.

'Launch aid' is part of the flood of cash which regularly goes to aerospace companies. Its purpose is to help set up the production lines and tooling needed for 'high-risk' civil aviation projects. British Aerospace and Rolls-Royce get the lion's share of the £650 million the DTI is currently spending, for new planes and engines. It is supposed to involve a 50–50 split of the risk between government and the company.

In fact, Westland persuaded the Government to hand over their £40 million share before Westland was required to contribute its own, and it spent the lot. As a result, the Government carried all the risk. If nobody ordered the plane once a prototype was developed, then Westland could simply cancel the project. There was some small print saying the Government could demand its money back, but nobody was particularly worried about that. Once the money was gone, experience tended to show, it was gone for good. On the other hand, if the project succeeded, Westland would not have to start paying back its loan until it had sold about a hundred helicopters.

This was the first major decision on Westland taken by Mrs Thatcher's government. It hardly squared with the Prime Minister's publicly proclaimed slogans about good housekeeping, the thrift of the corner shop, and standing on one's own feet. But at the time, Jenkin boasted there would be 'a fair return to the taxpayer ... We are delighted by this example of partnership between the Government and the private sector'.

Westland's next port of call was the Foreign Office. In Autumn 1983 a sales team had demonstrated the original W30 in New Delhi to the Indian government. They hoped to sell a fleet to service the new cluster of oilrigs off the coast of Bombay. Mrs Gandhi was well-disposed to the deal, and big military sales, including Westland's own Sea Kings, were being made already to India through the MoD. The Indians were also keen to acquire a small fleet of helicopters to ferry V.I.P.s about.

The Westland W30 was, in commercial terms, a poor proposition for India – just as it was for most other people. In normal conditions, a twenty-seater passenger craft was too big; in the 120-degree heat off

Bombay, the thin air cut its power and increased its fuel consumption drastically, so that it was too thirsty and could not carry full loads.

But this deal was more concerned with politics than commerce.

Westland had little cause to complain about the Government's sales service. The Foreign Office offered to give Mrs Gandhi £50 million of 'aid', provided she put it all towards buying Westland's helicopters. A sales team led by the junior DTI minister Geoffrey Pattie flew to India in early 1984, with a long list of arms it hoped to sell. It had the Westland package tacked on to the end, and the Indian cabinet acquiesced 'in principle'.

Their bitter competitors, the French, riposted with cheap credit at two and a half per cent, and a 'special offer': if India bought twenty-one of their own Dauphin helicopters for the oilfields, France would throw in six V.I.P. helicopters absolutely free. Westland returned to its Whitehall lobbying, and Mrs Thatcher authorised another remarkable deal. India's 'aid' allocation would be raised another £15 million. This would now cover the entire cost of twenty-one oilfield helicopters with their basic spares; the whole lot were to be a free gift from Her Majesty's Government.

In July 1984 the Indian High Commission in London wrote to Westland, agreeing to buy provided the helicopters passed the Indians' engine tests. Westland was so confident that the politics of the sale were stitched up that it immediately started to manufacture five W30s and the spares to go with them, as well as a test machine to be shipped to Bombay. It ran up huge bank overdrafts. The factory was eventually to be crammed with no less than £42 million of W30s – all unsold. Treacher later explained this extraordinary gamble by saying, 'It was the elusive large order for which we had hoped so long, which was going to get us off the ground.'

But while the Indian deal hovered on the brink, the big target remained Britain's own Royal Air Force. If the RAF bought a version of the W30 and paid for its development, it could be worth £500 million. There was a different Whitehall group to be lobbied for this – Westland's main customer, the Ministry of Defence.

What Aldington and Blackwell never realised was that, in the words of one of their lobbyists, 'the MoD had gone sour on Westland.' An important omen occurred in 1984 when Michael Heseltine cancelled a long-standing Westland helicopter maintenance contract. He put it out to competition and received a much cheaper bid from an entrepreneur called Alan Bristow. It was true that the Army had, since the 1970s, had a request in to order some new medium transport helicopters. But helicopter-buying was particularly prone to inter-service squabbles. The Army, the Navy and the RAF all operated them. Helicopters thus had no one backer to give them bureaucratic clout.

The Navy had already sabotaged one attempt to devise a joint order by insisting on its right to order separately the big, expensive EH101 offered by Westland as a specific replacement for the old Sea King. The RAF, for its part, insisted on the right to fly the Army around in RAF helicopters. To do otherwise would be to lose prestige. The Army was only permitted to operate very small machines for itself. This meant that transport helicopters fell on the RAF budget, although it was the Army that was lobbying for them. And naturally the RAF was never interested in sacrificing part of its main budget to someone else's unglamorous demands...

Westland offered the Army the W30, but the Army, with a normal military preference for more elaborate machinery (known in the Services as 'gold-plating'), reported that compared to the equivalent US and French craft the W30 was cheap and nasty. Admiral Treacher bravely described it as 'cheap and cheerful'.

The Army then announced that it was thinking of changing its mind altogether. After the 1982 Falklands experience, and the September 1984 NATO exercises called 'Lionheart', it said it now wanted to carry a whole platoon of thirty-two men at once. Any helicopter it bought would have to be twice as big (and almost certainly twice as expensive).

This delay and bickering was handy for Heseltine and the MoD's defence secretariat, which had huge cash problems trying to pay for Tornadoes, the £10 billion Trident nuclear force, and the other hardware swelling the defence estimates. If they let the whole helicopter idea slip quietly out of the bottom of the programme, who would care?

The answer was that Lord Aldington cared – almost to the point of panic. In October 1984, just after 'Lionheart', he wrote a long letter to Michael Heseltine. It contained elements both of pleading and menace. Westland had to have some cash to develop its helicopter to sell to the RAF, he wrote, or the company would face a 'financial predicament'. He demanded a meeting with the Defence Secretary. He also raised the hope of turning to the Americans for assistance. There was a possibility, he wrote, that the only way out would be 'an association with a US manufacturer'.

It was the first time that an American partnership had been proposed – and, in the light of subsequent events, it is notable how little concern it provoked.

One possible US partner whom Aldington almost certainly did *not* have in mind was a man called Columbus Iselin. Iselin had the iron-grey hair, the impeccable cuffs and the chunky gold jewellery of the typical US multinational executive. Previously in Saudi Arabia, lobbying for the big defence contractor Rockwell, Iselin had been regularly over the past two years in London. He was now working for Sikorsky, the world's biggest military helicopter manufacturer and Westland's old mentor. His job was to break into Europe and sell the Black Hawk helicopter.

This was Westland's most feared military rival. The Black Hawk had been designed ten years earlier, after the Vietcong had demonstrated how easily they could shoot down existing US 'air cavalry'. Sikorsky boasted of its ability to soar straight up, even in hot weather, carrying eleven troops or three and a half times its own weight. It could fly practically upside down, hug the ground at night below enemy radar, fit into a Hercules transport plane, or cover 1300 miles with extra fuel tanks. All its systems were in triplicate: 'There is no way a single bullet travelling in a straight line can pass through this helicopter and bring it down,' said George Price, Sikorsky's director of international business.

Nonetheless, Sikorsky had considerable trouble and delay in getting the Black Hawk accepted into production for the US Army. Corporate heads rolled, and matters were not helped when a 1978 prototype plunged into the Housatonic River, killing two company test pilots and a flight engineer. Blame fell on the 'stabilator' – a stubby wing near the tail which swivels from horizontal to vertical depending on whether the craft is hovering or moving forward. (Six years later, the stabilator was again suspected when the entire Black Hawk fleet was temporarily grounded after a crash. Pilots were to lodge at least seventy complaints about stabilator problems.)

It was not until 1982 that the Connecticut plant was solidly established, with the eventual prospect of selling as many as 2,500 craft to the US military. Only now could they turn to an overseas sales drive. But it was bitterly hard going in the recession, particularly against the French. Sikorsky had only sold forty-two Black Hawks abroad. They had shipped a test machine to Tibet and persuaded the Chinese to buy twenty-four. They then covertly sold another dozen to be painted with the garish blue and yellow sun of China's traditional enemy, Taiwan. Switzerland ordered three after a high-altitude fly-off with the French Super Puma. President Mitterand of France personally intervened and the US order was cancelled.

Sikorsky had set out to penetrate this political ring-fence in Europe. Bill Paul, the apparently mild, lean and bespectacled boss of United Technologies, Sikorsky's parent company, appeared in London at a conference during the 1982 Farnborough Air Show to make sweeping offers of 'collaboration'. 'We can share each other's markets,' he said. 'This is the strategy I think is essential since the helicopter industry is so small.'

Columbus Iselin was hired to find a cooperative European helicopter firm. 'The first thing I realised was that our invitation was being rebuffed. Everybody said, "Thanks, but no thanks."' Aldington and Blackwell at Westland were among the first to be sounded out. Would they build the Black Hawk under licence?

They were not interested in a partnership. They were excited about the prospects of the W30 for the British Ministry of Defence. They were saying they were going to dominate the civilian helicopter industry through the W30 contract in Los Angeles. They said they were going to use their influence to force the RAF to accept the W30.

Sikorsky went instead to the Belfast manufacturers Short Brothers, and persuaded them to apply, reluctantly, to the MoD to offer the Black Hawk under a Sikorsky licence. But Michael Heseltine told Shorts tersely that he had no requirement to buy it – and no funds.

Enthused by a belief in the power of their political influence, Blackwell and Treacher spent the next two years fighting it out aggressively for foreign sales with both Sikorsky itself (in Australia) and the French in India. By the time Aldington approached the British Government for help, Sikorsky had become well aware of Westland's current plight. The Farnborough Air Show only three months earlier had been the venue for another quiet Iselin approach, again turned down flat. 'Those guys in Yeovil haven't come to their senses,' Iselin reported.

It was shortly before Christmas 1984 that Aldington, accompanied by Blackwell, entered the Ministry of Defence to confront Michael Heseltine. In an obvious piece of 'softening-up', the chairman of the Tory back-bench aviation committee, John Wilkinson, had already been invited down to Yeovil and duly reported that 'something urgent must be done to save the company'.

Heseltine, however, with his Permanent Secretary Clive Whitmore and his new Junior Minister Adam Butler by his side, had looked at the briefs and did not see it as a major problem. Besides he had another, more pressing matter on his mind: a bitter argument he had begun with Mrs Thatcher and Norman Tebbit's Trade Department over their refusal to let him help Merseyside by ordering a £140 million frigate from Cammell Laird. The DTI wanted to have the yard closed for good to save money, but Heseltine was eventually to persuade Mrs Thatcher that the 'good' trade unionists who had recently crossed picket lines there deserved to be rewarded. He had to act tough, telling Richard Mottram, his private secretary, that he would resign if he lost. But that had proved unnecessary.

At the same time he was addressing meetings of the Independent European Programme Group, an organisation set up in 1976 to pursue the goal of greater cooperation on defence projects, which he had done much to revive and which was now taken seriously by most European defence ministers.

Heseltine did not like Aldington's manner, and he did not like Blackwell's lack of realism. He suspected that Westland was inefficient and did not deliver promptly. It was said to be too soft on the unions. Futhermore – and this is something never to be underestimated in British politics – there was the question of the constituency. A Liberal, Paddy Ashdown, had appalled Conservatives by snatching Yeovil from them in the 1983 election, and was leading the bell-ringing to save Westland. Heseltine is said to have remarked he was not going to do anything 'to cement that so-and-so in his seat'.

Westland was not given top priority. The suggestion of an American tie-up – 'I want a piece of the US defence budget and a piece of NASA,' said Aldington – was countered by a heavy hint about pursuing the possibilities in Europe. But no pressure was brought either way.

The Chairman came back to report failure; Blackwell, of Westland, increasingly in debt to the banks, had believed he could defy the wishes of a big US manufacturer and force the Defence Secretary's hand. What happened instead was that both men – apparently independently – took concealed steps to oust him.

Chapter Four

EXIT THE FAIRY GODMOTHER

*'Ministers do not really control their vast
departments. Problems are handled by a mixture
of dilettante dabbling and crisis management'*

– Clive Ponting, March 1986

In the spring of 1985, two secret moves took place in London which
were to bring the Westland crisis to a head. On 18 March, three men
gathered at the Green House restaurant in Mayfair, accompanied, for
'cover', by their wives. A little earlier – 5 February in High Holborn – a
phone-call to the offices of stockbrokers Hoare Govett placed orders
with them to start buying discreet parcels of Westland shares on behalf
of a foreign company called Baynards Holdings AG: 50,000 on that
day, another 50,000 a week later, and more than £1 million worth in
total by the end of the fortnight.

The plots had begun.

The host at the Green House lunch was Columbus Iselin of
Sikorsky. He says that the two men he was secretly talking to were
anxious members of the Westland Board – Bob Miller, a long-serving
technologist and Sikorsky supporter, and Geoffrey Jones, former
professor of aerospace studies at Southampton. The man who had
brought them together was Peter Bloomfield, hired by Iselin as
Sikorsky's London public relations consultant. A potentially friendly
MP, Bill Walker, Tory member for Tayside and vice-chairman of the
Conservative aviation committee, was also contacted. Thought was
given to making a quiet approach to the Junior Minister at the MoD,
Geoffrey Pattie.

The Americans were losing patience. The previous month, Shorts
had finally ruled themselves out of the ring as an alternative 'front' for
the Sikorsky Black Hawk; Heseltine had given them a healthy

contract to make RAF trainers instead. Within two hours of that announcement, Bill Paul himself was on the phone from Connecticut to Basil Blackwell. For the last time, would Westland drop the W30 and take the Black Hawk? Blackwell stubbornly said no.

The secret share-buying started at the same time. Baynard Holdings AG was a company owned by the family trust of Alan Bristow, a colourful millionaire tycoon. Bristow intended to take Westland over. He knew about helicopters and he knew that the MoD liked him and that the DTI would back him. On 5 February he had phoned his brokers after a confidential meeting with Geoffrey Pattie to ask what the Government's attitude would be. 'You'd be a fairy godmother!' Pattie had said.

Blackwell, unaware of any of this, was himself stepping up the lobbying of Whitehall, though with growing desperation. A naval administrator, Captain Bill Gueterbock, had been hired from the MoD by Treacher as a lobbyist. And he in turn hired the London firm of GJW, run by three former ministerial political advisers. Their job was to identify potentially sympathetic MPs and officials.

None of it did any good. The MoD – 'the men with the cheques' as Treacher put it – remained flint-hearted. 'I'm not doing anything with the present management,' Heseltine told his colleagues at the Ministry. His junior colleague Adam Butler advised Aldington to kick Blackwell upstairs into the chairman's post and hire 'an effective chief executive'.

It is unlikely Heseltine knew that he was pushing Westland steadily into the arms of Sikorsky, because, as far as he was aware, there was no immediate crisis. No one in Whitehall had fully grasped that Westland had taken some terrifying financial gambles which were about to come crashing down.

Probably the first outsider to begin to suspect was the 'fairy godmother', Alan Bristow.

Bristow was a self-made Tory tough guy. He was short, chunky, bald and loud; he also had about £17 million in his pocket from the recent sale of his stake in one of the world's biggest private helicopter fleets to his backers, British and Commonwealth Shipping.

Bristow was a Westland *bête noire*. At the age of twenty-six, as Westland's chief test pilot, he had taken a swing at the firm's commercial director following a furious altercation. 'I knocked him out too,' said Bristow later. 'He had been extremely rude to me.' His private firm, Bristow Helicopters, was built up by hiring out machines for surveys and oil exploration, after a period spent air whaling for Aristotle Onassis in the Antarctic, and flying as a mercenary for the

40

French in Indo-China. They gave him the *Croix de Guerre*. 'Yup,' he says, 'I enjoyed it.'

Bristow was consistently rude about Westland, grounding their Wessex helicopters in 1981 after a spate of company accidents and ostentatiously replacing them with French Pumas. He said, 'Helicopters are ten times less safe than planes. Manufacturers are reluctant to admit their products are defective... We are very perturbed with the Wessex.'

At Westland, they muttered that rather more maintenance of his machines would have helped.

His public image as a union-basher followed an inquiry by Lord McDonald into a pilot's strike, which observed that many of his employees feared him. Calling his staff relations 'lamentable', McDonald said, 'He has a turn of phrase more suited to the barrackroom than the boardroom.'

Bristow had good contacts, as millionaires tend to do. They included Lord King, influential Tory chairman of British Airways, and Lord Forte, who frequently shot on Bristow's Surrey estate.

One millionaire who was slightly out of his league, however, was Lord Hanson, who controlled the enormous Hanson Trust. Bristow approached the peer, who had a small helicopter charter company, Air Hanson, for possible support. Although known for his takeover activities as 'the predatory peer', Hanson responded that he did not know Bristow, and was not interested in Westland – a position he was later to change dramatically.

In fact, one of Hanson's analysts, Philip Turner, was asked on 4 February to write an analysis of the prospects for Hanson himself to mount a takeover. Remarking that Westland was in 'deep trouble' and the share-price seemed lower than the assets would justify, Turner concluded, 'Any interest?' In a second memo on 7 February, he said Westland's future depended on whether the MoD gave it orders. Hanson took the opportunity of a visit to Michael Heseltine at the MoD to raise the question of Westland. Hanson's friends claim that the response was, 'Westland can go bust as far as I'm concerned.' Defence Ministry accounts say that Heseltine did indeed privately summon Hanson, but only to see if he was interested in buying the Royal Ordnance Factories; any words about Westland were therefore brief and casual.

The takeover plot itself was, in the end, inspired and backed by one of Bristow's customers, Sir Philip Shelbourne, chairman of Britoil; by his stockbrokers; and by Alan Curtis, former owner of Aston Martin and deputy chairman of Lotus Cars, who had good contacts with the Ministry of Defence.

Heseltine himself was later to lay great emphasis on the claim that Bristow was a patriotic British buyer. This was mere propaganda. As events were later to show, Bristow was perfectly prepared to do deals with Sikorsky himself if the need arose.

At the same time as the Bristow bid was being secretly hatched, Westland's fortunes took another lurch downwards. On 13 March, 1,500 miles away in the bitter cold of Moscow, the leaders of the world's nations were gathering for the funeral of the Russian leader Chernenko.

These global wakes are frequently the scene of much informal summitry, and it was in the course of a private tête-à-tête between Mrs Thatcher and the young Rajiv Gandhi, who had succeeded to the premiership of India following the assassination of his mother, Indira Gandhi, that the question of Westland's W30 helicopters was raised. Gandhi, a qualified pilot himself, turned to Mrs Thatcher and said, 'I don't want the W30s. They're not in the slot. They're too expensive to run.'

This desperate piece of news was brought back to London just as Lord Aldington was arranging his retirement. Suddenly it seemed as if all Westland's chickens were coming home to roost.

Gandhi had been proving a testing ally ever since his mother's death. He had been trying to force Britain to clamp down on emigré Sikh extremists in London, and was highly critical of the Government's response. Now he had detected the weaknesses of the W30 which Mrs Gandhi had said she would buy.

This was far more of a disaster than the Foreign Office and the DTI realised at the time: if India pulled out of the deal, Westland faced not only a grave strategic problem, but, because of its borrowings from NatWest and Barclays, the prospect of imminent bankruptcy. The Board of Westland did not wish anyone outside to know, but some, including Admiral Treacher, plainly grasped that the jig was up.

It was five days later that Columbus Iselin had his secret meeting with two of the Westland directors. Eight days after that, Michael Heseltine made the long-feared public announcement that 'Air Staff Target 404' – the defence helicopter contract – had been officially withdrawn. He said he was forced to abide by the advice of the military on such issues. Few people at Westland believed this novel claim that ministers were powerless before the whims of the Chiefs of Staff. But the effect was immediate: the Zimbabwe Army, which was thinking of buying some W30s, was dismayed by the lack of British endorsement, and withdrew.

At the beginning of that month, Westland's share price had been

115p and falling (it was already down from 143p the previous year). By the end of March, it had slid again to 103p, the price at which Baynards Holdings AG decided to buy another 200,000 shares.

Meanwhile, Mrs Thatcher had thrown herself into the role of international lobbyist for British industry. In April, she diverted from a planned tour of the Far East to make a hurriedly-arranged trip to India. There she lectured Gandhi on the need to 'honour his promises', reminding him that his mother had virtually contracted to buy the helicopters. Gandhi complained again about Sikh terrorists at large in Britain, and did not appear keen to dwell on the topic of W30s. His officials raised yet more technical complaints about the machine – the safety margins on takeoff, for example.

Two days later, messages arrived back in London from the PM's entourage in New Delhi, and Junior Defence Minister Adam Butler, accompanied by Air Chief Marshal Sir John Rogers, went to see the Westland directors at their London headquarters in Carlton Gardens. They broke the news that Gandhi was still being difficult, and offered a sop: the RAF was prepared to buy another twelve Sea Kings and find a use for them in Northern Ireland.

Westland was less grateful than ministers might have expected. Admiral Treacher commented, 'We said, "Twelve more Sea Kings is fine, but it doesn't help our liquidity with the £17 million inventory we have for another kind of airplane... What we need is orders for the W30. Can you find some way in which you can use these twenty-one W30s which are marching down the production line?"'

At this point the spectre of Sikorsky was specifically raised. The MoD were told that if Westland were not bailed out 'a possible consequence... might well be a link with Sikorsky, and Sikorsky taking a stake in Westland.'

Treacher says that the RAF at least were impressed by this: 'We got to the point where Sir John Rogers actually put forward a proposal that the military might take the twenty helicopters we hoped to sell to India. So there was clearly thinking and dialogue between ourselves and the Ministry.'

Eight days later, the Foreign Office minister in charge of aid, Timothy Raison, was sent to India in Mrs Thatcher's wake. This time there were British threats. If Gandhi would not buy the helicopters, then Britain might not give him £45 million of the 'aid' he had been offered. Gandhi replied that, despite Westland modifications, the helicopters were too big, and too costly to run. Why couldn't he spend the 'aid' on buying some distinctly overpriced British Harriers for his Navy? The Overseas Development Administration were genuinely taken aback: aid was charity to be spent on, well, development. Not on military purchases...

43

Progress on the helicopter front, therefore, had been minimal by the time Alan Bristow, after some final confidential talks at the MoD with Clive Whitmore and Adam Butler, unveiled his bid to a shocked Sir Basil Blackwell at the end of April. Butler, son of the former Home Secretary 'Rab' Butler, and a man whose expertise lay in administration rather than the more flamboyant approach to politics, found Bristow altogether too maverick a character for his taste. But Heseltine thought of him, according to his friends, as 'the ideal market solution'.

Bristow's new company, Bristow Rotorcraft, offered the equivalent of 150p a share, or £89 million for Westland. Bristow himself and his institutional backers were going to put in another £60 million cash to bail out the company, and, although he did not mention it at the time, they had another £30 million available for any eventualities.

What Bristow intended to do was make a deal with Sikorsky, and scrap the W30. As he said at the time, 'The entry into the civil market with the W30 has been very costly and ill-conceived ... it is not competitive in price, performance, reliability or direct operating costs.' He promised 'to dispel any belief that the Government owes Westland a living'.

On any objective analysis, Westland were crazy to refuse him. Bristow knew to an extent how weak the company was, since Admiral Treacher had passed on some, if by no means all, of the awful facts. Aldington had retired, leaving Blackwell to inherit a bed of nails as new chairman. There were no counter-offers available.

But Blackwell did refuse, indignantly. He announced, 'The Board intends to oppose the offer vigorously, and believes its own strategy for Westland is in the best interest of the shareholders.' In order to bolster that strategy, Blackwell tried to find a white knight. He went to Raffaello Teti, head of Westland's Italian partners Agusta. 'We had always had a magnificent relationship with Westland,' Teti says. 'A stupendous relationship, a gentlemanly one. We were all technicians, not politicians.' Agusta certainly wanted to keep two joint Euro-projects alive, the big EH101 and the Anglo-Italian battlefield helicopter, a deal for which had just been signed in the Mediterranean on the decks of the Royal Yacht *Britannia*. (The yacht is freqently hired out these days to impress foreign businessmen.)

But Agusta had no money. Smallest of the European firms, it was in crisis too, with 4,000 of its 10,500 workers on state-subsidised lay-off and the Italian government involved in a vigorous rescue operation, raising its own shareholding and pumping in funds. Teti recalls, 'Blackwell shouted S.O.S.! Agusta is a state company ... I had to pass on the file to the holding company EFIM to get the opinion of the ministry. This was going to take a long time.'

So Blackwell tried two British giants, GEC and British Aerospace, who supplied millions of pounds worth of weapons and electronics for Westland helicopters. But neither was in a charitable mood.

GEC, headed by the former Cabinet Minister Jim Prior, and Lord Weinstock, said it was not interested. (It had previously refused to invest in Bristow's bid too, on the grounds that 'Westland is a very shaky company.') On 15 May, Sir Austin Pearce of BAe said the same. The newly-privatised company saw no point in a takeover, which would merely lead them to sack everyone at Yeovil, and move what work there was to their own factories. Sir Austin now says, 'It was not right to use BAe shareholders' money, first to take Yeovil over and then spend a lot of money closing it down.'

The Prime Minister of India chose that month to demonstrate publicly that he shared Bristow's lack of faith in the W30. He announced for the first time that India had definitely cancelled its order. The Prime Minister of Britain demonstrated publicly that she was not going to be pushed around by Rajiv Gandhi. She announced that Britain had definitely cancelled its allocation of 'aid'.

This was of little help to Blackwell, who announced disconsolately, 'We are surprised and it would not be going too far to say we are hurt by the loss of the order.' He made yet another, more desperate approach, in secret, to Lord Hanson, the 'predatory peer'. Having previously turned down Bristow, Hanson proceeded courteously, in the course of a half-hour meeting, to turn down Blackwell.

Only one bitter course remained. At the end of May, after Bristow had published his full offer, with the capture to date of 17 per cent of the shares, Schroder Wagg, Westland's bankers, had urged the remaining shareholders to hold on. The company planned links, they said, with 'a substantial international organisation'. Blackwell was finally going cap in hand to the company he had shrugged off so impetuously – Sikorsky.

He was too late. The following day saw the opening of the Paris airshow. Alan Bristow flew there and put his own deal to Sikorsky. 'He told us that if he succeeded in acquiring Westland, he would have a company with no product,' says Iselin. He wanted a licence to build the Black Hawk. 'We said yes. After all, we had been actively soliciting Westland since 1982.' Bristow also asked if Sikorsky were interested in an 'equity position'. Sikorsky said they would wait for the full figures on Westland's finances.

When Blackwell himself asked Sikorsky for a takeover bid, he was refused out of hand. Columbus Iselin says, 'Westland came to us to stop Bristow. But we were not prepared to make an investment in the old management . . . The board did not understand what was going on in the industry. They should have cut their losses on the W30 at an early stage, but they were ensconced in an ivory tower.'

Blackwell surrendered on Wednesday 13 June, recommending shareholders to take Bristow's offer. But if Ministers thought their problem was over, they received a shock that weekend. Bristow, in meetings with Norman Tebbit, suddenly threatened to withdraw his bid, and the Prime Minister herself was forced to intervene, calling two crisis meetings.

'Bristow got cold feet,' one Minister says. It was scarcely surprising. Bristow could not get answers to his financial questions. He was receiving leaks from within Westland, and sources in Rolls-Royce had tipped him off that the company had ordered unsuspected dozens of helicopter engines from them. There were heavy commitments on helicopters leased, rather than sold; most ominous of all, Bristow was becoming aware that Westland owed the Government £40 million 'launch aid' for the W30 which he intended to scrap.

Bristow demanded that the Government, in turn, bail him out. He asked them to waive their rights to the return of the 'launch aid', and also to buy up to twenty-five of the redundant W30s. This was a total package in the region of £100 million, although Bristow pointed out the Foreign Office would save the £65 million free gift it was originally going to make to India. If Westland was not bailed out, there would be no cash in the firm to fund the big EH101 helicopter project for the Navy. For the first time, the full Thatcher 'economic squad' was forced to bring its views to bear on the problems of Westland helicopters.

Five departments were involved on the following Monday morning: the Prime Minister; the Treasury, headed by the Chief Secretary John MacGregor; the 'super-ministry' of Trade and Industry, headed by Norman Tebbit; and, relatively low in terms of political influence in this gathering, Heseltine's MoD. The Overseas Development Agency, administering 'aid' under Foreign Office control, was last and least of the political actors. Accounts of the meeting suggest there were certain dogmas taken as read – 'No Nationalisation', 'No Hand-outs' and 'No Lame Ducks'.

Beyond that, there were competing departmental interests. The Treasury did not wish to hand over money. Mrs Thatcher was irritated at the appearance without warning of a crisis, which seemed intimately connected with the troublesome Heseltine. Tebbit's department had paid out the generous 'launch aid' in the first place, and could scarcely have wished to lose face by writing it off. It was difficult to justify aid to industry at all in terms of pure Thatcherite theology. Heseltine, Bristow's main backer, wanted to establish that the crisis was either the fault of the DTI for failing to monitor the company, or of the company itself for keeping quiet. He also feared that the two dozen helicopters – whether for a 'strategic transport reserve', or use in Ulster, or for famine relief – would end up on his budget.

The Ministers met and wrangled, under Mrs Thatcher's chairmanship. Heseltine had a positive proposal. Up to £40 million would be put in, he suggested, provided it was split fifty-fifty between his department and the Treasury. It would include an 'incentive element' for Westland to carry on trying to sell helicopters. The meeting adjourned until the next day, to await developments.

But by then, the Bank of England, in close liaison with the Treasury, was making its own move. Alan Bristow had not increased his credit with City 'insiders' by what Westland called his 'unprecedented act of irresponsibility' in making and then withdrawing his bid. It would have been surprising if NatWest and Barclays, the two big clearing bank creditors, had not registered alarm.

David Walker, head of the Bank of England's industrial advisory unit, a body set up to keep a 'watch list' of strategically important British companies which run into financial difficulties, was due for a meeting with a banker who had some experience of rescuing large companies. Walker did not give away any names, but said to him, 'Some British clearing banks are particularly exposed to a major British company... And there's unease among the institutions about the quality of its management. Are you interested?' Yes, said the banker, he was.

On Tuesday 19 January, the Treasury turned down a Government rescue. Tebbit refused to write off the launch aid either. Heseltine's proposal was squashed.

Mrs Thatcher's final conclusion was that the Government should do precisely nothing. Let Bristow pull out, she argued. It was the banks in the City of London who were owed money, so the City could find its own way of getting it back. Tebbit, the same night, boasted to Chingford Tories that subsidies to British industry were being dramatically cut. It was a claim that Ministers would have cause to reconsider.

There was only one real recovery possibility, apart from bankruptcy; this was that Sir Basil Blackwell should be removed and Westland's future be handed over to a US company. Mrs Thatcher may have realised this, because shortly afterwards she circulated departments with her scribbled view that a Sikorsky bid should be 'openly considered'. She has a high opinion of American management.

All that Parliament was told about the Westland manoeuvres was a curious statement by Geoffrey Pattie, in an adjournment debate immediately after the Bristow bid's public collapse. He affected surprise at complaints that the Government had apparently remained silent: 'What else would have been proper for us to do? When a private company is the subject of a bid, there is no way the Government can take a view one way or another.'

The Government was to pay a high price in the end for its policy of concealed manoeuvre. NatWest and Barclays, through the Bank of England, egged on by Treacher and a number of anxious Westland directors, promptly had Sir Basil Blackwell deposed. In his place they put a man whose formidable single-mindedness was, in the course of the next six months, to topple two Cabinet Ministers and lay waste the public image of the Thatcher Government.

His name was Sir John Cuckney.

Chapter Five

THE COMPANY DOCTOR

'I hate being bullied by Ministers'

– Sir John Cuckney

Sir John Cuckney's professional career began with a secret. He was a member of MI5 for ten years, leaving the service only after Suez in 1957. For some of the time, he was posted abroad. MI5 controlled 'internal security' in all the then British colonies such as Malaya, and had liaison men in the capitals of the white Commonwealth. It was not all that unusual a career for young men of the right family who had done bravely in the war. Cuckney's father had been an Air Vice Marshal and he himself had served as a paratrooper.

But to spend several years 'attached to the War Office', working from the old Leconfield House building in Curzon Street during the Burgess-Maclean-Philby era, must have been an odd experience. It was a world where everything was done in obscure Whitehall corridors by secret connections. Those who have worked there say the greatest danger is that one develops an unrealistic sense of one's own superiority.

Cuckney may have felt the pressures. He left saying that one should not be a secret policeman too long, that it strained the sense of humour and did not give one enough freedom. Curzon Street had widespread connections with merchant banks; he moved to Standard Industrial and to Lazards, and rose fast.

When he took over the chairmanship of Westland, Cuckney was at the peak of his powers. Sometimes referred to as the 'company doctor' who never had a patient die on him, he had just completed a complex company rescue involving the John Brown engineering company, eight major creditor banks and financial institutional shareholders in the City of London. The rescue had attracted less publicity than other

49

capital reconstructions achieved by Cuckney over the previous fifteen years – the Crown Agents, Mersey Dock and Harbour Board and the Port of London Authority – but it had given him personal satisfaction. John Brown he recalls as a model of how banks and the shareholders can cooperate to save a famous name. The Bank of England had pressed him, again, into service, and he thought that, with a little luck, he could expect a similarly smooth passage.

Cuckney was skilled in the ways of Whitehall. Not only was there his MI5 experience; his jobs for government had also included setting up the Property Services Agency which controls all government buildings, and dispersing the bureaucratic fog enveloping the loss-making Crown Agents which buys and sells for former colonial governments. Only the previous month he had relinquished, after ten years, the chairmanship of International Military Services, an MoD-owned company which specialised in arms production and sales. The experience had given him numerous contacts within Defence and the Cabinet Office at the highest level. It had also, ironically, given him an insight into European defence collaboration; during his stint at IMS, he had helped put together a Spanish-German-Italian-British venture to produce a medium-weight gun, the FH 70.

Conservative-voting, conservatively dressed, Cuckney may not have appeared a colourful character. But he was enormously effective at the job he had carved out for himself. When it came to mounting company financial rescues, he had drawn up a few rules of thumb, which, he now says, give clues to his own performance during the Westland affair: never conduct post-mortems on the previous management; beware of armchair strategies or self-proclaimed experts; make sure that you have a binding rescue package which can be delivered on time; and above all, try to act in the interests of shareholders, employees and the creditor banks. He was later to add a further, more personal observation: he had a passionate dislike of being bullied by ministers.

The Bank of England's intervention stopped NatWest and Barclays from forcing Westland into receivership. They accepted the nomination of Sir John as 'company doctor', and gave him six months, until the publication of Westland's accounts at the end of the year, to devise a reconstruction. But the banks were still, of course, ultimately calling the tune. Westland had huge overdrafts of £40 million, and total debts three times greater than their capital base. The company was in no position to pay them back.

The banks would be reluctant to let their loans turn into what would be, in effect, a forced investment in the company's future, unless they liked what proposals they saw. Relatively few people grasped later, when the political arguments raged, that Sir John had not been hired to further the 'national interest'. That was the Government's job – and Mrs Thatcher had just retired from it. Cuckney was there to protect the interest of the banks.

Cuckney moved into Westland's small headquarters in Carlton Gardens, near St James's Park, on June 25, as Sir Basil Blackwell moved out. There was an atmosphere of considerable alarm at Westland and among its customers. The old board had commissioned a detailed financial survey from the accountants Price Waterhouse, and no one knew quite what horrors they would find as they poked about over the next six weeks. Cuckney kept Treacher on as his right-hand man. He also retained the lobbying firm of GJW Government Relations, who were to prove useful in providing contacts at the House of Commons. For the next three months he kept on most of the old board, including the Managing Director, Tony Reed, although their days were clearly numbered.

His first major axing was Westland's merchant bank, Schroder Wagg. He offered the business instead to Lazards. This was not merely because he had worked himself at Lazards in the past and was comfortable with them; the previous December, Lazards had promoted to chairman the merchant banker who was the immediate Tory predecessor of Michael Heseltine himself at the Ministry of Defence, John Nott.

It was the first of Cuckney's moves in building a powerful lobbying machine. Nott knew all the Cabinet personally. He also knew the Ministry of Defence inside out. Although remarkably few people spotted Nott's lean figure slipping in and out of Carlton Gardens, his ability to second-guess Michael Heseltine and read the minds of his former Tory colleagues was commercially invaluable.

Over the next three months, Cuckney looked around at his options. He then began to construct a draft deal with Sikorksy which was to infuriate the Ministry of Defence and appal every helicopter company in Europe. To begin with, it even made Mrs Thatcher blench.

Cuckney now says, 'Right from the first time I arrived, there was a possibility that Sikorsky would be a partner to consider.' Within three days of his arrival, the two pro-Sikorsky directors, Jones and Miller, were on the phone to Columbus Iselin with the new chairman's authority. Clearly, detailed negotiations would have to await the emergence of the Price Waterhouse study. But they responded. 'We want to talk,' Iselin says he replied. 'You know where I am. You call me.'

By the following Monday morning, Bill Paul of United Technologies had stepped off Concorde and was installed at the Inn on the Park in Mayfair holding two days of exploratory discussions with Jeffrey Jones and Admiral Treacher.

There was no doubt that Sikorsky would do a deal. But what sort of terms could a crippled company get? Cuckney had two possible levers to improve the company's bargaining position. The first was to get some backing and preferably some cash from the British Government. The second was to provoke a rival offer. There was another American firm showing interest, although its approaches to Westland were never revealed at the time. This was the Marmon Corporation of Chicago, a big mining and engineering group, which has a UK subsidiary, Kangol. Marmon also had an interest in a small US airline, but this was not the primary reason for sending its representatives to Yeovil. Marmon specialised in buying 'recovery situations' – turning round sick companies.

Cuckney was not enthusiastic, because they had no helicopter background; he wanted a compatible company, or in his own words, 'technological synergy'.

As far as Government was concerned, Cuckney had inherited from the Blackwell regime a pair of Departments – the DTI and MoD – who were ill at ease with each other but jointly had a low opinion of his company. 'They hated Aldington and Blackwell', one executive says. Cuckney puts it more delicately:

I was slightly surprised that there was not a closer and rather more friendly relationship between the company and its sponsor department (and indeed, its main customer department)... There was plenty of room on the company's side for a closer and improved relationship... it was largely a matter of personality.

Six days after the Sikorsky talks, Cuckney went to see Adam Butler at the MoD. Accounts there say Cuckney's tone was bland. He said he was not convinced he needed an outside partner; the City might put in some finance; his options were open. But what was the MoD's attitude towards Sikorsky? Butler said, 'The Government prefers control to stay in the UK. But it can envisage control passing to an international company. We want to see someone involved with experience of the helicopter industry, but we don't want a takeover. It's up to you really. The DTI is the "lead department", not us.'

Surprisingly little was said about Europe. The received MoD wisdom was that the idea of a single European helicopter industry was attractive, but unlikely.

Cuckney tried to mend fences with the DTI. The main thought in ministers' minds was the brief adjournment debate the Liberal MP Paddy Ashdown had obtained for 8 July, when something soothing would have to be said by a Minister in reply to him. Cuckney brought up with them the tricky question of the launch aid. He says:

> The problem was, we would never have got our accounts signed by the auditors nor embarked on a reconstruction, nor got it underwritten, if we had to disclose in our accounts that the DTI had the right of instant recall on that sum of money.

The DTI provisionally agreed to drop their right, set down in the small print, to demand immediate return of the £40 million. But they stalled on whether they would write the loan off altogether, talking of 'waiting for Price Waterhouse' – the full accountants' report on Westland. Cuckney did not know, of course, that Bristow had previously asked for the same government help and had been refused. Cuckney repeated another of Bristow's demands – that the Government buy up the Indian helicopters. Again he was blocked. 'It was understandable the Government wanted to wait,' he concedes.

In the 8 July debate, Geoffrey Pattie listened to a long complaint by Ashdown about Government harshness towards Westland, made with a clear eye to the reaction of his local voters. Pattie answered with the kind of remarks considered appropriate for the general public:

> Sir John has an outstanding reputation... His arrival has brought stability following the turmoil... we want a period of calm... the company believes there may be potential for sales of W30s in the US, Europe, the Gulf, Asia, Africa and Australia. We must not forget Westland is a private sector company. There is no government shareholding, and it is not for the Government to intervene in the management of the company or to seek to influence the form the company's future should take.

There was some truth in this version of the view the DTI had formed already of Cuckney. He impressed them, and they felt comfortable with him. But his early moves to find an alternative to Sikorsky were not productive. He tried to persuade British Aerospace to take him over, just as Blackwell had done earlier in the summer – an approach loaded with irony. Had Westland been nationalised along with the rest of the aircraft industry in 1977, it would by now have been the 'helicopter division' of BAe, safe from lean times, and in the same position as its big US rivals and the French.

The week after the parliamentary debate, Cuckney could be seen in the London offices of Sir Austin Pearce, BAe chairman, making his pitch. The two, who later became opponents, dispute what was said. Cuckney's version is:

> They were not interested in helping financially or in any participative way... I got the very firm impression they were very critical of Westland... They were not interested in contributing financially... They might have been prepared to help over management and other issues, but my impression was strong enough not to think there was any point in sending them a copy of the Price Waterhouse report.

Pearce says he told Cuckney, just as he had told Blackwell before, that BAe could offer a limited amount of cash, but no takeover:

> My recollection of that meeting is not the same as Cuckney's... I repeated my offer of financial help... I was not asked how much... Cuckney said one of his options might be receivership... I asked him to come back to us if we could help, but he did not.

Then, two days later, Cuckney presented himself in the office of Michael Heseltine at the MoD. His main tactic seems to have been to determine whether the Defence Secretary would respond any better to lobbying from a new chairman for the elusive RAF order. After all, Heseltine had publicly professed his 'warm support' for the appointment of Sir John Cuckney.

But things did not go particularly well. Heseltine was somewhat brusque. The last time he had been round this particular course with Westland, he had seen his ideas voted down by the DTI and the Prime Minister. Yet here he was, once again, being asked to raid the MoD's purchasing budget on behalf of the importunate helicopter-makers. Cuckney recalls:

> I knew there was a rather forlorn hope that the AST404... was then still a potentially live issue, and there had been talk, certainly in Westland, hoping that the W30 might meet it... I had only been a few weeks in office.

He says he told Heseltine how things looked, that Westland was too small, lacked financial muscle and needed an international partner. Cuckney did not ask at this stage for any government cash and he did not bring up Sikorsky. Instead, he dwelt on the idea of looming bankruptcy: 'Heseltine made it quite clear he had his own budget problems... His attitude was he did not particularly mind if we went into receivership.'

According to Cuckney, the Defence Secretary said that if Westland went bankrupt, GEC and BAe could 'pick up the pieces'. 'He made it quite clear he was not our sponsor department.'

Heseltine was bluffing to an extent. After Cuckney had left, he told members of his own department, 'I know I'll have to put some MoD money in at the end of the day.'

One of them says, 'He and Cuckney had a big row about Heseltine's attitude, with Cuckney accusing him of wanting to see Westland in receivership. Well, that was all part of the game.'

The question of Europe did not figure largely in this poker session, although it was certainly made clear that the Government's helicopter policy, insofar as it had one, was European. Cuckney equally made clear that he preferred a 'pragmatic approach', which seems an understandable attitude for a banker.

As the summer wore on, and Sikorsky spoke ever more openly in Washington of its plans, Heseltine became increasingly active in other big European deals. There was certainly very little competition for this task within the Thatcher government, and he did display an impressive talent in the field.

It was on 2 August that Heseltine finally secured the European Fighter agreement which ensured a new generation of expensive fighter-planes would be built collaboratively, giving Britain the prospect – say his friends – of saving £1 billion. It cost him another bruising collision with Tebbit's DTI, which was prepared to abandon a 'European deal'. And it was the following month, after repeated trips to the Middle East, that Heseltine sold an enormous batch of the existing European Tornado fighters to Saudi Arabia for $4 billion. Characteristically, he did not think it necessary even to send the papers to the DTI, although they 'sponsored' the British firms who would benefit.

The European fighter was regarded by Heseltine as one of his major triumphs, and indeed this is the sort of government buying spree which explains Cabinet Ministers' condescending references to Westland as a '£30 million company'. But while Heseltine's mind was elsewhere, Sikorsky was moving at high speed. It mounted a direct lobby of the MoD on 1 August, and appeared to win over Heseltine's purchasing chief, Peter Levene. If Sikorsky is to be believed, he was accommodating. Iselin recalls, 'We wanted to know what their reaction would be. Were they enthusiastic? Did they want us to disappear? Shall we stick the end of our elbow in the water to see whether it's too hot for baby?'

He says Levene told him the Defence Ministry would support a Sikorsky investment of any level, provided Westland still 'appeared to remain British'. Sikorsky groped for a ceiling of acceptability: they agreed on 40 per cent. Levene demanded a 'floor' of a 15 per cent minimum stake, 'because less would be meaningless, and would not represent a genuine commitment... These were the guidelines on which the British government said it would sanction our involvement and agree to a Black Hawk licence.'

Geoffrey Pattie at the DTI recalls similar approaches. But he emphasises, 'There was no suggestion then that we should contribute'. On 8 August, Cuckney met Tebbit to probe the DTI's attitude.

What is fascinating about these summer manoeuvres is that they demonstrate, just as Alan Bristow's earlier soundings had, that the notion of 'market forces' was seen, by Government and companies alike, as a complete pretence. In the real world, no big company would dream of trying to take over or join forces with a firm like Westland unless it got discreet government permission. To all intents, the Government is the only 'market force' in the game.

On 15 August, a week after preparing the ground with Levene, the eight volumes of the Price Waterhouse report arrived at Westland, and Sikorsky was able to get down to the serious consideration of a deal. Cuckney says:

> The United Technologies reaction was immensely professional. They appointed bankers, brokers, solicitors, very quickly. They flew a team of about sixteen over and they invited us to visit their factories. There was another team of about eighteen shortly after that.

Whitmore and Hayes at their respective departments were told by Sir John, 'There seems no viable alternative to Sikorsky.' Cuckney had not approached the disliked French, the Germans or the Italians.

The Price Waterhouse report was later presented as a document which gripped everyone with a sense of dire emergency. In fact, it told Cuckney little that was not already clear. He would soon run out of cash, because up to £90 million was being thrown away on stocks for apparently unsaleable W30 helicopters. And what would occupy Westland workers for the rest of the 1980s?

It was true that, by the year's end, Westland would be moving into what Cuckney calls 'technical insolvency', exceeding borrowing powers in the company's Articles, and breaching the terms under which it had raised £30 million in an issue of debenture stock (entitled to priority payments over ordinary shareholders). But 'technical' is the key word. The banks had agreed to put Cuckney in, and the banks were not going to rock the City boat by refusing to refinance him. 'Bankruptcy' was not an impending natural catastrophe; it was merely the final weapon in the hands of the creditors.

Over the next six weeks, a deal was sorted out which might suit the two key parties to the negotiations, Sikorsky and the bankers. If it had gone through, it certainly would not have suited either the British taxpayer or the European helicopter industry.

Further work on the W30 was to be scrapped. The medium-term Westland problem was to be solved by making American Black Hawk helicopters under licence. They would be 'anglicised' by installing a more powerful Anglo-French engine from Rolls-Royce and Turbo-meca.

The question of who would buy them was never finally spelled out. But continued pressure could be put on the British Defence Ministry. The deal would probably also kill off the embryonic project for a European transport helicopter. This would open up the rest of the European market. Sikorsky would have got through the stockade.

The second half of the deal was more delicate. Something like £75 million would be raised to tide Westland over its immediate cash crisis. The three parties concerned – Sikorsky, the institutional shareholders and the banks – would each chip in and share future control of the company. But all three intended to take care that they got their money back, and had no liability for any further expense. How was such a conjuring trick to be performed?

Once again, it was the British Government that was to be expected to pay for the 'private sector solution'. The Government was to spend more than £120 million to buy up no fewer than forty-five of the redundant W30 helicopters: this would clear out all Westland's useless stock. After all, Britain might still manage to give twenty-one of them away to the Indians. Furthermore, the DTI was to forget the debt of £40 million for the futile 'launch aid'. And workers would still need to be sacked to make ends meet. The Department of Employment would find £25 million for their statutory redundancy pay.

In return for this largesse, costed later by Heseltine as more than £200 million, the Government was not to take any shareholding. Westland was to remain an 'independent' private enterprise, controlled only by the banks and the Americans. It could be argued that it was a high and, indeed, a bizarre price to pay to preserve the dogmas of Thatcherism. Cuckney was forced to resort later in the autumn to one of the oldest tricks in the defence lobbyist's book in an

57

attempt to sell the proposition – that the 'national interest' demanded it.

Meanwhile, the Westland unions – 11,000 people at Yeovil and its satellites at Weston-super-Mare and the Isle of Wight, some making even more unsaleable hovercraft – faced uncertainty and secrecy.

Sir Robert Armstrong, the Cabinet Secretary, later told the little story of the hen and the pig to explain why civil servants should be allowed to keep their secrets from an investigating committee. The hen and the pig, said Sir Robert, were on a journey and stopped at a motorway café. The hen wanted to order eggs and bacon, but the pig refused: 'For you,' said the pig, 'it's just a contribution. But for me, it's a total commitment.'

The story fits the plight of the workers rather better. For the bankers and indeed the Government, the affair was just about a contribution and who should make it. For the workforce, the very nature of their lives was at stake. This human dimension is lacking from the Whitehall documents that emerged from the Westland affair: the nearest Leon Brittan, the Trade and Industry Secretary, came to it was to write a report to Mrs Thatcher giving as the very last reason of all for agreeing to a package deal: 'POLITICAL: that if the Government does not help, it will be blamed for allowing the company to go into receivership.'

Unfortunately, the unions, egged on by the company management, knew of nothing better to do than lobby for government purchases. During August, union delegations travelled up to Whitehall once again to plead the case, which they had put to a succession of ministers down at Yeovil. They wanted the MoD to buy at least eighty of the W30 helicopters which the Yeovil management had once assured them would sell in their hundreds. 'We would have preferred ... that the Government place further orders for the W30 and that we have the Indian deal,' the unions were later to testify. 'We would have looked to retain our independence.'

A fortnight later, Mrs Thatcher reshuffled her Government. It was an event which led some wits at the MoD to claim that Sara Keays was to blame for the subsequent Westland affair. Mrs Thatcher was anxious to bring back Cecil Parkinson, who had been forced to resign after the disclosure of his relationship with his secretary, Sara Keays. The scheme was now that Parkinson should return to the DTI.

A few days before the reshuffle, however, Conservative Central Office realised that Miss Keays was about to publish her memoirs, reminding the world of Parkinson's behaviour. Mrs Thatcher reluctantly dropped the plan. In a last-minute decision, Leon Brittan, the most loyal Minister available, was moved from the Home

Secretaryship and drafted into the job. Tebbit took over the Party chairmanship, but remained a member of all the key economic committees. There was no question of Heseltine being allowed to take over the DTI.

Despite the changes in Whitehall, the Sikorsky lobby proceeded cautiously but steadily. On 3 September, Heseltine, still at work on his Oxfordshire garden, was rung at home by Bill Walker, the Tory MP whom Sikorsky used as an intermediary. 'Bill Paul wants to meet you,' he said. A meeting was fixed for a couple of weeks ahead.

But Cuckney may have begun to fear Sikorsky were cooling. For on the same day, he belatedly sounded out the Italian company Agusta on a rival tie-up. The head of Agusta was due to arrive at his office for routine talks on their joint EH101 scheme... It was the first approach Cuckney had made to them, and was to lead Raffaello Teti of Agusta to accuse Cuckney of double-dealing. For Cuckney left Teti with the impression that no one else had been approached. Cuckney says:

Agusta had financial constraints... At that stage they were not empowered to contribute, though they did, much later. Teti understood our problem, and said it was a fraction of the size of his own but he understood the difference between being nationalised and not being nationalised when you get into financial problems. He did not have any money immediately to hand.

Teti's version is different in tone:

He asked me if I would participate in increasing the capital of Westland. I asked if he had any information to evaluate the company. Either at that meeting or later, he said, "No. First you tell me if you are interested. After that, I'll show you the documentation."... To tell the truth, he wasn't very polite...

Little more than a week later, Admiral Treacher must have been feeling the situation called for desperate steps. He made a second visit to British Aerospace, this time begging them, not to mount a takeover, but to become a 'major industrial partner'. Treacher may not have realised that only two days earlier, Lygo could have been seen in Stratford, Connecticut, saying to Sikorsky, 'Are you really serious about Westland? Have you seen the accounts?' Sikorsky had said, 'Yes. But we want a base in Europe.'

So Lygo's reply was blunt: 'How much?'

'Thirty million. We'll recover. It will be a bargain. You'll be able to aquire more shares.'

'Pay thirty million for a bust company with an option to buy more shares at the full price if it recovers? You must be mad.'

Over the next fortnight, Sikorsky's parent company's top men, Bill Paul and Hubert Faure, the UT president, were closeted with John Nott and Marcus Agius at Lazards merchant bank. Cuckney found their teams of financial advisers 'very impressive ... They impressed us as people who would be capable of taking quick decisions without any political issues ... The professionalism was comforting when we were drifting on to the financial rocks.'

The possibility revived after all that the Indian deal might be resurrected; Gandhi was to visit London the following month, and promising preliminary talks were held. Sir Clive and Sir Brian at the MoD and the DTI were circulated with memoranda from Lazards urging the Government to underwrite the Indian deal, as Yeovil technicians flew out to Bombay to try and modify the craft. Relations between Westland and Whitehall were humming.

Before he presented his scheme for government subsidy, Cuckney made some moves which were to be of crucial importance in the battle that developed. He cleared out some of the old guard from the board, including the managing director, Tony Reed. He brought in three men: Charles Verrall as finance director from the Midland Bank; Sir John Maldwyn Thomas, deputy chairman of John Brown and former head of Rank Xerox – and a third, key appointment.

This was the former Tory MP Anthony Royle. Royle was 'wired in' as a potential lobbyist to the City, Westminster and the Government. An Old Harrovian, he had sat for the safe seat of Richmond in Yorkshire for twenty-four years, turning it over to the present Trade and Industry Secretary himself, Leon Brittan, only at the previous election. Royle had served for several years as a Conservative Central Office vice-chairman. He was a close associate of Lord King, the British Airways chairman whose expertise at political infighting was legendary. Ennobled by Mrs Thatcher as Lord Fanshawe on his retirement in 1983, Royle was on several City boards, including Brooke Bond, where he had worked with Cuckney.

Fanshawe made a proposition to Cuckney: that Westland should hire, on a confidential basis, the flamboyant Tory propagandist, Gordon Reece. Many people in the company had no idea Reece had been hired, and nor did Michael Heseltine. Reece had made his name as Mrs Thatcher's personal adviser on public relations, and had lately been running Conservative Central Office publicity. He was an intriguingly Americanised figure – a TV producer who had graduated from *Emergency Ward 10* and the Eamonn Andrews show to the selling of Margaret Thatcher. It was he who was credited with teaching Mrs Thatcher to lower her voice and concentrate her propaganda on women's magazines and the Jimmy Young radio show. It was he who recommended the *Sun* and the *Daily Mail* as better indicators of public opinion than the heavier papers, and who struck a new note in two victorious election campaigns by suggesting 'photo-opportunities' of Mrs Thatcher touring chocolate factories or cuddling calves. It was he who is said to have told Mrs Thatcher to refer to troops in the Falklands as 'our boys'.

Reece now sold images from an office in Park Lane. But his buyers tended to be of a peculiarly political kind. Lord King of British Airways was one of the first; he had a major fight to prevent ministers giving lucrative routes to the rival airline, British Caledonian, and, with Reece's help, it succeeded.

In August 1985, the chief executive of Guinness, Ernest Saunders, hired Reece to promote his controversial attempt to take over Bell's, the Scottish whisky distillers. If enough political support was not maintained, there was a danger of a monopolies investigation. To the accompaniment of an extravagant advertising campaign, Guinness won over the Scottish press and the politicians; Saunders kept Reece on the payroll while he successfully pursued a second contentious takeover bid – this time for the bigger whisky firm of Distillers.

If a tycoon had business anywhere near Whitehall, the odds were that Reece would pop up, if not as a 'confidential adviser' then – as in the case of the Egyptian Al-Fayed brothers, successful buyers of Harrods – as a personal friend.

What exactly was it that Reece had for sale? His PR slogans were regarded by his rivals as somewhat banal – they could be seen throughout the Westland affair, in the recurrent claims that the firm was only interested in commerce, not politics; that Sikorsky represented a 'NATO' solution, unlike the French; and that a Sikorsky tie-up had something to do with 'high-tech'. But this public advertising came much later in the affair.

Cuckney himself says he had been through politically disputed rescues before in his career, and he needed somebody who knew the ropes. Reece offers the public thought that he 'manages political risks' for big companies. His usual response to inquiries about Westland is that he was hired to 'get the climate of opinion right' to promote government underwriting of the Indian deal. It is probably true that the average City businessman is impressed by someone who appears to have an easy intimacy with Mrs Thatcher – Reece was regularly invited to spend Christmas Day with her and her family.

And, as one of Westland's PR team said, 'He could tell us how the PM was likely to be thinking.' It is also true that Mrs Thatcher's attitude was to turn out to be absolutely vital to the outcome of the contest.

Cuckney's team now represented a formidable challenge to any Cabinet Minister. It was almost American in its lobbying 'clout'. Senior military men and government politicians were on the board. At executive level, former ministry officials like Gueterbock worked with the Parliamentary lobbyists from GJW. Their merchant bank was run by John Nott, a recent member of the Thatcher cabinet. And the chairman's personal adviser was Mrs Thatcher's own publicity man. It had a striking resemblance to the kind of team assembled so successfully by Lord King himself to force his views on recalcitrant ministers.

On 21 September Walker the MP took Paul of Sikorsky along to Heseltine's office. He wanted to suggest to him that Sikorsky only wanted to help. Walker says, 'Heseltine told Paul the MoD had no requirement and no money for the Black Hawk – and no money to put into the rescue package. Paul assured him, "We are prepared only to take a minority stake in Westland, and we are prepared to give them work." We left believing that at the very least we had a fair wind for this.'

Heseltine described this meeting later to the Commons in diplomatic terms: 'I told them we had to preserve all options.' Privately, he described it to colleagues as the moment the scales fell from his eyes. One says, 'Heseltine maintained his officials had been briefing him that Sikorsky seemed to be the only way. He says that meeting had a significant effect on him. He realised for the first time that all they were in it for was to find an outlet for the Black Hawk. All the emphasis throughout was on the Black Hawk and their new US project, the LHX. Sikorsky were embarking on a conscious sales effort.'

Heseltine much later vigorously denounced the Sikorsky approach to the Commons Industry Committee: '... Sikorsky were going to use every device known to man to get the British government to buy Black Hawk... they were deeply embarrassed how unsuccessful it had been, how few they'd sold. They'd tried all over the place.'

It is clear that Bill Paul had failed to soften Heseltine up. Three days later, a draft proposal from Cuckney arrived on Heseltine's desk, via the DTI. There was a mention of contacts with Agusta, but Sikorsky was plainly the only real contender.

'I'm appalled!' Heseltine told Whitmore and Richard Mottram, his private secretary. 'Completely appalled!' He scrawled emphatically on the dossier, 'No option except receivership to be discussed without my express authority!' Privately, he announced that if the company was going to demand such monstrous sums from the public purse, it could go bust instead as far as he was concerned.

Cuckney's propositions were laced with heavy references to this 'strategic company' on which Britain's armed forces depended for their vital flow of spares, and the aircraft of the future, with the clear message that the MoD should provide the equivalent of £20,000 per head of the company's workforce, in the 'national interest'. Heseltine, who is prone to inveighing against 'the City' and its interest in short-term profits, was scornful.

Whitmore, only too aware of his master's remarks about putting the firm into liquidation, prudently decided to hang on to a cheque – for £6 million – scheduled to be sent to Westland as one of the generous advance payments on their military contracts to supply Sea King spares. The money was not legally due to Westland, in the MoD's new, cautious view. If the creditors were to be left high and dry, he did not want the Public Accounts Committee icily inquiring at some embarrassing future interrogation, 'And whatever possessed you, Sir Clive, to hand over £6 million of the taxpayers' money to a firm which you knew was about to go bankrupt?'

To Heseltine, it was Cuckney and the Americans who were the manipulators, trying to use their backstairs influence with the MoD. But the decision was officially in the hands of another Minister – his colleague at the DTI. A ministerial meeting between them would have now to take place to fix the Government's 'line' and give Sir John an official response.

For Leon Brittan, the new Secretary for Trade and Industry, Westland was something of a distraction from the main affair on his agenda; the attempted sale of the motor company Austin Rover lock, stock and barrel to the US. It was a project of which Heseltine was kept in ignorance.

When, therefore, the two met in the first week of October, their attitudes were very different. Neither of them had any sense that this was a particularly significant meeting, however. And there was certainly no indication that this was the beginning of a collision that would eventually cost them both their jobs.

Chapter Six

THE MATING DANCE OF THE SWAN

*'People who have a burning sense of mission are
the most dangerous of all'*

– Leon Brittan, January 1981

There was no doubting the legal expertise of Leon Brittan. At one of
the most critical stages in the Westland drama, on his feet in the House
of Commons, he was being pressed to confirm or deny whether the
Prime Minister had received a letter.

It was a matter of the utmost delicacy. To admit to knowledge of the
letter would expose Brittan to difficult and possibly damaging
questions about its contents. To deny it altogether would be to risk
misleading the House – an unforgivable parliamentary sin.

Brittan chose instead to fence with his questioners. Asked whether
he had received a letter, he denied it; asked whether any *other* member
of the Government had received one, he said he could only speak for
himself; pressed to say whether the letter came from the *Chief
Executive* of the firm involved, he said he was 'not aware' of it.

Technically, Brittan had got away with it – he did not lie to the
House. But within a matter of hours he was back in the Chamber,
apologising contritely to MPs 'if I have given a misleading
impression'. There had indeed been a letter from the *Chairman* of the
company, but he had not been able to confirm that because it was
marked Private and Confidential to the Prime Minister.

'The extraordinary thing about his performance that afternoon',
said one MP present, 'was his demeanour. Here was Leon in a
desperately tight spot, but I could swear he was actually enjoying it all.
He was back in court fencing with a clever witness and scoring all the
points.

'It was completely the wrong approach.'

The episode sums up three qualities which have marked the rapid rise and equally sudden fall from power of Leon Brittan QC, MP. They are an undoubted cleverness, tinged with arrogance; unquestioning loyalty to his leader; and a flawed judgment when it comes to political pragmatism. 'He possesses an unfortunate tendency to talk himself into trouble,' said one commentator.

Until he became Home Secretary at the age of forty-three – the youngest since Winston Churchill – Brittan's career had been dazzling. President of the Cambridge Union, a double first (English and Law), Chairman of the Bow Group, a brilliant libel lawyer, QC at thirty-nine, Junior Minister at forty.

Some observers found it hard to say precisely where he stood on the political spectrum, although his patron and friend was Sir Geoffrey Howe, Mrs Thatcher's Chancellor, a lawyer of liberal inclinations, but a firm monetarist. He himself refused to be classified. 'If you ask my views on a particular subject I will tell you them,' was his favourite response.

His family was Lithuanian. His grandfather had been a doctor in the Lithuanian capital of Vilna, and his father studied medicine in Berlin before emigrating to Britain and setting up in practice in Cricklewood, North London, where he and his elder brother Sam, the *Financial Times* columnist, grew up in an Orthodox Jewish household.

Success at Cambridge and the Bar led finally to success in politics, though he applied and was rejected for fifteen seats before he was chosen for Cleveland and Whitby, entering Parliament for the first time in 1974. Almost immediately he showed his grasp of political and legal detail when, as opposition spokesman on the complex issue of Devolution, he steered his party's case through the House of Commons. His promotion thereafter was rapid.

Monday 5 January 1981 was a red-letter day for Brittan. A party for two hundred guests was thrown by Geoffrey and Elspeth Howe at No 11 Downing Street to celebrate his marriage two weeks earlier to Diana Peterson, who had been married previously and had two daughters. Relatively late in life, Brittan had become a husband and stepfather.

In the middle of the party, Howe clapped his hands and called for silence. He wished his guests to know that that morning Mrs Thatcher had promoted Leon Brittan to be Chief Secretary to the Treasury. After less than twenty months' experience in government, he was now a member of the Cabinet. Beaming, Brittan acknowledged the applause. It was, he admitted later, the happiest evening of his life.

The new job was a testing one: to keep the spending Ministers in line with the Government's strict financial targets, and bully them if they rebelled. Brittan performed it tactfully but firmly, joining battle with, amongst others, Michael Heseltine at Environment and John Nott at Defence. Although in Round One of the exercise they got away with £5,000 million more than the Treasury had hoped, Brittan came back next year and did a brilliant deal with Heseltine, whereby £7,000 million of excess bids at the MoD were knocked out.

His speeches during this period were regularly in favour of tough budget policies, and privatisation, against state spending. As a 1974 entrant to Parliament, he was untainted by service under Edward Heath, and his Thatcher credentials seemed impeccable. He was one of the Prime Minister's blue-eyed boys. Whether he had sufficient popularity to go further was, however, still in doubt. Brittan has never been at ease amongst the wider electorate, and he had no obvious power-base in Parliament.

'He hasn't got the large body of friends you need when you run into trouble,' said one Tory MP.

But he was quite capable of looking after himself. His toughness showed when his constituency of Cleveland and Whitby was divided up by the Boundary Commissioners, and Brittan had to find another seat. He opted for Richmond in Yorkshire where the local squirearchy opposed him as an alien and an interloper. But Brittan refused to back down. He fought for his adoption, and appealed to another of his patrons, Willie Whitelaw, who put it about that 'the North needs another senior Cabinet Minister'. Finally, Brittan was in.

His reward for admirable service came after the General Election when Mrs Thatcher promoted him to Home Secretary with a brief to tackle the growing problems of law and order.

It was in this office, for which, as a lawyer, he was apparently so well qualified, that Brittan stumbled for the first time. A debate on the reintroduction of hanging was due that winter, and the Party looked to Brittan for a lead. He had previously voted against the death penalty, but had then modified his position to favour its reintroduction for terrorist murder. Attempting to stick to this dual approach, he gave a floundering performance in front of MPs. Worse, he showed that he was unsure of the legal status of the 'Diplock' courts in Northern Ireland, where there is no jury. He was greeted with hoots of derision from the Opposition benches, and his own side looked embarrassed.

'The trouble with Leon is that he sticks relentlessly to his brief,' said one Labour MP. 'If he'd been captain of the *Titanic*, you'd have heard reassuring messages over the tannoy about the time of arrival in New York even as the ice was crashing into the hull.'

The trouble on this occasion was that even the brief was defective.

'The Home Secretary has hanged himself,' said the *Guardian*.

Over the next eighteen months, Brittan managed to redeem himself by demonstrating a firm line on law and order, and promoting a policy of longer sentences for violent criminals; his interventions in the miners' strike, sending police reinforcements to keep the pits open, were decisive.

But in June 1985, he stumbled again, and this time the reasons were different: an over-zealous interpretation of the Prime Minister's wishes. Ironically, he was to pay the price for his mistake by losing her favour and his job.

The *Real Lives* controversy involved a BBC television documentary on Northern Ireland featuring an interview with Martin McGuinness, alleged to be the Provisional IRA's Chief of Staff. Tipped off in advance about the programme, a *Sunday Times* journalist asked Mrs Thatcher, in the course of a trip to Washington, what her views would be about interviewing terrorists on television. Not surprisingly, she said she was against it.

Back at Westminster, Brittan took up the case and wrote a letter to the Chairman of the BBC in which he said that, while he did not wish to interfere, he would be delighted if the programme were scrapped.

It was at best a clumsy intervention. The BBC found itself in the position of trying to maintain its independence while being leant on heavily in public by the Home Secretary. Brittan was accused by Lord Annan of behaving like 'a demented poodle' or alternatively 'a charging rhinoceros', who had 'trampled on the delicate relationship which should always be maintained between the Government and broadcasting'.

The BBC duly postponed the programme, but Brittan had been politically damaged. In that year's Autumn reshuffle, Mrs Thatcher shifted him firmly sideways to head the Department of Trade and Industry. The one thing Brittan had no experience of was Industry.

Summing up his virtues and his failings, one fellow-MP put it this way: 'Leon has too many brains and too little sense. He does the wrong thing for the right reason, or the right thing for the wrong reason. He is forensic rather than political.'

The Prime Minister, who greatly admired him as a Minister, acknowledged that he might not have possessed 'enough subtlety'.

Thus, when it came to crossing swords with Michael Heseltine, the contest was always going to be uneven.

There was something about the physical contrast between the two – the tall, blond, good-looking Heseltine, and the short, round, less well-favoured Brittan – that caused one maliciously-inclined Tory MP to say that the contest reminded him of the classic story of the school prefect roughing up the swot behind the bicycle shed.

There was, however, one crucial difference; in this case the swot had a determined ally in the headmistress of the school.

Both Michael Heseltine and Leon Brittan are credited with having clear and powerful memories. It is hard, therefore, to explain why their recollections of the meetings that took place on 4 and 17 October in Brittan's office at the Department of Trade should differ so crucially on the central issue that was discussed.

The first of those meetings was Brittan's baptism into the Westland affair. Although he was in the chair, he was very much the junior partner, as Heseltine, with his greater experience, outlined the problem the way he saw it.

The main item on the agenda was the prospect for sales of the W30. With Rajiv Gandhi expected soon on a visit to Britain, the Prime Minister would need a briefing on the latest position.

There was a testy discussion about how much money was needed to underwrite the sales, and where it would come from. Each Minister was anxious that there should be no drain on the resources of his Department, with Brittan in particular arguing that there could be no commitment 'from the DTI's financial resources which were very scarce and indeed decreasing'.

He conceded that if the Indian order could be firmed up, there was a case for some support, though it would be a great deal more limited than anything Westland had in mind. Much of his own Department's chances of getting back its 'launch aid' would depend, in his view, on the MoD coming in with an initial order for the W30's military version.

Heseltine was having none of that. He wanted to ensure that the original promise of £65 million British 'aid' from the Overseas Development Administration to prop up the Indian sale would be put back on the table. The MoD was not going to be stuck with a situation where collapse of the Indian order led to unsold helicopters and unpaid bills.

A lengthy discussion about the real possibility of the company going into receivership showed that Heseltine was prepared to envisage it without too much concern, while Brittan thought that on balance it should be avoided if an acceptable rescue package could be put together. Neither appeared to find the idea of Westland going bust disastrous – it was an unsentimental discussion.

They then turned to the prospects for partnership with a foreign company, and it is here that accounts differ sharply. Heseltine was later to say that Brittan expressed a clear preference for a European partner. Brittan rejects this angrily. He claims he stated only one preference, and that was for the company 'to have a genuine free choice'.

The minutes of the meeting, prepared for the Prime Minister, tend to support Brittan on this point, though the distinction is a narrow one:

> Mr Brittan noted that at that stage Sikorsky appeared the company most likely to be prepared to come in. There were no proposals from British companies. Westland were in contact with MBB, Aerospatiale and Agusta. Mr Brittan considered Westland should be encouraged to pursue the possibility of a European solution... If, however, it became clear that Sikorsky was the only practical possibility, he did not consider the company's proposals should be rejected on the sole ground that they involved an association with Sikorsky, provided the required assurances were given by the company.

Brittan was to be pressed later by the Defence Committee examining the Westland affair to say whether he did not incline just a little bit further at that stage to the European option.

'Did you not have any feeling inside you that it might be better?' he was asked.

'Feeling is nothing to do with it,' he snapped. 'I was following the policy of the Government.'

Brittan wound up the meeting by saying that the Prime Minister might like to have a meeting before she saw Mr Gandhi. But in the event she did not – she had more pressing matters than the relatively minor one of Westland. It was decided to wait and see if Gandhi became more cooperative after his trip. There would then be a full ministerial meeting before Brittan informed Sir John Cuckney officially about the Government's position.

Cuckney found out, in fact, long before that. In one of his own phrases, he liked to deal with the organ-grinder, not the monkeys. On the first of what were to be several key occasions, he used his connections to go over the heads of both Heseltine and Brittan, straight to Downing Street to find out what was going on.

Cuckney has never said exactly which lever he was able to pull, but the available evidence shows that shortly after Brittan had written a confidential report on Westland for Mrs Thatcher following the 4 October meeting, Cuckney got back detailed private 'guidance' on its contents. It could only have come from inside Downing Street.

Cuckney's 'contact' was his most important secret weapon throughout the Westland affair, as events were to demonstrate.

The guidance Cuckney received said:

> The level of unsold helicopter stocks you have built up is regarded as staggering; receivership for Westland is not ruled out; it is most unlikely the Government will underwrite anything; it is Ministers who are taking the tough line, not officials; it is not the role of the MoD to rescue companies; nor does the Government as a whole intend to step in and save you.

It is safe to assume that Cuckney took a fundamental decision after this 'intelligence report'. The effort by Westland to secure a new government subsidy now seemed bound to fail. So he would have to deal with any prospective commercial partner from a position of weakness, not strength. This meant that he was no longer in a position to pick and choose: his ideal partner would have to match enthusiasm to join Westland with the resources to make it possible.

The option that seemed to him to lack both was the vague prospect of an offer emanating from Europe. The truth of the matter was that the European alternative which both Brittan and Heseltine were so confidently advocating simply did not exist.

It was a cause for considerable frustration to Raffaello Teti, President of Agusta of Italy, that ever since his meeting with Cuckney and Treacher the previous month, he had been unable to prise any financial information out of Westland to use as a possible basis for future partnership. His inquiries, he says, had met with a complete blank.

'I never succeeded in getting one single sheet of paper from Westland,' he complained.

The contacts with MBB and Aerospatiale referred to in Brittan's minute to the Prime Minister were equally insubstantial. Cuckney's brief encounter with Teti had not impressed him, and he had made no proposals at all to the French and Germans. Treacher and the rest of the Westland executives regarded them as cut-throat rivals, not potential European partners.

At this stage, however, the French picked up rumours of an unspecified American tie-up with Westland – and became deeply interested. They dispatched their top men, Pierre David of Aerospatiale, with Karl Fiechtmueller of their German partners MBB, to London to talk business. On 8 October they sat down at Westland's headquarters in Carlton Gardens.

Again, accounts of this meeting differ considerably. MBB and Aerospatiale are insistent that they came prepared to discuss a rescue deal, and that they were prepared to come up with a sensible offer as soon as they had had time to study the books.

'Aerospatiale's reaction was slow, but slowness is a weakness particular to partnerships,' says Admiral Henri-Jean Dugage, the company's international director. '... In truth, it *would* have been in Aerospatiale's interest to see Westland sink. But we knew the British Government would never let the business go down. It was going to be taken over either by Europeans or Americans... We have never been taken seriously because Westland never wanted to take us seriously.'

To Cuckney and Treacher they were merely French-led predators, interested only in keeping the Americans and their Black Hawk helicopter out of Europe. In his evidence later, Treacher characterised the European companies as 'a shifting team of people, none of whom spoke with one voice, none of whom understood how to do it.'

Cuckney was even more scathing:

> I felt their motives were obstructive and negative rather than positive and forward-looking. I did not think they were negative to the point where they wished to see us in receivership, though I had heard in the past that those views had been expressed by them...

He also accused them of making a deeply cynical suggestion at the confidential October meeting: that their price for a link with Westland would be its betrayal of Agusta, the remaining and weakest European company. Westland would have to ditch its existing deal to make a battlefield helicopter with the Italians, and throw in its lot with the rival Franco-German machine.

Such back-stabbing may have put Cuckney off. But it was scarcely because he had an exalted view of the ethics of the industry. Cuckney, too, had been less than straight forward with the absent Agusta.

Teti of Agusta had not even heard that there was an American bid in the offing. He learnt about it first, not from Westland but from Sikorsky themselves, soon after the London meeting, when he received a telephone call from Bill Paul. It was a message which thoroughly alarmed him: 'He told me that he was in the process of entering Westland, and that I shouldn't be worried about this because our programmes with Westland would not be touched.'

Teti was far from reassured. He asked for an urgent meeting with Sikorsky's executives, and began working out the implications of the

American bid. The more he thought about it, the angrier he became. He explains:

> I discovered that Cuckney was playing a double game, and was working out a deal with Sikorsky. I found his behaviour unpleasant in that he was dealing with the Americans at the same time that he was dealing with me. It's perhaps too much to talk in terms of betrayal. Rather, let us say it was extremely discourteous.

In London, Cuckney relayed his scepticism about any of the Europeans to Clive Whitmore and Brian Hayes, the senior civil servants at the MoD and the DTI. Whitmore, taken aback by the damning terms in which he spoke of the European companies, reported to Heseltine that the prospects of an alternative bid to Sikorsky were beginning to look bleak. He added that he felt Cuckney was being unnecessarily pessimistic about it.

Westland's plight was now beginning to creep into the financial columns of the newspapers. Cuckney's meeting with the French and Germans was reported, as well as renewed interest in the company from Alan Bristow. The shares of the company rallied to 83p, but the price was only just over half what it had been the last time Bristow took a serious interest.

On 14 October, Rajiv Gandhi arrived in Britain and was met at Heathrow Airport by Mrs Thatcher who made a flattering speech of welcome. 'India', she said, 'is the greatest democracy in the world.'

Most of the Indian Prime Minister's concern appeared still to centre on the threats his Government faced from Sikh militants, and on the apparent freedom with which they were allowed to operate in Britain. But in briefings to Indian journalists, Gandhi was now prepared to be affable about the W30. The problems of finance and of performance had been resolved, he said, and some sources said there could be sales of as many as forty-eight machines.

Heseltine put the Defence arguments himself to Gandhi, but the true sales figure remained twenty-one helicopters, and nothing was actually signed.

That evening in London, as Gandhi was being entertained at Downing Street, Heseltine attended the first of two private meetings at the Carlton Club to listen to and commend the enthusiastic arguments being put for a European strategy in arms procurement. Two days later, he was seated round a table at the Department of Trade with fellow Ministers, discussing the future prospects of Westland and the potential for a European deal.

This time there was a rather more heavyweight gathering at the DTI. Heseltine and Brittan were joined by the Party Chairman, Norman Tebbit, by MacGregor from the Treasury and Raison from the Overseas Development Administration.

Again, the meeting appears to have been dominated by the Heseltine argument on Europe, supplemented this time by a strong attack on the Sikorsky bid. He repeated that it was a 'bargain basement' deal for Sikorsky. Westland would be turned into nothing more than 'tin-bashers' – building helicopter bodies for an American firm which would be dictating terms from across the Atlantic.

In this, surprisingly, he was backed by Tebbit who was also suspicious of Sikorsky's motives. He thought they were probably leaning hard on Westland to get into the European market to sell their Black Hawk helicopters. As a former airline pilot himself, Tebbit had some knowledge of the business from the inside.

Heseltine now made an offer which sprang partly from his distrust of the Sikorsky bid, and partly from his belief that the European alternative would be more than just a commercial venture. It had, in his view, wider goals, with far-reaching defence implications for Britain and Europe. Given these, it was probably beyond the capabilities of Sir John Cuckney.

He was speaking very much in the language of the Carlton Club. But when he went on to suggest – in a deceptively casual fashion – that he himself might explore the possibilities of putting together a European consortium to make an offer for a Westland partnership, he was inspired as much by the success of his European Fighter deal as by any vision of the future. He saw no reason why something like the EFA deal should not be repeated.

And Brittan saw no reason to object. As he told the Defence Committee later:

[He] expressed the view, very fairly, if you are talking about a European partnership, it is not something that a private sector chairman, however able and experienced, could effectively pursue, and he offered to join the hunt himself. I was more than content he should do so, and he did so with enthusiasm and verve ...

It is, therefore, a little surprising that Brittan made no mention of this proposal to Sir John Cuckney when he met him the following day, 17 October. Or rather, there is no mention of it in the brief summary of that meeting, sent to Heseltine's office by John Mogg, Brittan's Private Secretary. The memo is intriguing in several other respects.

On the surface, it presents Cuckney with a bleak picture of the Government's position. There is no guaranteed offer of underwriting for the Indian order, no help with Sikorsky, and an instruction to pursue the European alternative, however unpromising it looks.

Brittan later made much of his reasons for proposing this. He insists that he wanted a European offer because the Sikorsky bid still involved the demand for Government money to underwrite the Indian helicopter. Any alternative proposal which might avoid a Government shell-out would be welcome:

> I myself felt that [Sikorsky] was the only offer at the time and although I wanted a rescue I was extremely reluctant to proceed with a proposal which involved a risk of public money being spent if an alternative could be found, and it was for that reason that I asked Sir John Cuckney to see whether it was possible to get a European minority shareholding either as an alternative to the Sikorsky one or to supplement the Sikorsky one...

This explanation is not reflected at any point in the official minute of the meeting – largely, it appears, because Brittan did not disclose it as his real reason for pursuing the European option. And Cuckney himself gives an entirely different version:

> I recall Brittan making the point that there was a Government preference for a Euro-solution, but I was of course by then well aware that the Government preference lay in the Ministry of Defence... it never came to me as *the* Government preference. Brittan's attitude was that it was entirely up to the board.

There was, therefore, considerable ground for misunderstanding, since the three parties in the matter had totally different perceptions about what was required: Heseltine was pursuing his ideal of European cooperation; Cuckney was paying lip-service to it just to keep the MoD happy; and Brittan thought it could save him money.

Cuckney did promise to pursue Agusta, who seemed the least unattractive of the three Europeans, and to renew contact with the others. But he grumbled that it would seem like 'importuning'.

In return, he hoped that Brittan would lean on Heseltine to get him to stump up the £6 million which the MoD still owed Westland, and which they were holding back.

Brittan said he would do what he could. Despite his recommendation of a European alternative, he had been impressed by Cuckney's assurance that Sikorsky offered the best, indeed the only, chance of saving Westland, and his gloomy assessment of the opposition. It was an impression that would grow rapidly in the next few weeks.

All of which left Michael Heseltine, apparently alone, out on a European limb. Which is exactly the way he later claimed to have seen it when he received the DTI's note on the Brittan-Cuckney meeting:

> It was only then that my anxiety began to grow ... my willingness to support the DTI turned to anxiety that the preference for Europe was being choked off. I told my colleagues privately that Cuckney had the wrong experience to give him an insight into how European collaboration works ... Collaboration is actually led by governments and not by companies.

And he intended to lead it. Happy as Leon Brittan had said he was in supporting Heseltine's enterprise, he must have had some misgivings. For a Government Minister to take time out to put together a commercial bid for a private company is unusual to say the least. And since Heseltine would doubtless be using contacts at Government level, the possibilities for confusing commercial and political goals were enormous.

It was not a confusion that particularly worried Heseltine. Indeed he thought the commercial and the political, in this case, were indivisible. He did, however, instruct Clive Whitmore 'on a power of direction' – as Ministers can do – to hand over the £6 million owed to Westland.

For the time being, other hands were at work to start the ball rolling. It is one of the many ironies of the Westland saga that Heseltine's famous European consortium was not actually begun by him at all, but owed its origins to the behaviour of Sikorsky and Westland themselves.

On 18 October Signor Teti of Agusta kept his urgent date in Paris with the Sikorsky team. He told them he was considering putting together a bid for a minority stake of 29.9 per cent of the company, and asked them whether there was any chance of their joining him. Sikorsky's response, as Teti recalls it, was diplomatic: 'They replied: "Because Westland will need a lot of money, you go ahead with your offer of 29.9 per cent and we'll make our offer of 29.9 per cent." It was an elegant way of saying to me that they wanted to do it their own way.'

Teti's intuitions may not necessarily have led him to realise at once that Sikorsky had other Italian plans in mind which excluded Agusta. But he realised that if Agusta was to stand a chance, it would have to find others to confront Sikorsky. The resulting consortium, with MBB of West Germany and Aerospatiale of France, was not an original idea, more, as Teti explains it, a sort of spontaneous combustion between the three firms:

> The European Consortium began after we three telephoned each other. It was very simple, between friends and completely unbureaucratic. We said, we must intervene in this case to help Westland, otherwise Westland will end up building bits of machinery – exactly what Agusta were doing thirty years ago. Above all, we didn't want the European market invaded by the Americans.

The first meetings were set up by MBB and Aerospatiale alone. Agusta was still very much in the hands of its own government. Lazards, Cuckney's bankers, told the other two that if they were serious, they had better find a British merchant banker to represent them. They offered them a list. Aerospatiale say, 'We wanted Lazards. But they were committed to Sikorsky already. So we took MBB's choice of Lloyds.'

On 20 October David Horne, Managing Director of Lloyds Merchant Bank, flew to Munich with a colleague, Peter Thompson, to attend the first meeting of the new team. He met Karl Fiechtmuller of MBB and Pierre David of Aerospatiale and began to read himself in. He was alarmed to learn that the only documentation available was the summary of the Price Waterhouse report. A bid, he was told, would have to be in by the end of November. There was no mention of Heseltine, of Government interest, or indeed lack of it.

'As far as I was concerned, it was just a normal job,' said Horne.

It would not stay normal for long. One of the many things Horne did not know was that, even as he sat on the plane to Germany, his potential clients had already been outflanked in Italy. While Lazards had been advising the Europeans how to proceed, Cuckney had taken a phone-call from Hubert Faure, president of Sikorsky: 'Our intelligence is that there is opposition building up within your Defence Ministry to Sikorsky. We are worried about this anti-Americanism and we're going to have to do something. You leave it with us.'

Within a week, Colin Green, the Englishman on the Sikorsky team, returned from Milan with a proposition designed specifically, Green says, to give the Sikorsky deal 'a European flavour'. They would sell Whitehall the idea of an explicit tie-up with the automobile giant Fiat. The thought was not a surprise to Cuckney; one element of previous negotiations had always been that Fiat would eventually appear on stage, possibly because there were subterranean plans in Italy for Fiat to take over Agusta itself.

These dealings between Sikorsky and Fiat have always been one of the murkiest areas of the Westland affair. Sikorsky are uncharacteristically loth to go into any detail, and Heseltine later accused them of constructing a unique deal in which Sikorsky, although supposedly putting up half the cash, were to continue to exercise all the votes. This said much about Fiat's willingness to pay through the nose for the arrangement. It is something which has never been fully explained.

Unlike Agusta, Fiat was a highly successful company with both political and financial muscle. One observer of the Italian scene said of it, 'Fiat is to the Italian state what the Duke of Burgundy was to the mediaeval kings of France, technically part of the kingdom, but barely less powerful than they were.'

As a private company owned by the Agnelli family, Fiat could move faster than Agusta. Its interest in Westland was purely mercenary; its air division, Fiat Aviazone, specialised in making transmission systems and accessory gearboxes for all the Aerospatiale helicopters, but it needed new markets, and was eager to sell them not just to Westland but also to Sikorsky itself.

The finding of Fiat was a shrewd political move as well, since the Italian company had important NATO contracts, and a wealth of experience in supplying them with vehicles and weapons systems.

On 24 October Westland made a full presentation of its position to Sikorsky – revealing information the Europeans would dearly have liked to see. Westland had prepared for it seriously, even holding a dress rehearsal the previous day at 4 Carlton Gardens.

The meeting took place at the City office of Lazards, Westland's merchant bank, and the presentation was made by the full Westland board, headed by Cuckney. Watching intently was the Sikorsky team: Bill Paul, Colin Green, Hubert Faure and Columbus Iselin. Paul later recalled the occasion:

What we wanted was Westland's view of Westland. Was it the same as ours? If not, we would walk away. We were in an asking and listening mode, not a dictating mode... we were extremely delighted that Westland was telling us exactly what we ourselves thought of the company in terms of its short-term problems and long-term development. It was as if we had given the presentation, not them, so we left the meeting giving no commitment but saying to ourselves that we were absolutely enthusiastic.

The full negotiations were now to last for three months and were described by Iselin as 'a mysterious exercise, like the mating dance of the swan'.

They were to prove very complex, involving meetings of up to forty people, which frequently continued until 2 am. In addition to the Sikorsky and Westland teams, there were two merchant banks, the lawyers and the two creditor banks, Barclays and NatWest.

Many of the problems revolved around technical details, like persuading the banks to convert their loans to Westland into Westland shares. Great secrecy surrounded the negotiations. Westland was codenamed 'Buffalo' – later, inexplicably, changed to 'Wren'. Nothing was leaked to the City, let alone the Europeans.

In the course of the discussions, the Sikorsky executives grew to like and admire Cuckney.

'I have nothing but admiration for that man,' said Iselin. 'He knew nothing about helicopters. But he recognised that the first thing you have to do in business is find a product. He's a consummate business-man, and he's a gentleman.'

Cuckney, knowing that there was still great pressure from Heseltine for 'a European solution', could now say, 'We have one with Fiat.' And he would say to Leon Brittan, who wanted a deal that would not cost the Government anything extra (beyond the probably irretrievable £40 million 'launch aid'), 'We have that too.' He claimed to the Defence Committee later:

> We found a private sector solution, not costing the taxpayer a penny... to what we have been told is a private sector problem. [It was] essentially a NATO solution, and European, not just American. We attach a lot of importance to the Italian involvement.

Brittan too claims to have been impressed by this 'European solution'. He said later, 'There was European co-operation, in that Fiat is a major European company and cannot just be written off as a sort of tag-end.'

It had, however, nothing to do with Heseltine's pan-European ambitions for an industrial grouping which would build up European technology, keep out the Americans and make helicopters together.

For David Horne, struggling to put together an offer on behalf of the real European team, without access to data, things were depressing. As he told colleagues:

> By the second week of November, I felt we were on a loser... The

Price Waterhouse summary wasn't worth the paper it was written on. It related to history, to forecasts from April and May. But it was very hard to get more information.

'I assumed that everyone was being treated equally. I simply didn't know that Sikorsky were getting privileged information. We've always been able to believe each other in the City. But this was different. Later Lazards admitted they had given Sikorsky more information than us.

Horne was worried, too, about a lengthy submission drawn up by MBB and Aerospatiale. It was, he thought, long-winded and high-flown. He would have preferred something more down-to-earth. Two meetings at Lazards convinced him things were going badly.

Help was at hand, however – in the shape of Michael Heseltine. It is from this point that Heseltine's practical interventions in the chancelleries of Europe really begin, and, in terms of events at Westland, they did begin very late. The Sikorsky scheme was streaking down the track and the Europeans were still at the starting gate.

The Defence Secretary had been out of the country for most of early November. He had flown to the Far East for the fortieth anniversary of World War II's end, to visit the graves of war victims with a group of their widows and relatives.

But on the way back, on 14 November, he stopped off in Rome to talk to his opposite number, the Italian Minister of Defence Giovanni Spadolini. Three days earlier he had already despatched his Junior Minister Norman Lamont to Rome, to take soundings. Now he weighed in himself. It was not a particularly fruitful discussion. Spadolini's mind was on the political crisis left in the wake of the *Achille Lauro* hijacking, and he could devote little attention to Westland or its problems.

But Heseltine was determined that at least he would sow some seeds of interest. He flew back to whip up interest amongst defence ministers in France and Germany. It is a testament to his creative energy that, once he had focused on the idea, he was able, within less than eighteen days, to bring it to the point of causing a national crisis.

Chapter Seven

UP THE WALL

'One man's vision is another man's nightmare'

– Sikorsky executive, January 1986

Sir John Cuckney's Whitehall intelligence had correctly identified Heseltine's involvement on the European side as a major obstacle. Without him, the Consortium was a feeble competitor; with him, it was unpredictable and threatening.

On 20 November the Westland Board confronted the Consortium in the boardroom at Lazards, and were far from impressed. Once again they seemed to be talking in high-flown but unspecific terms. The European team for its part was lectured about short-term work problems and shown an immensely complicated chart drawn up by Sir John Treacher which none of them could understand.

Cuckney summed up their efforts as he saw them: 'All [they] did was that, in effect, we put forward a capital reconstruction scheme, and *they* came along and said, "Drop Fiat-Sikorsky. We will come into that little slot." That is not a competitive situation.'

In the background, however, larger wheels were beginning to turn. On 23 November the *Financial Times* revealed that Heseltine was making a 'last-ditch' effort to save Westland by means of a European deal. 'There are too many manufacturers chasing too few orders in the teeth of efficient US competition,' he was quoted as saying. Aerospatiale's president had asked to see both Heseltine and the French Defence Minister, Paul Quiles, in the hope of political intervention.

The British Defence Secretary told the French and German helicopter companies that they could come and see him in London on Friday 29 November. But he insisted that their Italian counterpart, Agusta, be invited too.

He then asked for another meeting with Cuckney. It was fixed for 26 November at the MoD.

It was the first time the two had met since July, and there was a certain wariness as Cuckney walked into Heseltine's office, accompanied by Lord Fanshawe. Heseltine, in an elegant blue pullover, lounged in his usual way on the office sofa underneath a portrait of Lloyd George.

He wanted to know how the rescue was going, and why Cuckney did not seem to be making progress with the Europeans. He said he was concerned about the absence of a strong offer from Europe, and wanted to help one along. But if he was to do so, he wanted to be certain that it stood a chance:

> I was not prepared to use up any of the good will I had got in the European negotiating situation if there was no serious interest . . . So I put the position to Sir John. I said I would like to help, could I help, to which he said, 'I haven't the staff to go round Europe chasing the Europeans. They are all fully stretched with the complex negotiations for a capital reconstruction. But if I had a choice, that would help me because it would obviously, by having a choice, strengthen my negotiating position with Sikorsky.'

Cuckney largely accepts this account, though he says the argument was put in a jocular manner by the Defence Secretary, and not by him: 'I agree. I do remember Heseltine saying at least it gave one a stronger bargaining position, or words to that effect.'

'In that case, I will make a major effort,' said Heseltine.

'Splendid, excellent,' replied Cuckney.

His colleagues now argue, 'He would have been a bloody fool if he had not agreed to this. There was always the chance that the Sikorsky/Fiat deal might fall through.'

Heseltine asked what kind of deadline Westland had, and was told that they had wanted to make an announcement on 11 December. However, Cuckney was prepared to postpone it until 18 December. Heseltine took it as a commitment to give him three weeks which – he would later claim – was broken.

One intriguing incident at the end of this meeting might have shaken Cuckney's complacency. As he stood up to leave, Heseltine picked up the phone and ordered two of his civil servants to go round at once to Lloyds Merchant Bank, headquarters of the European operation. Events seemed to be moving very fast indeed.

Next day Manfred Woerner, the West German Defence Secretary, was due in London for the annual Anglo-German summit. Heseltine, accompanied by Sir David Perry, his European procurement chief, seized the chance of proposing that they put their weight behind a European partnership with Westland.

It was, he pointed out, a real opportunity to give some substance to European cooperation in armaments and to follow up the 1978 agreement they had all signed to rationalise the helicopter industry. There was a sweetener; perhaps it would be possible to reopen stalled talks about merging the two wasteful rival projects in which the Germans were involved...

Heseltine explained that he was bringing the French, German and Italian companies together in his office in forty-eight hours' time.

Woerner was enthusiastic. He pointed out that Perry and Karl Schnell, the designated civil servants at each Minister's side – the 'National Armaments Directors' who dealt with joint procurement – were also due to meet Admiral Mario Porta, their Italian opposite number in Bonn that very Friday. Why not ring the Italian up and get them all to meet jointly in London instead? They would be crucial if the consortium was to be given the political clout it clearly needed.

It was the kind of opportunity Heseltine welcomed. A series of telephone calls from Perry rounded up Emile Blanc from France as well. That Friday the three European company heads and the three international civil servants all flew into London. They assembled in Heseltine's office at the MoD, accompanied by David Horne, the French and German merchant bankers, and Sir David Perry. Alistair MacDonald, the senior official from Leon Brittan's Trade Department, was prudently invited as well.

By bringing in the National Armaments Directors, Heseltine was significantly changing the rules of the game. They are responsible to their respective Defence Ministers, and their job is to push ahead with the elimination of waste and rivalry in European defence procurement. These four men had been key figures the previous year in pushing through Heseltine's prize project, the European fighter.

For the first time, the putting together of a commercial proposition was to be backed by heavyweight statecraft. It is clear with hindsight that Heseltine had conceived an ambitious project, with a very specific ideal in mind.

Of all the turning points in the Westland drama, Heseltine's conference on 29 November is the most critical. From it flowed actions which were to end in political turmoil.

One of its more intriguing effects, however, was also its least publicised. The National Armaments Directors' agreement was to convince John Cuckney and his team that if they were to win the

Westland battle they might have to bypass both Heseltine and Brittan and take their case to the very top. The time was about to come when it would be necessary to win the backing of the Prime Minister herself.

For Cuckney, the challenge was to exert more political influence in this matter than the Secretary of State for Defence. He had his 'secret source' with access to Downing Street; and he had in his pay the services of Lazards, headed by John Nott, the former Cabinet Minister, the wily Tory politician Lord Fanshawe, and Gordon Reece.

As it happened, Reece had just received private confirmation of the favour in which he was held in the loftiest political circles. He had received a letter from Nigel Wicks, Mrs Thatcher's Principal Private Secretary, asking him if it would be 'agreeable' to him if Her Majesty the Queen was pleased to grant him the honour of a knighthood. The answer was, it would. He was now Sir Gordon Reece-in-waiting, though the elevation would not be gazetted until the New Year's Honours List.

His 'K' was for political services. They were to Tory Central Office and to the Prime Minister herself. From now on, his intimate knowledge of the workings of Downing Street and his close friendship with the Prime Minister would be even greater assets in helping to steer Westland through the political manoeuvrings that lay ahead.

Given the consequences of the NADs' agreement, the actual meeting on Friday 29 November was extremely straightforward – save for one curious fact. Given that there was, effectively, just one word on the agenda, and that was 'Westland', where was Westland itself? One person not present was Sir John Cuckney. Heseltine explained later, somewhat unconvincingly, that everyone had been rounded up at the very last moment, so there was hardly time to invite him.

This was not so. The businessmen who marched up the steps of the big MoD building in Whitehall remember quite clearly the name 'Sir John Cuckney' on the security guards' list of invitees at the door. Even before the meeting began, there had been some explosive noises off.

The Cuckney camp say his invitation to a meeting was withdrawn by Sir Clive Whitmore on the Friday morning itself, and they were left seething at the snub. Heseltine gave the Commons a different part of the story. He says Cuckney rang Whitmore about what appeared to be the true nature of the meeting:

He said he had learned of [the NAD group's] existence in the *Financial Times*. He said he was expecting a telex within hours from Sikorsky and that as soon as it came, he would convene a board meeting which would confirm the Sikorsky deal. So much for the man who, only a few days earlier, had said he would welcome a choice... The only excuse would be that even knowledge of such a deal would frighten Sikorsky off – a miscalculation of historic proportions.

Cuckney was perhaps annoyed because he realised he had misjudged Heseltine. Not only had the whole thing been arranged behind his back, it seemed to have nothing to do with preparing a commercial proposal for Westland. Instead it bore the hallmarks of a political move to outflank Sikorsky and possibly destroy the best chance he had of rescuing the company.

Cuckney's threats to do a quick deal with Sikorsky had, however, to be taken seriously. There were two choices for Heseltine: call off the NADs meeting and talk Cuckney round, or press ahead and meet him head on. One of Heseltine's close friends said later, 'It was bluff, of course, but Michael's got terrific nerve. To him, it's all poker.'

The meeting went ahead. Heseltine addressed it himself in his most statesmanlike manner, reminding those present of the 1978 agreement, and the need to get a deal over battlefield helicopters that would take Europe forward into the 1990s. There were echoes of his Carlton Club speech as he went over the proposals he thought should emerge at the end of the day.

Then, late that morning, he left to travel to Rochford, near Southend, where he was due to speak on behalf of the local MP, Michael Clark. The others got down to business.

In front of them was a proposal to combine two rival helicopter projects; the PAH-2, which is Franco-German, and the A129, which is Anglo-Italian. The resulting machine would join the EH101 and the NH90 as Europe's three main helicopters. Once that was agreed, it followed that members of the Consortium would only buy these and would not compete with rivals of their own.

While the officials negotiated in one room, the helicopter companies sat in another. For what was effectively the first time, Agusta was persuaded to throw its lot in irrevocably with the consortium, and effectively abandon the A129 for the good of all. There was some talk of the Germans joining in the Anglo-Italian EH101 as a quid pro quo. Agusta was none too happy with this 'EEC development policy for the European helicopter industry'.

Agusta's private diary of events, kept in Milan, records, 'Agusta declared it was not in complete agreement... because there was not time to modify it, Italy said it wanted to rediscuss the agreement document at a later date.'

But it was effectively swept into the full-scale Consortium. A scheme was outlined for a £25 million joint cash injection into Westland and guaranteed sub-contracting work to tide the British company over; as good an offer in their eyes as that of Sikorsky. The MoD proposed to boost it by ordering some extra helicopters from a Europeanised Westland. They would be paid for – in a remarkable touch of creative accounting – out of the notional savings from the future European helicopter policy.

By the time Heseltine returned, late that afternoon, there was an agreement on the table. In the space of just five hours, the defence officials and senior executives of four countries had proposed and agreed on the creation of an exclusively European helicopter business. Whatever else was later said about it, the NADs' agreement that day was a remarkable achievement.

Heseltine was delighted. It was, in his view, a major step along the road to European defence unity, and a natural projection of a policy that he himself had long argued for. He put it, inevitably, in the broadest of political perspectives:

The essence of the agreement we reached with the National Armaments Directors is that the four Ministers had before them a set of proposals whereby... there would be three helicopters with which no one in Europe would compete and, if they had a requirement, they would buy. That was the logical step to which the 1978 helicopter agreement was designed to take us. It had already taken us there in respect of the EH101 and the NH90. In the negotiation of the final deal, which I was entrusted by my colleagues to do, we added the third leg of the triangle and found the three helicopters upon which Europe could cooperate for the rest of this century.

It was visionary stuff, and, as Heseltine shook hands that evening with all those who had contributed to the agreement, he had every reason to be pleased. Early the following week he would present it to his Ministerial colleagues. He hoped that they would be as delighted as he was.

He could scarcely have expected Cuckney to share his pleasure, but he rang him on the spot and described the agreement in detail in a thirty-minute call. Westland tried to ring up Jean Martre of Aerospatiale at the MoD building to check what had been said, and was told he had already left for the airport. Cuckney promptly went round to the MoD building with Treacher, and the British official team showed him the paper headed 'Final Agreed Copy'. Finally, in another call that night, Whitmore clarified the remaining uncertainties in Cuckney's mind.

Cuckney's reaction was far from mild. In the words of one of those involved, 'Sir John went up the wall.'

Chapter Eight

'WE'LL TAKE CARE OF HESELTINE'

*'I make up my mind about people in the first ten
seconds and I very rarely change it'*

– Mrs Thatcher

The alarm bells started ringing before the weekend was even over.
Cuckney told colleagues, 'Heseltine's gone for the jugular.' An urgent
telephone call from Lazards alerted Bill Paul of United Technologies
to the NADs agreement and all it stood for. He was as shocked as
Cuckney:

> Frankly, I was startled and stunned by this development. Doors
> were being closed in our faces in an emotional anti-American
> way... I contacted top Government officials at the Pentagon and
> alerted them to the situation, and I contacted a number of
> Europeans whom we are close to.

Those Pentagon contacts were to result, some weeks later, in discreet
American pressure on the British Government, when it was intimated
that a multi-million dollar contract for British Rapier missiles might
be at risk if the Sikorsky deal did not go through. But for the time
being, Paul was ready to be reassuring. Cuckney's first question, when
they spoke on the telephone, was, 'Will you back off because of this?'
'No,' said Paul.
'If the European decision sticks, will it be a show-stopper as far as
you're concerned?'
'I won't back off. We'll still proceed.'
With that reassurance, Cuckney could turn his mind to how best to
fight back. On Monday he would make the formal approach to the

DTI. For now, however, there was a more immediate route to take. The time had come to go straight to the top.

Mrs Thatcher's personal involvement in the Westland business had been, up to this point, cursory. Save on two important occasions, she had left it to the Ministers involved. Now she was beginning to regret it.

The first time she had chosen to intervene had been when the Bristow bid collapsed and she had vetoed Heseltine's scheme for a joint MoD/Treasury subsidy for Westland, thus inviting the Bank of England rescue. The second time had been when she ticked off Rajiv Gandhi for going back on his mother's word and failing to buy the W30 helicopters.

Neither intervention had helped Westland particularly, but both had shown the Prime Minister in characteristic form – saving the taxpayer's money at home and 'batting for Britain' abroad.

Of far greater importance had been her unspoken but ever-present influence on the way her Ministers had reacted. Each response to the Westland crisis had been made in the name of Thatcherism, which defines an attitude not only to Government spending, but to the role of management. It was best summed up recently by Mrs Thatcher's Education Secretary and economic mentor, Sir Keith Joseph:

> She saw [our economic decline] stemming from successive governments which, by increasing the money supply, kept on rescuing managements and labour from having to become more competitive... She saw it infecting management which was allowed to be flabby.

And she saw it in a very personal way. As Lord Harris, founder of the Institute of Economic Affairs, put it: 'I quite like the way that she regards it all as her money. She sometimes talks about *my* industries and *my* budget.'

From that weekend it was, increasingly, to be *my* helicopter business.

The first detailed version she heard of that Friday's meeting, and the implications of the NADs agreement, came not from her Defence Secretary, who was responsible for it, but from Sir John Cuckney, who was deeply opposed to it. He made it his business to see that she was informed directly about what was happening.

Cuckney makes no secret of his belief that, since two of her Ministers now appeared to be pulling in different directions, it was right that she should be asked to step in and sort matters out. Using the links with Number Ten that he now had at his disposal, Cuckney relayed to the Prime Minister not only the facts about the proposed European intervention, but the grave misgivings it was causing.

His message pointed out to her that far from giving Westland's shareholders a choice, the NADs proposal was effectively closing off the best offer they had – the Sikorsky-Fiat deal. By laying down conditions in which only European helicopters would be bought by European governments, it was setting up a protected market which would prevent Sikorsky or any other US helicopter company from selling into Europe. The very existence of the agreement, in his view, carried the risk of frightening off the Americans, who were offering a sound and privately financed deal. The Europeans, for their part, had come up with nothing solid enough to put to the shareholders, let alone offer the rescue for which he, Cuckney, and not the MoD had responsibility.

The appeal touched several immediate chords with Mrs Thatcher. To begin with, Cuckney was her kind of businessman – someone who, in her own favourite phrase, presented 'solutions and not problems'. He was seeking a private deal which offered the prospect of saving Government money, and he was talking to a hard-headed American company with the sort of know-how essential in the international marketplace.

The other side appeared to have everything wrong with it. The NADs agreement sounded monopolistic and anti-competitive. It was dreamed up by Michael Heseltine, who had an irritating habit of causing trouble, and who this time sounded as if he was endangering a perfectly reasonable rescue package.

And it was European.

Mrs Thatcher is not an enthusiast for Europe. She is immensely critical of the Common Market's institutions and bureaucracy, and spent the first five years of her Government in a long and bitter dispute about Britain's contribution to the EEC budget – a process which soured relations between her and the European leaders with whom she was dealing. Her relations with two of them in particular, Helmut Kohl of West Germany and Bettino Craxi of Italy, are based on a lack of admiration which she has found it hard to disguise.

By contrast, she has never disguised the warmth she feels for America, her friendship for President Reagan and her admiration for the energy and expertise of US companies.

From the very beginning, therefore, her instincts, based on this preliminary, and, of course, one-sided assessment of the Westland crisis, were to favour the American solution. Although in public and to her Ministers she was always to maintain a position of evenhandedness towards the two contenders, she herself was never in any doubt that the Sikorsky proposals contained the best deal for Westland and its shareholders.

There is on the Whitehall files from this period a note which records her determination that nothing and nobody should be allowed to undermine the American bid. It reports her as saying, in response to Cuckney's complaint about the intervention of the Defence Secretary, 'We'll take care of Heseltine.'

What Mrs Thatcher learned early the following week from her Trade Secretary Leon Brittan served only to reinforce these views.

Brittan was telephoned by Cuckney on Monday 2 December and told that Heseltine's draft NADs agreement amounted to 'sabotage'.

That call was followed up by a letter from him which stressed the need to have the terms of the agreement lifted as soon as possible and the danger of Sikorsky withdrawing if they were not. Talks on buying a Black Hawk licence from Sikorsky were far advanced, he said, and his best hope.

The letter went on to threaten the real possibility of Westland going into receivership, and said that losses currently amounted to £100 million. More significantly for Brittan, Cuckney repeated the demand that a commitment must be given to write off the £40 million launch aid for the W30. He implied that the Europeans were still deeply divided, saying the French and Germans had hitherto only made an offer which had not been approved by Agusta.

Cuckney's fundamental point was that the banks would not tolerate the NADs agreement because it would make a Sikorsky deal too risky. He therefore ran the risk of 'falling between two stools' and losing his company.

There is more than an element of hyperbole here. Cuckney ought to have been aware from his conversation with Paul that Sikorsky were not on the point of withdrawing. And he must have known that the NADs agreement had no legal force unless it was signed and agreed by the Cabinet, as well as the other European defence ministers. But its very existence horrified him.

He was, therefore, leaving nothing to chance. That Monday he went round to the MoD for a face-to-face briefing from civil servants, then called in at the DTI to lodge a complaint in person.

Brittan had already been briefed by his own Department's man at the NADs meeting, Alistair MacDonald, but the language of civil servants tends to be restrained, and there is no evidence that MacDonald saw the agreement in quite such apocalyptic terms as Cuckney. However, by the time Brittan had heard Cuckney's version, delivered in person, by letter and by telephone, he can have been in little doubt about the seriousness of the situation.

His own instinct was automatically to sympathise with Cuckney and think the worst of the NADs agreement. As the sponsoring Department, the DTI would be left to pick up the pieces if the Sikorsky deal fell through. And he himself had no enthusiasm for the broader European goals Heseltine had espoused; indeed, he says bluntly that he 'did not happen to agree with [them]'.

More important perhaps, in a personal sense, was Brittan's intense irritation with Heseltine's meddling. Here was a man for whom he felt no personal warmth and who was, in his view, erratic and unreliable, interfering in the most outrageous manner in an issue which was his, Brittan's, responsibility. The fact that he had encouraged him to go and drum up a European bid in the first place was no excuse for this kind of behaviour.

He was later to describe the agreement that Heseltine had fixed with the Armaments Directors as a 'pistol pointing at the company', a 'half-Nelson' and a 'knock-out blow'. Members of the Defence Committee who heard these terms coined a phrase for his tussle with a fellow-Minister. They called it 'mud-wrestling'.

Brittan's arguments echoed directly what Cuckney had told him:

[The NADs agreement] seemed to me to be going beyond providing a European alternative, it seemed to me to be carrying partisanship into that alternative to the extent of saying, 'Not only have I brought together this alternative but I have also given it a knock-out blow which will make the other option no longer feasible... the Europeans came up with an alternative attached to a half-Nelson if I may put it that way. That seemed to me to be ludicrous...

This then was the message Brittan passed on to the Prime Minister, reinforcing her own view. Officially, she felt that the NADs recommendation went 'far beyond the 1978 declaration'. Unofficially, she decided that Heseltine would have to be stopped in his tracks. She called a Ministerial meeting to be held on Thursday 5 December.

Michael Heseltine, the object of all this vilification, was professing injured innocence. A request from Brittan that Friday's agreement should be withdrawn forthwith was rejected. 'Not until the European offer is properly considered,' he said. His response to the charge of sabotage was that there was nothing in the agreement which could possibly be regarded as a threat because it was merely a recommendation. He was later to argue that it was only a basis for discussion, and its status had been misunderstood: 'I came back with a piece of paper which was that offer from the European Ministers. I never said, "This is set in stone. You have to go that way. It can never be amended." But it never got to be discussed.'

He was quickly made aware, however, of the strength of feeling on the other side. Briefed by his own officials following their meeting with Cuckney that Monday, he realised that the Sikorsky deal was probably nearer fruition than he had realised, and that the effect of the NADs recommendation might have been to speed it up rather than the reverse. He also learned to his concern that there had been detailed discussions over the granting of a licence for the Black Hawk – the very thing he was so opposed to. He suggested that Brittan be asked to write to Cuckney requesting further details of the Sikorsky offer to demonstrate why it was a better deal than anything the Europeans could offer. The suggestion was ignored.

The two meetings chaired by Mrs Thatcher on 5 and 6 December were fractious and bad-tempered, revealing for the first time the deep divisions that the Westland debate was beginning to cause.

Although the meetings were simply ad-hoc discussions by Ministers and had no official Cabinet status, the line-up was high-powered. Apart from the Prime Minister, Heseltine and Brittan, there were the Deputy Prime Minister, Lord Whitelaw; Geoffrey Howe from the Foreign Office; Norman Tebbit, Party Chairman; John MacGregor and Nigel Lawson from the Treasury; and John Biffen, Leader of the House.

They were told that the deadline for publishing the Westland accounts and concluding a deal was just one week away, and losses were predicted to be as much as £100 million. The issue of the £40 million launch aid remained to be considered, and a Government agreement to waive repayment was now seen as a condition for any successful deal.

Leon Brittan then outlined the DTI's view of the main issue to be decided. The NADs recommendation, with its flavour of protectionism, was, he believed, a major obstacle lying between the Westland board and its attempt to reach a conclusion with Sikorsky-Fiat. The choice should be left to the Westland shareholders, but until the recommendation was lifted that was impossible. In his view it should not be allowed to stand for a moment longer than was necessary.

Put like this, there seemed little argument. The Prime Minister made it clear that she wanted a decision, and made it equally clear what she thought that decision should be. Virtually all those present were prepared to agree in principle that the NADs recommendation should be scrapped, and for a time Heseltine was in a minority of one.

But his argument – one that was to be heard many times by ministers over the next few weeks – was hard to reject out of hand. He said that European defence ministers had gone to a great deal of trouble to put a bid together and it would be a grave discourtesy to reject it out of hand without even seeing it. The very least they could do was discuss the NADs agreement at a full Cabinet economic committee. As he said later, 'If Ministers enter into agreements, other Ministers must respond properly and collectively.'

It was an argument that was to be used against him later by Mrs Thatcher, but it carried some weight. Both Norman Tebbit and Geoffrey Howe found it convincing enough to give their support, and it was quite clear, as one of those present put it, that, 'Michael had the bit between his teeth. He was banging on and on. He wouldn't take no for an answer, and everyone realised there was no shaking him.'

The first meeting was adjourned, but by the end of the second there was still an impasse. Reluctantly, Mrs Thatcher agreed that there would be a full meeting of the Cabinet's Economic Committee the following Monday, 9 December.

Not all the arguments were going on in the upper echelons of British politics. That week saw the first concrete proposal from the European Consortium. On 2 December David Horne of Lloyds Merchant Bank had sent a letter to Lazards saying that the Consortium was now in place and he proposed to put up £25 million, with more if desirable. There was no intention of trying to gain control of Westland and they were flexible on the question of share capital. They would eventually sell back to British shareholders once the company had been stood on its feet.

The offer was noted by Lazards, but got scant respect from Westland. Treacher commented, 'It was their first effort... none of them understood how to do it... I took them through step by step on how to get their act together. One of the most destroying things was that they had no act to get together.'

Michael Baughan of Lazards informed Horne that the code-name for Westland had been changed again because of an unfortunate leak. It was not now Buffalo, but Wren. The new name was not intended to be any reflection on the size of the problem.

An inconclusive meeting with Lazards that Thursday was followed, however, by excellent news for the Consortium next day, when Clive Whitmore at the MoD telephoned Horne to inform him that British Aerospace was now prepared to join up.

The arrival of a major British firm was to have a significant impact on the Consortium's prospects as well as causing some heavy political waves. It was Teti of Agusta who had urged that a British 'front' be found for the Consortium, and the first approaches to BAe were not quite as casual as they were later described.

There is evidence that BAe had already been sounded out in November. One senior source from GEC, its eventual British collaborator, says, 'BAe was approached in November, but the figures didn't appear to come out right to them and they refused.' British Aerospace had, in the course of 1985, turned down first a full takeover, then a £30 million 'partnership' and finally a relatively small investment. No one could accuse BAe's Chief Executive, Admiral Lygo, of being keen on Westland helicopters.

Austin Pearce, Chairman of BAe, recalled the circumstances of the remarkable change of heart between one ministerial meeting and another:

> It may sound a very strange situation, the way this arose, but I actually rang Clive Whitmore in the afternoon to talk, believe it or not, about the trusteeship of the RAF Museum. At the end of the conversation, he said, 'What is your interest in Westland?'

That call was promptly followed by another. It was from Michael Heseltine, who urged on him the idea of European cooperation. If it was put like that, Pearce was in favour. BAe, already involved with such European projects as the Tornado jet, the European Airbus and the European Fighter Aircraft, knew more about working in Europe than most British companies. He now said he was prepared to be involved if the helicopters could be built on 'a sensible basis'.

Heseltine asked him how much he was prepared to put in, and Pearce responded with a modest £5 million. Heseltine said he thought it ought to be more. Eventually BAe was to go up to £6.75 million. BAe also said it wanted GEC, the huge electronics supplier which was, if anything, even less enthusiastic about a rescue, to be asked to join in and pull its weight.

It was not an enormous gesture of confidence, but BAe's importance went far beyond its financial commitment. It became the spokesman for the Consortium. Admiral Sir Raymond Lygo, bluff and down-to-earth, was chosen to put the case for Europe to the press.

The case needed putting. Westland had announced 750 redundancies, and predictions of what the company report would reveal on 11 December were grim.

The row between Heseltine and Brittan had now become public, and Westland's version of events, including its hostile attitude to the European bid, had been aired in the press.

There was a distinct confusion over what the aims of the European bid really were; a confusion that still exists, though each party to the argument has given his or her public explanation.

Heseltine himself was quite clear. It was a matter of strategy, a way of advancing towards a joint European defence policy, of 'seeking to enhance the defence industrial base of this country' which would contribute to its long-term security.

Brittan considered this suggestion 'inherently incredible'. He said he had never heard anything about the European offer 'which was ever presented as being necessary for the defence of the realm'. Instead it was 'motivated, with perfect sincerity, on broader European and industrial grounds which I do not happen to agree with.'

Mrs Thatcher saw it as a way of improving the range of options open to Westland's shareholders, but only *without* the NADs agreement. If that remained in force, she said, Sir John Cuckney 'would not be able to recommend to the company shareholders any reconstruction proposals involving Sikorsky and Fiat'. What this appeared to mean was that, if the Europeans did not pull back, there would be no proposal at all for the shareholders to consider. In other words, the choice was Sikorsky or nothing.

But if that line of argument was confusing, the Europeans themselves seem to have been under an even deeper misapprehension. Raffaello Teti of Agusta explained:

> We thought that the European offer was solidly backed by the British Government. We believed at the time of the London meeting that Heseltine expressed the official British position. We thought we were acting as part of an official European policy, and for this reason we were later very upset.

In the light of all this, it was not surprising that the European team should have felt the need of a clear and influential voice to speak up for them and plead their case with the voting shareholders of Westland helicopters.

For the moment, however, all the talking was being done in Mrs Thatcher's Cabinet Committee.

Until recently the very existence of 'EA' – the Economic Affairs Committee of the British Cabinet – was a state secret.

When Mrs Thatcher came to power she, like all her predecessors, distributed copies – classified 'Confidential' with each one numbered –

of the first secret document her Cabinet would be privileged to see. Headed 'Questions of Procedure for Ministers', it contained miscellaneous instructions for the use of scrambler phones, and relics of past Whitehall internal battles, such as this gem: 'The Junior Minister is not subject to the directions of the Permanent Secretary. But equally, the Permanent Secretary is not subject to the directions of the Junior Minister.'

One of the main sections is headed 'Cabinet Committees'. It explains:

> [These] relieve the pressure on the Cabinet itself by settling as much business as possible at a lower level; or failing that, by clarifying the issues... even though an important question may never reach the Cabinet itself, the decision will be fully considered... appeals to the Cabinet must clearly be infrequent...
>
> Decisions... are binding on all members of the Government. They are, however, normally announced and defended by the Minister concerned as his own decisions... it is important to avoid giving any indication of the manner in which the Minister has consulted his colleagues... discussion will be hampered if the processes by which it is carried on are laid bare...
>
> [If Cabinet Committee decisions] were announced as such, [it] would lead to the embarrassing result that some decisions of government would be regarded as less authoritative than others; critics... could press for its review by some other committee or the Cabinet itself...
>
> It is therefore undesirable in principle to disclose the existence, composition and terms of reference of Cabinet Committees and the identity of their chairmen, since ill-informed speculation about the status and authority of individual Ministers may well result...
>
> Government policy should not be discussed with persons outside Government service... care should be taken that no discussions of Government policy are held in places where they might be overheard.

Answering a request for information in 1983, the Cabinet Secretary, Sir Robert Armstrong, had written, 'Neither I nor any of my staff would be in a position to say anything about the Cabinet Committee system in this country which went beyond what the Prime Minister herself has said...'

But it had been Mrs Thatcher herself who first referred to EA –

along with three others – in the course of a parliamentary answer given in 1979. Since then the secrecy protecting the names of 25 standing committees and more than 100 *ad hoc* committees of the Cabinet has been broadly ignored. The edifice of the state has not noticeably crumbled as a result.

And certainly the rules were never applied to Sir John Cuckney. As usual, he was excellently briefed from Downing Street sources about the 'status and authority of individual Ministers'. Westland's own intelligence material, which was, in the words of a company source, 'conveyed to Sir John', shows that by the night before the crucial 'EA', he had been helped a lot.

The note records that there were 'deep divisions within the Government'. Heseltine was prepared to travel 'all over Europe' to sign the necessary international protocols. And there had already been two Cabinet Committee meetings to try and resolve the matter.

Anyone reading it could only deduce that someone must have been holding 'discussions of Government policy... in places where they might be overheard'.

The Economic Affairs Committee which met that Monday 9 December at 4.30 pm was also not to remain secret for long. The cast-list of the previous week had been swollen by the addition of several Ministers: Kenneth Clarke, assisting Lord Young from Employment; Peter Walker from Energy for part of the meeting; Michael Spicer, standing in for Nicholas Ridley, Minister of Transport; Kenneth Baker, Secretary for Environment; and John Wakeham, Chief Whip, the last a figure of great importance in subsequent weeks as he monitored the reactions of backbench MPs to this increasingly puzzling affair. The original group of Tebbit, MacGregor, Heseltine, Whitelaw, Biffen, Howe and Brittan himself were, of course, also present.

It was chaired by Mrs Thatcher, who had personally ordered the calling of all the meetings to date. She began, as she usually does, by laying down the line she expected to be followed by those attending. In this she may not be notably different from her predecessors, but unlike them she does not respond kindly to those who broaden it.

Her view, backed strongly by Brittan and MacGregor, was that the NADs agreement was an interference in the free choice offered to shareholders, and should be lifted at once. She wanted a decision that day.

Sir John Cuckney, accompanied by Marcus Agius from Lazards, was now invited in by Mrs Thatcher to address the Committee and give Ministers the view from the front line. This was a remarkable event. Even departmental officials do not attend Cabinet Committees. Occasionally an outside 'expert' is called in, but never one who has such a partisan role. Heseltine, who was constantly urging the introduction of businessmen into government, was unlikely to object in principle. But, once again, Cuckney was closer to the heart of things than many a member of the administration.

He had been well briefed about the position, and had decided what to say in order to outflank Heseltine. After studying the Westland 'intelligence', the line he chose was that he could only consider a European rescue that was 'fully underwritten' by the British Government. This was calculated to make ministers shudder at the potential commitment and expense.

Westland, he began by saying, was in a 'fabulously weak' position, about to declare a £95 million loss and demonstrate that it was effectively insolvent. Sikorsky was the only rescuer of substance in sight. Apparently setting little store by bullish reassurances Bill Paul had given him, he warned Ministers that Westland risked Sikorsky backing away from its bid if they were threatened.

As for the European proposal, said Cuckney, it was totally unrealistic. He recalled a remark made by Sir John Treacher that 'if we had eighteen months and £85 million, it might well be worth trying to participate in a reconstruction of the European helicopter industry'. Short of that, it was irresponsible to pursue it.

The argument was a powerful one, but Heseltine, again, had a simple and persuasive response; so far, he said, the Europeans had not even been given the chance of presenting the board of Westland with a proper proposal. The shareholders deserved to have a choice. Surely it was worth giving the Consortium at least until the end of the week to come up with a firm offer. If they could not, so be it, Sikorsky would win. But until that time, the NADs recommendation should stand.

The Westland team left at 6.10 pm, and the atmosphere began to deteriorate. Mrs Thatcher continued to insist that a decision was needed that afternoon, and that the NADs agreement must be thrown out. Equally insistently, Heseltine refused to budge. He and Brittan exchanged angry words across the table as other Ministers tried to find a way out.

Heseltine was later to claim that he had a clear majority in support of his proposal. That was true, since most of those hearing the argument for the first time found it relatively easy to back, but their motives for doing so were varied. Clarke, Baker and Spicer were indeed pro-European. Tebbit wanted a genuine choice for the shareholders. Wakeham thought the only way of getting Heseltine to shut up was to give him his head and let events dictate his fate.

Few of those present had ever seen Mrs Thatcher so embattled amongst her own Ministers. As the meeting went into its third hour, she slammed the table in front of her and said, 'Very well, we'll have to meet again on Friday at 4 o'clock, after the Stock Exchange has closed.'

This simple statement and the events which flowed from it were to lead directly to Heseltine's resignation. He himself points to it as the turning point in the whole affair; since it has been endlessly disputed, it is worth examining precisely what was said and what was meant by it.

Mrs Thatcher is unequivocal on the subject:

The conclusions of the Cabinet Economic Committee on December 9 laid down a clear policy, and that made a further meeting unnecessary. No decision to hold a further meeting was taken or recorded. No meeting had been agreed, so there was no meeting to cancel.

Heseltine is equally definite:

We know that it was the Prime Minister who said there would be a meeting on the Friday and we know it was the Prime Minister who cancelled the meeting. So there is no doubt who is responsible for the decision.

The facts are as follows: late in the meeting, as irritation mounted on both sides and the clock moved past 7 pm, Mrs Thatcher did indeed make a statement that there would have to be another meeting on Friday to resolve the matter.

That was noted by the Cabinet Office civil servants present, who duly minuted it as a meeting which they would be responsible for setting up. The undertaking to hold a meeting was not, however, seen by everyone as such a cast-iron proposition as Heseltine believed it to be. The proposal was not, for instance, included in Mrs Thatcher's summing-up, but was made in the course of an intervention just before her final statement.

One Minister recalls it as the kind of remark an angry school-mistress might have made: 'You'll all have to come back on Friday... keep you in after school... that kind of thing.'

When she did come to her summing-up, Mrs Thatcher's conclusions were that the European Consortium should produce a firm proposal to put to the Westland Board by Friday. It would then be up to the Board to decide whether the proposals were acceptable or not. Until then the NADs recommendation would be allowed to stand.

She had, for the time being, lost the argument, and she was not best pleased.

The meeting came to an end at 7.20 pm, with Brittan and Heseltine still arguing furiously about the precise terms of the Prime Minister's conclusions and their implications for the NADs agreement. Their colleagues stole away, reluctant to prolong what had already been an exhausting session.

Brittan came out and gave his version of events privately to Westland, telling Marcus Agius of Lazards that the Europeans had been given until 4 pm on Friday to make the best offer they could. If that offer was not acceptable to the Board, the Government would no longer consider itself bound by the NADs agreement.

'Is it indeed going to be left up to the Board?' asked Agius.

'Yes,' said Brittan. The message was passed to Cuckney.

Heseltine reported back to his civil servants with a rather different account: there would be a meeting at the end of the week after the Stock Exchange had closed, he said, by which time the Europeans should have a firm offer on the table. At that point a decision would be taken by the Cabinet Committee on the NADs agreement.

Plainly, some civil servants at least shared Heseltine's view about the Friday meeting, for at ten o'clock that Tuesday calls were made from the Cabinet Office fixing arrangements for it. Friday afternoon is not a favourite time for MPs to be detained in London. There is no business to attend to in the House of Commons, and most Members leave for their constituencies or their country homes, or both.

There was, therefore, some irritation, as Ministers were contacted and told to make themselves available. Nicholas Ridley, although he had not been at the Economics Committee, rearranged his diary to attend what sounded like an important occasion. David Young also noted it.

Brittan, however, did not. And it seems that some time on Wednesday morning Downing Street was alerted to the fact that a meeting was being arranged which the Prime Minister did not wish to take place.

Again there are two theories as to what happened. One – the Downing Street version – is that a mistake was made by civil servants, and the meeting was unscrambled as soon as that was realised.

The other theory, suggested by the timing of the cancellation, is that as soon as the DTI learnt that another meeting was being planned, they tipped off Downing Street with a warning about the grave implications if it went ahead. On past performance the voting might well go Heseltine's way, they pointed out, thus throwing the Sikorsky bid out of court. It might perhaps be better if it were called off altogether.

Whatever the explanation, countermanding instructions were rapidly sent round, and the wretched civil servant at the Cabinet Office who had been carrying out what he believed were his Prime Minister's instructions was given a severe ticking-off by Sir Robert Armstrong for exceeding his brief.

Most Ministers, on learning that there would not now be a meeting, were profoundly relieved.

Not so Michael Heseltine. The Defence Secretary was first given the news that morning by his private secretary, Richard Mottram, as he sat in his office at the MoD. He was, in his own words, 'absolutely shattered'.

Until that point he had been supremely confident that the European offer, once properly presented, would be welcomed all round. Doubts would disappear at what he was sure was 'a superb bid', better all round than Sikorsky's, and absolutely suited to Britain's role in Europe. He was well aware that he faced deep opposition from the Prime Minister and her Trade Secretary, but he was certain – perhaps arrogantly so – that he would be proved right in the end.

Now he seemed to have been outflanked by the cancelled Cabinet Committee. He had not properly appreciated quite how much hostility he had incurred, nor the lengths to which his opponents would go to defeat him. On a more personal level, he may have begun to consider what effect the affair would have on his reputation with the European defence establishment if he was publicly repudiated by his own Cabinet. In his view, the rules had been changed again and a tougher, more ruthless game was being played.

From that point on, he began to consider seriously the possibility of resigning. That night, he discussed with close friends in the House of Commons whether he should not leave the Cabinet and bring the issue into the open from the back benches.

'But that's crazy,' said one Tory MP. 'You've got to stay and fight.'

Heseltine agreed.

Chapter Nine

CRISIS IN CABINET

'Ministers do have rows, one has to face that'

– Michael Heseltine, February 1986

There were now two people in town who reckoned they were being cheated. One was Michael Heseltine. The other was David Horne, the beleaguered banker in charge of putting together the European bid.

Horne was a terrier-like Aberdonian, brought in from Warburgs the previous summer to head Lloyds' new merchant bank organisation. The world of 'corporate finance' is notoriously one that encourages machismo – the big deal, the triumphant bid – for all that its players are mostly, like Horne, pleasant men who play golf and have suburban houses in Guildford.

Nevertheless, Horne had never faced a problem quite like this one: in the space of just four days he had to turn his Consortium's proposals, already scorned by the Westland Board, into the 'super-bid' that Heseltine had in mind, without any of the financial information from Westland to which, under City rules, he believed he was entitled.

From Monday 9 December, when he submitted an 'amplified' offer from the Consortium, up to the deadline of Friday 13, when he made its finished submission, he worked round the clock.

He did now have the valuable assistance of British Aerospace, whose board had decided officially that Monday to join the Consortium. This had caused considerable irritation to Leon Brittan, who had immediately passed a message to BAe's Chairman, Sir Austin Pearce, that he was 'upset' not to have been consulted beforehand. Pearce was sufficiently concerned to request a meeting.

In advance of the publication of the Westland company report Horne asked Thomson, his deputy, to go along next day to Lazards to go through the balance sheet. Even here, crucial information was missing.

Thomson found that the write-off figure – the total losses which the accountants had decided it would be prudent to cover – had apparently suddenly risen from the previously-stated total of £91 million to £106 million. This, said the accounts, was explained in 'Note 9'. But when Thomson turned to Note 9, it had been deleted because it was 'commercially confidential'.

Next day Horne himself called at the offices of the County Bank, merchant bank advisers to NatWest and Barclays, to try and worm some details out of them on the state of their loans to Westland. These were refused.

Thomson, with other European representatives, went to Carlton Gardens, armed with a list of questions for Westland about the Indian order, the value of the stock inventory, the state of the W30, and the breakdown of the write-offs. The answer to each question was a polite 'no', again on the grounds of confidentiality.

Raffaello Teti of Agusta was equally unsuccessful. He had tried a more direct approach, writing to Cuckney with a warning that the American offer might create trading problems for Westland in Europe, and asking him to give greater consideration to the European offer.

He was not pleased to be told in a reply from Cuckney, which may have sounded slightly less ungracious in Italian, 'You are reasoning with your heart, while I reason on the basis of money.'

Westland claims that Cuckney invited Teti to join the Sikorsky-Fiat combine, but Teti denies this. He says that not only has he no recollection of such an offer, he was so infuriated by hearing that Fiat was involved in the first place that there was a 'five-degree earthquake' at Agusta's headquarters when the news came through.

Back in London, David Horne was equally cross about the lack of cooperation. He wrote Lazards a formal letter of protest, with copies to Cuckney, Heseltine and Brittan, complaining about it:

Such a refusal is incomprehensible and certainly not justified . . .
we fail to understand how the Board of Westland . . . could discriminate to the extent, in our view, of depriving shareholders of a better and more soundly based proposal.

It got him nowhere. In the meantime the Sikorsky machine was moving smoothly towards its final offer. One result of the Cabinet Committee on 9 December had been a letter from Brian Hayes,

Permanent Secretary at the DTI, confirming that the launch-aid of £40 million would indeed be waived.

When added to the massive amount of organisation and expertise that Sikorsky had by now deployed, the resulting package was a formidable one, ready and waiting to be delivered on 'deadline Friday' – the 13th.

Heseltine, by now fully recovered from Wednesday's shock, was taking a close interest in the progress of both sides, and had decided that the time had come for a little delicate political bribery. He wrote to Cuckney, saying that if Westland would agree to take part in the four-nation European battlefield helicopter project, then the MoD would place an order with them for six Sea King helicopters. Of course this would also presume that future French, German, Italian and British helicopter requirements were met from within Europe.

The offer – or threat – was received by Westland together with another letter from the MoD pointing out the labour advantages inherent in the European offer. Neither communication went down well.

Heseltine also decided that he would protest, in full Cabinet that Thursday, about the matter of the cancelled meeting – despite the fact that Westland was not on the agenda, and was certainly not going to be put on it by Mrs Thatcher.

Brittan, somewhat apprehensively, asked John Mogg, his Private Secretary, to find out from Heseltine's Private Secretary what his intentions were, and was told that the Defence Minister would probably *not* intervene in Cabinet that morning. Brittan was, therefore, infuriated when he went back on this. But, as Heseltine told him airily later, he had decided to raise the matter anyway.

Waiting until Cabinet was well under way, he interrupted the discussion and announced slowly and deliberately, 'I want it recorded that a meeting planned for tomorrow has been cancelled.'

There was a stunned silence, then Mrs Thatcher snapped back that no meeting had been planned, and none cancelled. The civil servants, she said 'have no authority to fix a meeting'. A short and noisy altercation between the Prime Minister and her Defence Secretary ensued, with other ministers looking on in amazement. No one else joined in.

Afterwards Heseltine approached the Cabinet Secretary, Sir Robert Armstrong, to insist that his protest be recorded in the minutes; on discovering that this had not been done, he lodged a complaint. In what is described as 'a heated exchange', Armstrong told him later that there had been an error and he would see to it that a note was added. This was still, in Heseltine's view, inadequate. The matter remains outstanding.

'Such an error and correction were unprecedented in my experience,' he said, though other ministers are more familiar with the time-honoured expedient of 'editing' Cabinet minutes.

Two key Party figures, Lord Whitelaw and John Wakeham, the Chief Whip, did later try and intervene with Mrs Thatcher to persuade her to 'let Michael have his meeting'. They were overborne; a situation which, to judge by subsequent events, may have left both Ministers feeling Heseltine had been given rather a raw deal.

Friday the thirteenth, as a member of the Defence Committee later pointed out, was unlucky for a number of people.

It was, primarily, unlucky for the Europeans. David Horne had done his best to make the Consortium's proposal as convincing as possible, but the contrast between it and the Sikorsky offer was marked.

The size, for instance; when Sikorsky finally delivered its submission to Lazards that morning, it was contained in a pile of documents that weighed in at more than five kilograms.

The Europeans, by contrast, sent in a small sheaf of papers. Columbus Iselin of Sikorsky described it condescendingly thus:

We had a mountain of documents, whereas the Europeans never even generated a sandhill. It's difficult to think of anyone giving credence to something as sketchy as the Europeans put forward, especially when a lot of it was written by an avowed hyena [believed to be a reference to Heseltine]... It consisted of eight pages, of which three were written by Heseltine.

In fact Heseltine had not made a written contribution himself; but, as the 'avowed hyena' in question, he responded that, since he had been refused permission to report his proposals to Cabinet, he 'was required instead to report them to the board of a private company'.

The result, though thin, was strong enough to persuade Cuckney, of all people, that, as far as substance went, the differences between the two were 'qualitative, not just quantitative'. Both had come up with proposals on amounts of money offered, and man-hours of guaranteed work for the Westland plant, which were, in his words, 'beginning to equate'.

But that did not alter his basic attitude; he still disliked the European offer intensely. 'It was a minor adjustment to the offer made on the 9th... it was totally negative... not constructive and forward-looking.'

Sikorsky, by contrast, was 'immensely professional'. They had the 'ability to actually deliver on time'.

The Westland Board examined the European offer for forty minutes and rejected it out of hand.

At 2 pm Cuckney sent a letter round to Downing Street announcing the decision, and saying that Westland wished now to complete negotiations with Sikorsky-Fiat with a view to recommending a deal to its shareholders.

At 4 pm he rang Downing Street to confirm the position; the NADs agreement, he assumed, was now inoperative.

Both sides held press conferences. David Horne hung around long enough to hear Cuckney announce the Westland decision, then telephoned Sir Raymond Lygo at British Aerospace.

'Do we go on with the bid?' he asked.

'Go on!' said Lygo. 'Don't give up.'

Horne raced over to the MoD, where a rival press conference was being held. There he was asked by Bridget Bloom of the *Financial Times*, 'What do you do now?'

'We fight it, of course,' said Horne.

The other actors in the drama were mostly well content with the way things had gone. Heseltine, it seemed, had been properly put in his place, and the marketplace had given its view. As far as Mrs Thatcher was concerned there was 'no further issue to discuss'.

As far as Brittan was concerned, the Board had been 'perfectly reasonable' in rejecting the Europeans so peremptorily. And as far as Cuckney was concerned, Westland was now free to sign up with Sikorsky-Fiat as it had wa further issue toong.

There was, however, a dissenting voice.

Michael Heseltine announced that he intended to raise it again in Cabinet the following week, on 19 December.

That weekend the lobbying began. It took various forms, from the delicate to the devious.

Sir Austin Pearce, who had asked to see Brittan to find out why the Trade Secretary was 'upset' by British Aerospace's involvement, came away with a faintly uneasy impression, but little more.

Brittan, flanked by his Private Secretary, John Mogg, told Pearce that he felt he should have talked to the DTI before becoming involved with the Consortium. Pearce pointed out mildly that they were, these days, a private, denationalised company, and supposedly free to take their own commerial decisions as they wished.

He added that they had regularly told people like Norman Tebbit and Geoffrey Pattie, and even the DTI's Permanent Under-Secretary, Brian Hayes, about their well-understood attitude to Westland. He had intended no discourtesy. Brittan simply responded, 'That is your view. I still believe you should have talked to the DTI about it . . .'

Michael Heseltine was telephoned on Sunday evening by two lobby journalists, who said, 'You'd better know that they're leaking heavily on you. You're being rubbished by Number Ten. There's nothing you can do, but have a look at *The Times* tomorrow.'

Sure enough, there was a welter of stories next morning. *The Times* front-page account said, 'Reports that Heseltine has Cabinet support... are wrong. His tactics were reviewed last Monday by a Cabinet committee... he found little support.' It went on to say that Sikorsky had 'the Government's full endorsement... Ministers believe that the European offer... is a hollow one.' In the *Daily Mail*, there was a prominent report of Cuckney's attack on Heseltine's tactics as 'astonishing and distasteful'.

Not all the press comment was one way. The heavyweight *Daily Telegraph* and the *Financial Times* both carried leaders supporting the European initiative – indicating that this battle was more than just the Government against its maverick Defence Secretary. But in the meantime Heseltine was being made aware of pressure from other government departments as well.

His offer to Cuckney of a £25 million order for six Sea King helicopters if Westland went 'European' had been approved initially by the Treasury, provided it was met from within the MoD's existing budget. Now, however, there were second thoughts. That Monday Heseltine received a strong Treasury letter countermanding the previous one, and warning him that he had no authority to commit those funds. Cuckney, concerned about the implications for Westland in the future, was determined to have the political bribe withdrawn, or at least presented to the banks and other creditors in an 'even-handed' way as something Sikorsky was also entitled to, given equivalent circumstances.

Later that day Leon Brittan got to his feet in the House of Commons to deliver the Government's first parliamentary statement on the previous week's events. Matters were being left to the 'free market', he said; the NADs recommendation had lapsed; the way was now clear for a Sikorsky partnership with Westland. 'My statement is on behalf of the Government as a whole,' he added.

MPs watching the Tory front bench were fascinated to see Heseltine vigorously shaking his head in dissent. So public a mark of disagreement amongst Cabinet Ministers was unusual. Heseltine had moved from internal politicking to open rebellion.

The occasion was intriguing, too, because it was the first glimpse of an increasingly difficult role that Leon Brittan would now be required to play – one in which he had been firmly cast by Mrs Thatcher.

The Government's position, she had insisted, must be even-handed towards the two bids for Westland. Market forces must be allowed free play, and the shareholders should decide for themselves.

This was fine, provided both sides in the argument obeyed the rules. But Heseltine, of course, was making no pretence of being even-handed. And privately, if she was frank, neither was Mrs Thatcher. Her views about the importance of the Sikorsky bid were just as committed as Heseltine's were about the Europeans.

Brittan, who had begun by being agnostic, now found himself committed equally to the Cuckney position. But unlike Mrs Thatcher he had to join almost daily battle on the issue, without abandoning the pretence of being non-partisan.

It was an impossible position to maintain. It meant fighting with one hand tied behind his back as Heseltine outmanoeuvred him on the propaganda front. This helps to explain why the argument was conducted behind the scenes, with heavy reliance on leaks, arm-twisting and 'dirty tricks', rather than open political combat.

Heseltine himself was now a man with a mission. Baulked in Cabinet, he turned his attention to the House of Commons, a fertile breeding-ground for dissent. He now knew his argument backwards, and could make a powerful and convincing case of it. Behind him was a group of backbench supporters which included his long-serving ally, Michael Mates, and Dr Keith Hampson, his former PPS.

Heseltine started making phone-calls. The recipients were not only the board at GEC, who still had to be persuaded that they should join the Defence Ministry entourage and save Westland's technology for Europe. There were also Ministers, ex-Ministers and key Tory stalwarts to be persuaded.

To all, the message was similar. It was summed up by a Heseltine supporter as this:

Margaret and Cuckney have gone over to the Americans. Sikorsky will make the Black Hawk at Yeovil, and around 1987–9, when Westland reach the work gap, they will blackmail the British Government into buying it. Think of the political situation at that time. They start talking about 5,000 redundancies at Yeovil and Weston-super-Mare, and all those West Country seats are looking a bit dicky . . .

Next it was the Select Committee on Defence, an all-party group of backbenchers, prominent among them his own supporter Michael Mates. Another member was Michael Marshall, who was on the payroll of Consortium-member British Aerospace, as 'parliamentary adviser'.

Heseltine was invited to testify in secret session on 18 December. Although he faced some initial hostility, particularly from Winston Churchill, MP for Stretford, who accused him of 'cobbling together' the European deal at the last minute, his arguments went down well.

He spoke of the advantages of a European helicopter industry, and showed the Committee texts of agreements which the Defence Ministers of all three countries involved were ready to sign – agreements which would rationalise production and save the MoD £25 million right away.

The European offer – which he now referred to innocently as 'the British Aerospace solution' – would be an 'investment' in Westland whereas Sikorsky would have effective 'control' of the British company.

Furthermore, since Sikorsky's main interest was in selling the Black Hawk, and since the MoD had made it clear that it did not want to purchase the Black Hawk, the future for Westland under American control was not good. The British company would be simply turning out airframes rather than designing its own machine, and he could envisage circumstances in which Britain would be endangering its European helicopter projects and goodwill for the sake of an American machine which no one else wanted:

I do not see how a Black Hawk-led Westland revival is possible without the purchase of Black Hawk by the British Government, and I think every pressure will be brought on it to buy the Black Hawk. If the British Government buys the Black Hawk, that will be the end of the [European] NH90.

He was pressed to say what that implied. 'What do you see as the way forward if you lose your battle?' asked Mates.

'I see the future darkly,' murmured the Defence Secretary.

The Defence Committee was impressed. Word was put about that it was backing the Heseltine point of view.

At the same time Heseltine actively helped the Consortium prepare an improved offer for Westland and held a press conference at the MoD to announce it. Someone remarked that it looked like a Ministry of Defence team, rather than a group of European helicopter companies.

The Europeans, for their part, were determined to outbid Sikorsky. Their view about the NADs agreement was that since it had never been signed, it had not so far been operative, and so could not be withdrawn. It remained on the table, ready to be activated as soon as a European deal was struck.

They were fascinated, however, by the political battle which had resulted from it, and which they read about in the British papers. As Dr Teti of Agusta said:

> It was difficult for us to understand what was going on in the Cabinet. Certainly a similar row here in Italy would have led to the fall of the Government. We were not particularly worried. I imagine it was the English who were worried.

Aerospatiale took a darker view. Henri-Jean Roulleaux-Dugage, known affectionately amongst the Consortium as 'the little admiral', commented, 'The British Industry Minister switched horses in mid-stream. At the beginning he was European and then turned favourable to the Americans. Why?'

The 'British Industry Minister' and his leader were beginning to grow seriously worried about the Heseltine campaign and its apparent success.

Cuckney's lobbyist, Wilf Weekes of GJW, picked up from a friendly MP something of what was going on in secret session at the Defence Committee. Cuckney hastily sent word that he too was willing to give evidence; he was disturbed by the pro-Heseltine position they seemed to have adopted.

He telephoned Downing Street and protested about Heseltine's behaviour which, he said, posed grave threats to his final settlement with Sikorsky.

It was the day he was due to sign a 30 per cent share deal with the American company which he hoped would save Westland from insolvency. Figures to be released the following day would for the first time reveal the extent of the long crisis; the losses of £100 million in the year to September were many times worse than the City had predicted. 'The order of the magnitude of the financial problems is simply massive,' said Cuckney. 'People just don't realise.'

Mrs Thatcher took the matter seriously. She too was irritated by Heseltine's intransigence. More than that, she was beginning to feel that the whole authority of her Government was being undermined by the cavalier behaviour of one Minister. As for Leon Brittan, who was meant to be taking care of the public debate with Heseltine, he simply did not appear to be up to it. 'I wish Leon were as good at handling the press as Michael,' she said wistfully to her Chief Whip, John Wakeham.

Wakeham's subsequent instinct, as he pondered the problem, was to rally the troops and get a pro-Brittan lobby going. He thought he had better ask the Prime Minister first, but then dropped the idea. On the whole, perhaps, it would be better to let Heseltine have his head and allow his obsession to run its course...

That was not Mrs Thatcher's view. In her mind grew the conviction that the time had come for a showdown – one that might well result in the resignation of her Defence Secretary.

Two qualities which most people tend to associate with Mrs Thatcher now deserted her; in dealing with the Heseltine problem at the point where she could have disposed of it, she was neither tough nor sure-footed.

On Wednesday 18 December, as Heseltine was putting on his bravura performance in camera in front of the Commons Defence Committee, she summoned a meeting of her close advisers to consider what course of action she should take to limit the damage he was now causing.

Those present in Downing Street included Sir Robert Armstrong, Lord Whitelaw, John Wakeham and Bernard Ingham. It was a formidable line-up – the keeper of the constitutional conventions, the elder statesman; the head of what back-bencher Julian Critchley insists on calling the 'secret police'; and the master of propaganda.

The problem, as Mrs Thatcher saw it, was that Heseltine had now gone so far out on a limb in backing the European cause that he was endangering the credibility of the Government as well as posing a real threat to the Sikorsky rescue package for Westland.

The time had come, therefore, for an ultimatum to be put to him. She had failed to silence him in Cabinet, and failed so far to impose the normal disciplines of reticence which Cabinet Ministers are meant to obey.

Her inclination, therefore, was to write him a letter, containing conditions, which he would have to agree to in writing, governing the future handling of the Westland affair. She wanted to prepare a draft and to canvass opinion as to how it should be worded.

For the next two and a half hours her advisers pored over the letter and argued about its contents. Three different drafts were prepared and discussed.

It soon emerged that Bernard Ingham, her Press Secretary, with his responsibility for the Government's public image, was against sending it at all. Given the Defence Secretary's current state of mind, he argued, any such demand might have the effect of driving him into a corner and forcing him to resign in a cloud of recrimination. Friends of Heseltine had already been heard to mention it as a possibility.

That, in Ingham's view, would be a disaster for the Government. He pointed out that there was already quite enough criticism of what commentators called the Prime Minister's high-handedness. The last opinion polls had revealed again that she was seen as domineering. She had lost a large number of Ministers since she came to power, through sackings or resignations. The resignation of another one, especially one who was a Conference favourite and not noticeably 'wet', would have a deeply unsettling effect.

Ingham's influence on the Prime Minister, after six years of advising her on how best to respond to attacks on the Government, is considerable. Normally, his attitude to a problem was to 'tough it out', but in this case he urged caution, and, in the end Mrs Thatcher listened to him. She scrapped the last draft of her letter.

Instead, a decision was taken to seek a collective strategy at next day's Cabinet, whereby no Minister would lobby for either side, and Government unity would be preserved. The hope was that Heseltine would respect that.

In retrospect this decision – or the absence of one – was a grave error. From it flowed not unity, but an attempt at preserving the façade of unity, while at the same time seeking to undermine the Heseltine campaign at every available opportunity.

The man charged with this unsavoury task would be Leon Brittan.

Cabinet that Thursday was surprisingly calm. Westland was not a major topic, and most ministers were happy to steer round it. But it was perfectly clear that the problem had not gone away.

Mrs Thatcher laid down Government policy once again: it was up to the Westland Board to decide what was in the best interests of the company and its employees, she said. In those circumstances Ministers should avoid making any further public comment. She trusted that there would be collective Cabinet agreement to this.

Heseltine, to evecide what was in tappeared to accept that. He said it was right that there should be no 'advocacy'. But he pointed out that there would shortly be developments on the European front which would materially alter the situation, and he reserved the right to reply to factual questions if these were put to him.

Most of those around the table realised that this was a sizable loophole, but the matter was left there. That afternoon Mrs Thatcher told the House of Commons that there was now a united Government policy on Westland: 'The position [of Leon Brittan]... was reaffirmed by the Cabinet this morning... The position of the Cabinet is the position of the whole Government.'

This unity was to last approximately five hours.

That was hardly surprising, since others outside the Cabinet considered themselves under no restraint. Cuckney, announcing the Westland losses, said that Heseltine 'would not have minded the company going to the wall' in earlier months; lobby correspondents were briefed that Heseltine had been 'reined in' by Mrs Thatcher; and Sir Raymond Lygo pitched in on the other side, paying tribute to Heseltine's 'expertise' in putting together the European bid in rapid time.

That evening Leon Brittan, invited to appear on TV, was asked, inevitably, about Westland. He said that matters were up to the Board, but added that they should not have to negotiate 'with a pistol held to their head'.

Whether this was breaking the Cabinet embargo or not was debatable. The Heseltine camp did not stop to debate it. As far as they were concerned, the gloves were off again.

Brittan was certainly lobbying hard, if clumsily, behind the scenes. The next day, he ordered John Michell, the air division official who had been handling Westland, to ring up the Tory MP Winston Churchill, who had shown signs of wobbling at the Defence Committee. According to Churchill, Michell treated him to a long harangue in favour of Sikorsky.

Civil servants say it is questionable whether the Industry Secretary was actually entitled to ask his officials to do such political work. But, as events were to demonstrate, civil servants would increasingly be ordered to fling themselves into this ministerial contest.

In Downing Street Bernard Ingham was seriously worried. Two senior Ministers appeared to be breaking Cabinet rules at every opportunity, and he knew that the Sunday papers – ideal targets for ministerial briefings – would have more of the same.

That Saturday Ingham learnt that Brittan had been invited to appear on the BBC radio programme *The World This Weekend,* and realised that Heseltine would not be far behind.

Taking on the role of censor rather than disseminator of information, he set about trying to stop both men talking.

Heseltine, relaxing at home in Oxfordshire, had indeed been asked to contribute to the programme. The producer had telephoned to tell him that Brittan had recorded an interview, so perhaps he would like to do the same. Heseltine said he would.

Shortly afterwards Ingham called Heseltine and said they were trying to prevent Brittan taking part. Would he therefore also please stand down? Heseltine replied that he would wait to see whether Ingham had any success with Brittan first.

The next call from Downing Street informed him that even if Brittan's interview did go out on the programme he, Heseltine, must on no account say anything himself.

Heseltine smiled down the phone and hung up.

By Sunday morning there were distinct signs of desperation. When Heseltine arrived at the studio in Oxford to record his interview, he was told that Downing Street had been on the telephone trying to prevent the BBC using the Brittan interview. Senior producers were meeting to decide what to do.

As Heseltine waited, yet another call came through from Downing Street which he declined to take.

Finally the BBC decided to risk incurring the wrath of Ingham, and both interviews went out. Democracy breathed again.

Ingham had been right, however, to be worried about the Sunday papers. The *Observer* carried a front-page story revealing details of the meeting on 17 October between Brittan and Cuckney in which the Trade Secretary had apparently encouraged Cuckney to seek a European bid for Westland. The paper described Brittan as expressing a 'preference' for the European alternative.

A furious Brittan denied it outright, and described the story as 'a Christmas fantasy', though the dispute over what had or had not been said at the meeting was, as we have seen, open to interpretation.

Intriguingly, the same paper disclosed what was to be known as 'the Libyan connection' – the fact that Libya, with its terrorist links, had two directors on the board of Fiat, Sikorsky's partner. This too was seen by Brittan as black propaganda, though in fact the information had surfaced through routine inquiries. It was used gleefully by the Heseltine camp – 'Game, set and match to us' said one supporter. But there was always less to it than met the eye; the Libyans have never exercised any control over Fiat's policies.

The public squabble between two senior Ministers attracted far more coverage than the European Consortium which had, that Friday, lodged its new, improved offer with the Westland Board. It appeared to give more than Sikorsky, reaction was favourable, and Heseltine was said to be 'winning the battle'. That evening there was an atmosphere of cheerfulness amongst the team at the MoD, headed by Clive Whitmore, which had been working on the European campaign for the past six weeks.

The opposing 'team' was, however, much more formidable and tightly organised. It was to spend more than £4 million altogether on putting together the Sikorsky deal. Cuckney's small conference room in Carlton Gardens had by now taken on the appearance of a command headquarters. Every morning, shortly after 8 am, dozens of dark-suited advisers would join the Westland 'War Council'. They could be divided into different groups.

First came the 'City' directors who were handling the affair – three knights and a peer. There was Sir John Cuckney himself, Admiral Sir John Treacher, Sir John Maldwyn Thomas and, on most days, Lord Fanshawe, the well-connected Tory politician. The 'Yeovil' directors who made the actual helicopters only appeared from time to time. Their allies at United Technologies brought a team mainly led by Bill Paul from Connecticut – the lifelong Sikorsky 'company man'. Columbus Iselin and UT's president Hubert Faure also came when in London. Sometimes Fiat, the shadowy partner, sent two or three representatives as well.

Next came two merchant bankers' teams, both from the most influential City houses. John Nott, chairman of Lazards, only went to the war councils if they were held at Lazards itself, but he sometimes dropped in on Cuckney later in the day. His team consisted of Michael Baughan, the takeover expert Marcus Agius, and Michael Ross. Sikorsky's own merchant bankers were Morgan Grenfell, led by Peter Cadbury. Sir Peter Carey, recently retired Permanent Secretary at the DTI itself, was also on Morgan Grenfell's board, which must have been comforting for their customers.

There were two separate teams of lawyers to attend to the small print. Slaughter & May, one of the best-known solicitors' firms in the City, worked for Westland. Norton, Rose, Botterell & Roche represented Sikorsky.

And there were two sets of stockbrokers to handle the underwriting – and later the share trading. Peter Wilmot Sitwell of Rowe & Pitman was for Westland, and the firm of Cazenove for Sikorsky.

Finally came a considerable crowd of PR men and lobbyists. These were the responsibility of Admiral Treacher and, beneath him, Captain Bill Gueterbock of Westland. The firm's long-serving City PR firm was Lopex, led by Bob Gregory, who handled the dissemination of information, brochures, meetings and advertisements. A second 'Yeovil' PR team dealt with the helicopters themselves. Wilf Weekes represented the parliamentary lobbying firm of GJW, whose role was to bend the ear of friendly MPs and pick up Westminster intelligence. For Sikorsky, Peter Bloomfield of Bloomfield & Company was on the strength, while Morgan Grenfell sometimes brought their own Richard Shandwick along.

The last PR man was Gordon Reece, in many ways the most colourful of the crowd, though his role was still unknown outside Westland, even to Heseltine.

The War Council was often a big gathering, and most people would remain silent, collecting their briefings from Cuckney, Treacher, Baughan or Gregory, and working through a three-part routine: first, review of the morning's press; then announcements of 'today's actions'; and finally a tactical consideration of the forty-eight hours ahead.

But Reece would often hold the floor. 'He was a great one for grand statements, setting the scene in broad sweeps,' one of his audience says. 'He would tell us what the PM was supposed to be thinking, or look round, take off his glasses, bang on the table and say, "We mustn't get deflected today. We mustn't get swept into the political stream!" I remember once whispering, "But I could have said that!" and my companion whispered back, "Ah, but you're not Sir Gordon..."' With his big ties, his big cigars and his natural charm, he captivated his audience. 'One Saturday he appeared in a floor-length coat with masses of fur round the collar,' says one participant. 'I thought, my wife would give her eye teeth for that.'

Cuckney by contrast had a calm, low-key style. Emotional words about Heseltine were not heard, and he consistently refused to cancel his outside appointments, even at the height of the crisis: 'He would leave for the other City boards he chaired,' says one colleague. 'And keep in touch with his car-phone. He even went to the US for a week during the later share battle, on "routine business".'

There was one Christmas present for the taciturn Cuckney which further strengthened his team's hand. Frantic efforts by helicopter manager Don Berrington in Bombay secured an Indian agreement that the W30 had now been acceptably modified to carry loads in hot weather. They would still buy some machines from the rival French, but Westland would definitely get the order for the remaining twenty-one, 'probably by January'. The British Government was committed to paying for them out of its aid budget. (Later, an anonymous employee posted copies to the Opposition of a letter signed by Berrington. It revealed that Westland was actually paying the Indians a secret £10 million to take the helicopters, as an 'operating subsidy' to make up for the heavy fuel and maintenance bills.)

On the European side, David Horne of Lloyds was trying to co-ordinate a much more diffuse international team. He could not be expected to know what Westland was up to in Bombay. But he did eventually find out that it had brazenly ignored his new Euro-plan.

116

On the Saturday before Christmas, Westland sent out a circular to its shareholders containing details of the Sikorsky plan. There was no mention at all of the European bid; 'Not even a sticker,' commented Horne when he learnt about it that Monday.

Thus all the time, expertise and effort which had gone into the European bid was not even being presented to the men and women who would take the final decision – the shareholders.

Clearly, if the game was not going to be played by any of the normal rules, once again other methods would have to be tried.

Chapter Ten

TURKEY AT CHEQUERS

*'I don't accept that politics is a power struggle –
completely unethical and unprincipled'*

– Edward Heath

Heseltine now began to make a series of thinly veiled threats that were
to lead to Mrs Thatcher's final loss of patience. In the first of several
MoD messages, the deputy procurement chief John Bourn publicly
announced on Heseltine's instructions that – as far as the MoD was
concerned – a Westland in league with Sikorsky would face a bleak
future.

It would sell no Black Hawks to the Ministry, and would be blocked
from all joint projects in Europe. This government pronouncement
was a serious threat. Cuckney would find it hard to sell a deal to
shareholders in the teeth of such official hostility, when everything
depended on securing a full 75 per cent of their vote.

Heseltine coupled this pressure with a highly unorthodox private
approach.

This was to cause more anger than all the subsequent public
disputes and allegations of 'dirty tricks', although it was never more
than two telephone calls. He is said to have brought to bear on Sir
John Cuckney the full weight of his Ministerial pressure, and, whether
intended or not, what he said was interpreted as an open threat.

The episode began when Heseltine was lunching in a London
restaurant on 23 December. A 'leading member of Britain's defence
industry' – whom neither side will identify – came up to wish him a
happy Christmas. 'The best Christmas present I could have,' said
Heseltine, 'would be to get Sir John Cuckney in my office.' In a spirit
of goodwill, the industrialist rang Cuckney at home and told him to

expect a call. Heseltine's friends say, 'Michael was told, yes, there was possible common ground.'

But when Cuckney's phone in Kent rang, it was Heseltine in his most forceful mood. 'I want this conversation on strictly lobby terms,' he said, referring to the Westminster system whereby Ministers pass on information to journalists, safe in the knowledge it will never be 'attributed'.

Cuckney had promised himself a week at home over Christmas with his wife, who was recovering from a major operation. He himself had been feeling the strain after intestinal surgery earlier in the year. What Heseltine appears to have said to him – though accounts of the conversation differ – is that, since Cuckney's wife was ill, he was prepared to drive down personally to his home in Kent bringing with him documents and a 'team' if necessary.

His proposal to Cuckney was that they should cut through the arguments and the bureaucracy and sign 'heads of agreement' on Westland right away. The Heseltine camp put it more mildly. They say he merely wanted Cuckney to examine 'a programme'.

What the deal was to be is one of the more closely guarded secrets of the Westland affair. But there are some clues. Clearly, Heseltine had to offer an unpublicised 'sweetener' if there was to be any chance of succeeding in such a remarkable private approach. He is said to have mentioned that he had a great deal of influence with Manfred Woerner, the West German Defence Minister, and could push through the NADs deal.

This, according to the Westland camp, included a clause that was never publicly disclosed – and never, in the end, fulfilled: that the Germans, in addition to the other joint agreements, should return to the expensive EH101 helicopter project, with which Westland and Italy had been forced to struggle alone throughout the 1980s. Such a deal would have been very attractive to Westland and strengthened its future prospects considerably.

Whatever combination of carrot and stick Heseltine used, it misfired very badly. Cuckney resented his intrusion. Heseltine can be abrasive, his friends concede. 'Michael does believe you've got to talk tough to these City people,' said one. Cuckney was under the impression that the Prime Minister had repeatedly promised there would be no more ministerial campaigning.

His afternoon now thoroughly disrupted, he rang his lawyers at Slaughter & May, Lazards the bankers and members of the Westland Board to consult them about Heseltine's private approach. On their advice, he rang back Heseltine on the morning of Christmas Eve to tell him, 'I have no power to do as you ask.'

Heseltine returned his call around midday, and repeated at some length both his previous offer and the threat that Sikorsky would be 'shut out of Europe'.

Heseltine was certainly acting at this stage – as one of his colleagues puts it – 'like a man possessed'. On Boxing Day he made no fewer than three phone-calls to the chairman of GEC, his former Cabinet colleague and Thatcher critic, James Prior. Following his failure with Cuckney, he was now determined to persuade the huge avionics company, which had originally refused to have anything to do with the affair, to put all its muscle behind his Consortium.

It has to be said that the nature of the approaches to Cuckney is disputed. But one test can be applied by the political detective. In the course of the propaganda war, details about them – confidential as they were – have been passed more freely around by the Thatcher-Brittan-Cuckney camp than by the Heseltine side. This may suggest that Heseltine's supporters are more punctilious about confidentiality. Or it may be that they find the facts somewhat embarrassing to recall.

The news of Heseltine's phone-call spread through the Westland camp at speed. Cuckney rang Leon Brittan, who, according to Cuckney's friends, 'went berserk'. Someone also got hold of Gordon Reece, whose views of Heseltine were already harsh. Witnesses say he told one of the last Carlton Gardens War Councils before Christmas, 'We've obviously got to go for Heseltine. And it means going for the kill.'

Reece, who has been separated since 1977 from his wife and seven children, had once again received a private invitation to spend Christmas Day with Mrs Thatcher in the countryside at Chequers. As he explained to his Westland colleagues, 'The crowd comes on Boxing Day. But Christmas lunch is just a quiet family affair. We watch the Queen's Speech together, and talk about how we've all been doing...'

Given what was uppermost in Reece's mind that Christmas, it would have been surprising if he had not mentioned to the Prime Minister this latest example of the outrageous conduct of her Defence Secretary.

And whatever thoughts Mrs Thatcher had in response as she handed round the turkey at Chequers, it is equally hard to imagine Reece failing to make a mental note of her reaction.

For Gordon Reece, paid political lobbyist, on the brink of seeing the public announcement of his knighthood, it is hard to imagine a way of having a merrier Christmas.

It was as well for Heseltine that he had cancelled his planned

Christmas trip to Nepal with his family. For immediately after Boxing Day, in the slack period before the New Year festivities, Mrs Thatcher made a significant move to support Cuckney and contradict – finally and humiliatingly – the public statements made on Heseltine's authority.

A letter was arranged from the Prime Minister to Cuckney, one which he could publish. Its origins lay quite clearly with Number Ten. This was the first subterranean event in what might legitimately be called 'The Mysterious Affair of the Three Letters' – an affair in which the public perception of what was being done did not accord at all with what was happening behind the scenes.

On the morning of Monday 30 December, a day when there was little politics about and most newspapers were running on skeleton staffs, a major decision was taken at a small Westland War Council in the office of Lazards. Cuckney said he intended to send round by messenger the letter to Mrs Thatcher. This would demand official reassurance about Westland's future prospects after the Sikorsky link-up. Those present recall that Marcus Agius of Lazards seemed uneasy. There was a risk, he argued, that any Prime Ministerial reply would be too cautious to help. But Cuckney was remarkably confident. Gordon Reece was vague in his recollection afterwards to colleagues about whether he had helped Cuckney draft the text. 'I might have done, but I don't recall,' he told one.

Cuckney wrote:

Dear Prime Minister,
... It would greatly help my board to know if Westland would no longer be considered a European company by the Government, if a minority shareholding in the company were held by a major international group from a Nato country outside Europe.

This question is of fundamental importance in view of the statement... from the Ministry of Defence... that only by joining the so-called European Consortium would Westland be in a position to take responsibility for the British share of European helicopter collaborative projects.

The speed of the reaction in Number Ten suggests unmistakably that this letter of Cuckney's had been pre-arranged. On the same day Charles Powell, the Private Secretary concerned at Downing Street, sent round to Leon Brittan at the DTI a ready-drafted reply from Mrs Thatcher. An accompanying memo said the draft was to be checked with appropriate ministries and the Law Officers, and returned to Number Ten for signature by 4 pm the following day, New Year's Eve.

The draft said exactly what Cuckney wished:

> As long as Westland continues to carry on business in the UK, the Government will, of course, regard it as a British and therefore European company, and will support it in pursuing British interests in Europe.
>
> Government policy will remain that Britain should procure its helicopters from the most cost-effective source. Against this background, the Government would wish to see Westland play a full part in existing and future European collaborative projects.

The letter turned New Year's Eve into a day of high drama. Awaiting delivery of the Prime Minister's reply, Cuckney felt able to stall the European Consortium's offer of detailed further work-sharing. There was a choleric dispute between the two admirals, Lygo of British Aerospace and Treacher of Westland.

As Lygo recounts it, he rang Cuckney himself because he was becoming concerned. There had been absolutely no reaction at all. Failing to reach Cuckney he spoke to Admiral Treacher and said, 'Is there a problem? There must be a misunderstanding somewhere, because we have had no reaction from you at all. What is wrong with the offer? Is it something we have not recognised?'

'Yes. We really do not believe that at the end of the day the European Consortium will honour its obligations,' said Treacher.

'Well,' Lygo said, 'I must tell you that in today's meeting each company has bound itself severally to undertake its obligations in the event the Consortium offer is taken up. We are not a company that would put our hand to a document we do not intend to honour. I can well understand your suspicions and disbelief, but we would not do that. If you don't believe what we're saying, you'd better think carefully what you say.'

'I hear you and understand what you say.'

'Look, I have a lot of other things to do apart from Westland, and I can assure you this is a genuine offer. If you don't believe it, we'd better drop the whole thing here and now!'

Lygo was becoming cross: 'I didn't want to have a continuous series of meetings at which we were asked to appear as if we were the supplicants and then to be dismissed almost as if we were incredible. It was an embarrassing position to be in.' He attempted to persevere with Treacher: 'If you've got a problem, we stand ready to come and discuss it, or any other problems, with you...'

'Will you be available after New Year's Day?' asked Treacher.

'We shall all be here, and if you want further discussions, you shall have them!'

Lygo did not hear from Westland, however. He says, 'Our offer had not been properly discussed, not been properly put to the shareholders ...'

Meanwhile, Leon Brittan's officials at the DTI summoned the press. Every journalist covering Westland for the serious papers was invited to a briefing that afternoon, given by John Michell, the official who had earlier been set to lobby Winston Churchill on the Defence Committee. One of those present says:

Michell gave a pretty one-sided briefing in favour of Sikorsky, outlining the danger of retaliation from the US if they were rejected because we were already giving the European Airbus subsidies; he stressed the problems with the European state-owned helicopter industries and the protectionist leaning of the whole Consortium. He ended by saying that departmental differences with the Defence Ministry had been 'greatly exaggerated'. But he added that not a word was to be attributed to the DTI.

Further along Whitehall, in the main building of the MoD, Heseltine was brooding about Mrs Thatcher's latest move. A copy of the draft reply to Cuckney, apparently originating from the DTI, had been sent round to Heseltine that morning with inevitable results. 'Smoke issued from Heseltine!' recalls one of his colleagues. Mottram, his Private Secretary, rang his opposite number at the DTI, John Mogg, and demanded, 'What's this?'

It was during this call that Mottram discovered two things which, to anyone used to ministerial procedures, looked distinctly odd. Firstly Charles Powell, Mrs Thatcher's Private Secretary, had sent the original letter from Cuckney round to the DTI to handle. Letters to the PM about defence procurement questions are normally referred first to the Defence Ministry.

Secondly, the reply to Cuckney had not been drafted within the DTI at all, but had come in a memo from Mrs Thatcher herself. Mottram demanded the text of Mrs Thatcher's note, and Heseltine asked whether it had yet been copied to the Law Officers. Matters of this importance and sensitivity normally lead to the Attorney-General, wearing his hat as the Government's solicitor, being warned and approached well in advance. Indeed, the confidential ministerial regulations warn, 'It is essential that the Law Officers should be consulted *in good time*.'

It was a critical hour for Heseltine. Journalists who called on him for 'unattributable' briefings that day found him tense and – for once – silent. Finally, when they had gone, he picked up the phone.

There were few who could match Heseltine at this kind of in-fighting, and his next move was undoubtedly a smart one. He ordered his officials to draft an extra section for the PM's draft reply, repeating the MoD position: in the event of a Sikorsky deal, the MoD would not buy the Black Hawk and the European governments would probably refuse to collaborate with Westland.

Heseltine then telephoned the acting Attorney-General, Sir Patrick Mayhew (Sir Michael Havers was ill). The Solicitor-General was a barrister and a personal friend of twenty years' standing. He was not an enthusiastic admirer of Mrs Thatcher, who had moved him into what was essentially a dead-end legal job from a junior Home Office ministry. He had previously incurred Prime Ministerial displeasure for pointing out once or twice to Mrs Thatcher that he knew more law than she did.

Mayhew knew nothing so far of the contents of this important public letter. Heseltine told him the matter was urgent, and Mayhew agreed to come round to his office right away.

The result was exactly what Heseltine wanted. After studying the draft reply, Sir Patrick told the DTI that it might contain 'material inaccuracies' of a legally dangerous nature. Since the DTI had only shown it to their own, more junior, lawyers, before sending it on at the last minute on a Friday afternoon to Mayhew himself, they were outflanked, with the Prime Minister's deadline of 4 pm rapidly expiring.

By the time the bundle of papers arrived back at Number Ten, Mrs Thatcher found herself finessed. The telephone lines buzzed between Downing Street, the MoD, the DTI and the Solicitor-General's chambers. What did he mean, 'material inaccuracies'? Heseltine was ordered to send round to Downing Street and to Sir Patrick's office all the documents he had which showed what the French, Dutch, German and Italian governments were saying.

Sir Patrick, treading a narrow path of diplomacy, ruled finally that, while there was no need for the full panoply of MoD warnings, it was necessary for Mrs Thatcher to add one paragraph at least to her official letter, to read:

Some of these [European projects] are still at a very early stage and all of them require the agreement of the companies and governments – including HMG – concerned. In this connection you should be aware of indications from European governments and companies that they currently take the view that a number of projects in which Westland are expecting to participate in co-operation with other European companies may be lost to Westland if the UT/Fiat proposals are accepted.

Heseltine, expecting the Prime Minister to accept his counter-coup – albeit with bad grace – retired to a Fleet Street restaurant with his wife at 8 pm, all other plans for Hogmanay having long been abandoned. It was there that a frantic phone-call from Richard Mottram found him at 10.30. Mrs Thatcher would accept Mayhew's ruling. But she proposed to tack on her own final paragraph, in an attempt to dilute its impact. It read:

I can assure you that whichever of the two proposals currently under consideration the company chooses to accept, the Government would continue to support Westland's wish to participate in these projects, and would resist to the best of its ability attempts by others to discriminate against Westland.

Tired, and by and large content, Heseltine let it go. It had been a long day.

The affair of the Second Letter followed only two days later. If the first was a plot by Mrs Thatcher, the second was an unmistakable Heseltine 'dirty trick'. Even Heseltine himself has conceded that he was not exactly playing by Queensberry rules, though he claims he had been 'provoked' beyond endurance.

Essentially, what he did was to arrange another exchange of letters, this time between himself and the European Consortium, in which every word that Mrs Thatcher had refused to let him insert in the first was simply put out on his own behalf – as Government policy. 'It was simply outrageous,' say his enemies, and even some of his friends. However, Teti of Agusta says, 'It was music to our ears.'

Heseltine's justification for the Second Letter was that Cuckney had ignored in his public statements all the Heseltine qualifications so painfully inserted in the first. As a new eighteen-strong Sikorsky team flew in to London and resumed detailed negotiations, Cuckney said he was 'considerably heartened'. What he called 'the strength of the Prime Minister's letter' was bound, in his view, to weaken any European hostilities.

On the morning of 3 January Heseltine telephoned the office of David Horne at Lloyds, where the European Consortium had its headquarters. He dictated a letter with three 'questions' in it, which he wanted sent back round to the Defence Ministry forthwith.

Heseltine then went to a ministerial meeting chaired by Mrs Thatcher on another matter. Those present describe the atmosphere as 'surprisingly friendly'. Perhaps that is not so surprising. Mrs Thatcher would have felt ahead of Heseltine on points. And Heseltine knew that, when he returned to his office, he had a nasty surprise prepared for her.

As soon as Horne's 'spontaneous' letter arrived, Heseltine sent a ready-prepared answer. The first question was whether the MoD would buy the Black Hawk. Heseltine's reply was, 'The Government... has no intention of procuring the Black Hawk.'

The second question was whether Westland had ever exported a helicopter that had not been first purchased by the British military. Heseltine replied, 'I am advised that there has been no such export.'

Finally the letter asked what projects in Europe, 'further to the Prime Minister's letter', might be lost to Westland if it undertook the Sikorsky deal. Heseltine said:

> There are three future helicopters intended to form the core of the fleet of the British armed services in the longer term, all of which are planned to be produced collaboratively... [These were the battlefield helicopter; the transport helicopter, the NH90; and the big naval EH101 with Agusta.] There are indications available to HMG from both the other governments and the companies concerned that a Westland link with Sikorsky/Fiat would be incompatible with participation by that company on behalf of the UK in the collaborative battlefield helicopter and NH90 projects.
>
> There have been separate indications from Agusta that if the Westland deal with Sikorsky went through, Agusta would have to seek other partners.

Heseltine was exaggerating. In the event of a Sikorsky win, the all-European battlefield project might certainly collapse, but Westland could well still have expected to be left with the original, although less satisfactory, Anglo-Italian scheme.

The NH90 would probably fall too; but it was not very likely that the Italian government would dissolve the expensive and well-advanced Anglo-Italian EH101 scheme, whatever the outcome, and whatever the Italians currently thought it helpful to Heseltine to say.

The Prime Minister's reaction to publication of Heseltine's letter was, predictably, one of outrage. She later said frostily in public, 'The letter was never discussed with my office even though it dealt with points arising from my own letter.' The First Letter had complied, however artificially, with all the departmental protocol, even being circulated to MacGregor at the Treasury for approval before final despatch on New Year's Day. But Heseltine had simply ignored the conventions.

It was not long after the letters had appeared on the news-tapes that the phone rang in Brittan's private office. Westland, too, was furious that the Government seemed again to have failed to deliver the goods. Treacher and Fanshawe complained on Westland's behalf that Heseltine had gone far beyond the Prime Minister's text. This, they pointed out, placed them in 'some difficulty' about the documents being prepared to go to shareholders on Monday.

Brittan's staff assured them that despite Heseltine's letter no new information about European intentions had been received. Mrs Thatcher's original letter had been 'carefully drafted'.

That Friday evening there was a grim little meeting at Number Ten, as Mrs Thatcher and her closest aides, including Charles Powell, studied Heseltine's letter line by line. There was one section where he appeared to have gone too far in interpreting European reactions; there was nothing in writing from the Italian Government although there was from the others. Who spotted the omission is not known, but it is entirely possible that Mrs Thatcher, with her legal training, could herself have been responsible.

The charge of 'material inaccuracies' was now to be turned round, using the same weapon that Heseltine himself had brought into play – Sir Patrick Mayhew.

The scenario had one important refinement. It was hoped that Mayhew would agree that there were mistakes in Heseltine's document. He was then to say so formally, and *in writing*. The Solicitor-General was about to be manipulated in a way which would seriously embarrass him, and lead to a major political scandal when the resulting document was used to discredit Heseltine in public.

Afterwards, when the Third Letter became a political powder-keg, the blame was shuffled around amongst everyone involved. It is worth putting on record, therefore, that although Sir John Cuckney may have asked for a written rebuttal of the Heseltine document to satisfy his legal obligations to the shareholders, the instigation of this particular letter and the purpose for which it was intended can be laid at the door of the Prime Minister herself.

Mrs Thatcher admits that it was she who gave orders that Friday afternoon to Leon Brittan that he should find Mayhew and tell him that the letter appeared in her view to be 'inaccurate'.

Mayhew could not be found that evening, and, as the weekend began, the search resumed. Brittan tracked him down on Saturday, and pointed out to him the possible omissions in the Heseltine letter. Was there not a strong possibility, he asked, that the letter was inaccurate?

Mayhew was cautious. But he agreed that it might be so 'on a preliminary and provisional view'. (The words are those of the Cabinet

Secretary, Sir Robert Armstrong, reporting later.)

Brittan, having urged Mayhew to pass his views on to the Prime Minister, 'reported back' (his own words) to Mrs Thatcher in Downing Street at about 7 pm.

Charles Powell at Number Ten outlined on the phone to senior staff at the DTI the next phase of the scheme. Mayhew, he said, should be got to put his views in writing. The Cabinet Secretary was eventually to admit this awkward conversation too.

The Law Officers have an ambiguous position in government. Mayhew was a Conservative politician, and indeed had been a long-serving Junior Minister. But at the same time, when he took on his new job as Solicitor-General, he assumed a mantle of legal impartiality. This 'convention' cut both ways. It protected the Government from charges of abusing the law for political purposes (as for example when, the previous year, Mayhew had helped authorise the prosecution of Clive Ponting for 'leaking'). It also enabled Mayhew to be awkward when he felt like it, from a position of peculiar legal authority. He could not altogether be switched on and off like a political tap.

But the ground was now prepared for a formal request from the Prime Minister to the Solicitor-General that he should write a critical letter to her Cabinet colleague. It was conveyed through Powell to his opposite number in Mayhew's office, probably the Legal Secretary, Henry Steel, whose job it was to find Mayhew once again and convey the formal request.

It must have been as late as 10 pm when Mayhew was contacted at home and given his orders. Leon Brittan surprisingly told the Commons later, 'I did not ask Mayhew in any way to write the letter.' But the fact was that the Prime Minister did the asking with the specific knowledge of Brittan's own private office. This was after Brittan had personally established, at Number Ten's request, that Mayhew's attitude was going to be cooperative, and had rapidly told Number Ten so. Brittan's particular role, as events later that weekend were to confirm, was at the very least that of henchman.

Mayhew must have been concerned. Unbeknown to Downing Street, no sooner did he put the phone down late on that Saturday night than he picked it up again. He was alerting Heseltine.

On the available accounts of the conversation, it was relaxed and cheerful. The two were old friends, and called each other 'Paddy' and 'Michael'. Mayhew said that from what he had seen in that day's *Times* about Heseltine's letter, it went too far.

'It doesn't go far enough!' said Heseltine.

Mayhew replied that, on the evidence he had seen, there were inaccuracies. But Heseltine urged him to relax. It was just a matter of telling the PM the evidence was available, he said.

Mayhew said that, nonetheless, he felt obliged to have a formal exchange of letters with him on Monday after he had gone through the documents again at his office in the Strand. Heseltine agreed, cheerfully.

Heseltine has since emphasised that Mayhew never tipped him off about any instructions from the Prime Minister. This can be read as loyalty to an old friend who was taking a risk to help him. On the other hand, there was scarcely any need for Mayhew to spell out the situation. It was obvious what was going on.

The next morning, Sunday, word spread that 'Mayhew is willing'. A member of Leon Brittan's staff rang Sir John Cuckney at home, and told him 'in strict confidence' what had happened. Protocol would have demanded that someone at a senior level did this, which suggests it may have been Sir Brian Hayes, the Permanent Secretary.

There is no doubt that a call from the DTI was made. The Cabinet Secretary admits it. But Leon Brittan denies ordering the call or even knowing of it at the time. He has repeatedly said he had no idea of what occurred that weekend. If this is correct, then either his own officials were conducting a personal campaign against Heseltine, or they were by this stage taking their minute-by-minute instructions from Number Ten.

The Cabinet Secretary, Sir Robert Armstrong, claimed later that, in this phone-call, Brittan's staff had not betrayed any confidences about the Solicitor-General's intended letter; they had merely confided the fact that it seemed as if a 'material inaccuracy' might have been detected which was still 'under consideration' by the Government.

Even by Sir Robert Armstrong's account this incident is extraordinary. For a civil servant to tip off a company chairman about confidential government business is not what the Government's confidential regulations actually lay down:

Government policy should not be discussed with persons outside Government service unless this is *necessary* for the conduct of public business... serious leakages of information can occur when the press are enabled to piece together... items of information... It is therefore unwise to allude prematurely to... matters the disclosure of which has not been authorised...

In appropriate cases, it may be in the public interest to communicate certain information in confidence... but this is permissible only when it is known that such confidence will be respected.

Armstrong claims it was 'ethical' because Cuckney had a 'material interest' in knowing in general terms that there were possible inaccuracies in Heseltine's letter. But what was conveyed was in fact far from general. As later events showed, Brittan's staff 'leaked' quite clearly and specifically the fact that the Solicitor-General was to intervene. And that fact itself was immediately 'leaked' to the press before the weekend was over.

According to Armstrong's version, Cuckney's response to the DTI's leak was peremptory. He said he wanted the problem 'cleared up' by the time of his 4 pm press conference the following day. This timing was 'very important' to Westland, Cuckney reportedly said.

However, by lunchtime, Cuckney had also set out to ensure in his own way that the news quickly got out. A piece of 'strictly off the record' intelligence reached Peter Riddell of the *Financial Times*, a newspaper with whom Cuckney had good links. What his 'source' said was in these terms: 'The Solicitor-General is intervening. He is displeased with Heseltine. I don't know when, perhaps Tuesday. You can use this, but not from me.'

It was a sensational 'leak' and one that the Defence Committee, in their later laborious investigations of the history of the Mayhew letter, never knew of. It might have shocked them more than the subsequent leaks which caused such a scandal. But Riddell could not extract any corroboration from the MoD of the story, and the *Financial Times* never printed it.

Heseltine's own weekend had been spent privately attempting to lobby two figures who had kept out of all the limelight. But they had in fact always been in a key position to control Sir John Cuckney, and, to an extent, the Government. These were Lord Boardman, Chairman of National Westminster, and Sir Timothy Bevan, Chairman of Barclays. They were the ones who wanted their overdrafts back.

Furthermore, that very day, the banks were locked in tense and difficult negotiations with Sir John Cuckney, who was having a hectic Sunday. Sikorsky had been obliged to improve its offer to meet the Consortium bid, but the banks had to agree any changes to the package in which they took some of the risk by converting loans into shareholdings.

What Heseltine did was ring up James Prior, former Cabinet Minister and Chairman of GEC, who had already been enlisted as an ally and Consortium partner. Prior was entertaining to Sunday lunch at the time none other than Mrs Thatcher's arch-opponent, the fallen Tory premier Edward Heath.

As the Prior lunch cooled, Heseltine explained his needs. He wanted the two banks to come out in favour of the Europeans. Prior's leisurely Sunday was over; he must have spent at least seven hours thereafter on the phone. He rang his chief executive, Lord Weinstock; he rang Bevan; he rang Boardman.

Boardman was, of course, part of the political network; he had been a Tory colleague of Prior's when Boardman was a Minister at the DTI in Edward Heath's own government. Between discussions, there were no less than five more conversations with Heseltine himself. The banks would not play. As one of the chairmen said, 'Look, this puts us in a difficult position. Basically, what we want to do is secure our money.'

Cuckney had been more successful. By the end of the day he had secured agreement from the banks, called a snap Sunday-night board meeting to ratify the new Sikorsky deal, and put out the fact in time for the evening TV news. It was a dramatic pre-emptive strike.

Meanwhile on that same Sunday, Mrs Thatcher and a small knot of her most trusted colleagues were gathering in the countryside at Chequers. They were due to hold the regular 'beginning-of-term' informal conference of what might be termed the senior prefects, before full Cabinet meetings began again after Christmas. Among those present were the Chief Whip, John Wakeham, and Lord Whitelaw.

At least half the entire meeting was taken up with the question of Heseltine, and the atmosphere was ripe with expressions of loyal outrage. Whitelaw was particularly violent in his condemnation. Heseltine's unilateral public letter was 'outrageous' he said. 'I've never seen anything like it in my life.'

As a result of this hostility, the Prime Minister felt Heseltine had – at last – lost his friends at court. She confided that the Solicitor-General – an apparently impartial figure in the eyes of the public – was likely to object to the letter's contents. Those present now privately admit this. There is no evidence that she went further and told them to expect a letter from Mayhew the following day. She had asked him to write it, but she did not know when it would come or what it would say. Mayhew could not be pushed too far, and had to be allowed to write his own letter in his own time.

But the Chequers meeting proceeded confidently nonetheless to set the scene for a final confrontation with Heseltine. One assumption behind the discussion was that by the following Thursday's Cabinet Heseltine would have been deflated by Mayhew's criticisms. Wakeham, the Chief Whip, was clearly regretting his kindliness before Christmas in agreeing to let Heseltine have his head, and so was Whitelaw.

Mrs Thatcher said that a final ultimatum was to be presented to Heseltine at the Cabinet of 9 January. He was to be forbidden to make any more public statements whatever about Westland, unless he submitted them for approval in advance by the Cabinet Office. In other words, his campaign on behalf of the European Consortium was to stop. The decision was taken that had been shirked on 18 December.

A possible replacement Defence Secretary – George Younger – was designated. Mrs Thatcher was now prepared to challenge Heseltine to resign.

Typically, by the end of that Sunday, the first person to know that the secret Chequers session had decided – yet again – to stop Heseltine was Sir John Cuckney. He regularly knew more about the inner decisions of the Thatcher camp than did most other members of 'the Government'. He had become a very influential man.

Chapter Eleven

THE LEAK

'If the Right Honourable gentleman is unable to appreciate any of the consequences of receiving a letter that is marked strictly private and confidential... he is quite unaware of the normal obligations that exist in society'

– Leon Brittan, 13 January 1986

At 11.15 am on Monday 6 January, Sir Patrick Mayhew sat at his desk above the Law Courts in the Strand and inscribed his name at the foot of a letter classified as 'confidential' which was to cause a political convulsion.

It was not a particularly devastating letter, certainly not the one which Mrs Thatcher's friends had predicted would 'blow Michael Heseltine out of the water'. Indeed, 'cavilling' – the word the Labour opposition used about it later – seems about right. But it was the best the Solicitor-General felt prepared to do. Copies were run off for Mrs Thatcher herself, Leon Brittan at the DTI, the Treasury and the Foreign Office.

He had written:

Dear Michael,
I saw in the *Times* on Saturday, the text of a letter you are reported to have sent to the managing director of Lloyds Merchant Bank.

[He quoted Heseltine's passage: 'There are indications available to HMG from both the other Governments and the companies concerned that a Westland link with Sikorsky/Fiat would be incompatible with participation by that company on behalf of the UK in the collaborative battlefield helicopter and NH90 projects.']

This sentence, when read with the rest of the paragraph (in which the defence ministries of all four Governments apart from the UK are referred to) necessarily implies that *all* the governments and *all* the companies involved in the collaborative battlefield helicopter and NH90 projects have given this indication to HMG.

The telegrams (No 440 of 17 December from the Hague and Nos 1037 and 1083 of 5 December from Rome) and the record of your meeting with the W German defence minister in November – which were available to me when I gave advice on 31 December to the PM on the text of her reply to Sir John Cuckney – do not seem to me to support a statement that *all* the governments and *all* the companies have indicated that a Westland link with Sikorsky/Fiat would be incompatible with the participation by that company in the projects. The documents that I have seen contain evidence that the Netherlands Defence Secretary, the German Defence Minister and the Chairman of Agusta have commented to the knowledge of HMG in various ways, on adverse consequences which may flow from a decision to accept the Sikorsky offer. (In addition to Agusta, the documents disclose that Aerospatiale and MBB are additionally involved in the projects.)

It is foreseeable that your letter will be relied upon by the Westland Board and its shareholders. Consistently with the advice I gave the PM on 31 December, the Government in such circumstances is under a duty not to give information which is incomplete or inaccurate in any material particular.

On the basis of the information contained in the documents to which I have referred, which I emphasise are all that I have seen, the sentence in your letter to Mr Horne does in my opinion contain material inaccuracies in the respects I have mentioned, and I therefore must advise that you should write again to Mr Horne correcting the inaccuracies.

Yours ever, Patrick.

There was much speculation that morning amongst private secretaries at the DTI and MoD and at Downing Street about what Mayhew would say, and when his letter would arrive. And in any event, when Mottram at the MoD handed Heseltine his copy before lunch, he was forewarned. As soon as he had read it, he called Mayhew and told him he would give him a detailed written response by the end of the day. He seems to have regarded this correction of minor slips as no more than tiresome.

Over at Downing Street the reaction was more excited. Charles Powell read his copy in the office adjoining Mrs Thatcher's, and passed it, not to her – though she was in the building – but to her Press Secretary, Bernard Ingham, on the next floor.

Powell, a high-flying diplomat in his thirties on secondment from the Foreign Office with the equivalent rank of Assistant Secretary, was no mere clerk. His job was to interpret the Prime Minister's wishes and execute them efficiently in the overworked whirl of Number Ten, under his own boss, the Principal Private Secretary, Nigel Wicks. Much of his time at the moment was devoted to the political campaign against Michael Heseltine.

While Ingham, who outranked Powell, was studying the letter, Powell's phone rang. It was John Mogg at the DTI. He too had received a copy of the letter which he and his colleague John Michell had studied. He said that he had immediately tried to talk to Powell about it, but his telephone had been engaged. He had therefore telephoned his own boss, Leon Brittan, who had been attending a lunch engagement.

Brittan, he said, wanted Number Ten to 'put out' the letter right away.

Brittan was indeed out to lunch – and it was an important one. When Mogg rang him to report that the Mayhew letter had arrived, he had just arrived at a destination which he later went to notable lengths to conceal; at one point a story emanating from the DTI suggested that he was in his Yorkshire constituency on the day in question.

In fact, Brittan's private hosts were none other than Sikorsky's own merchant bank advisers, Morgan Grenfell. And the mandarin on Morgan Grenfell's board was the recently retired Permanent Secretary of the DTI itself, Sir Peter Carey, who was later also to be appointed to a Sikorsky directorship of Westland.

As Trade Secretary Brittan regularly lunched in the City, but it says something for the cosy relationship which Sikorsky now enjoyed with the Department that, at such a politically sensitive stage, the Minister should be enjoying the hospitality of its financial advisers. And cosy is the right word: as the Secretary of State left his office, an aide called out, 'Give my love to Sir Peter.'

When the call came through from his office, Brittan gave his view that the Mayhew letter should be issued via Downing Street. He no doubt kept the nature of this official business scrupulously from his hosts. But there is a rich irony in the fact that while he was presumably witholding from them information that was of direct and enormous interest to their bid, he was at the same time giving instructions over the telephone that the same information should be leaked to the press.

Brittan's instructions were to have far-reaching consequences, but the call itself lasted only a matter of minutes. 'How far Brittan addressed himself to the discourtesy or impropriety or unwisdom of what he was doing, I do not know', the Cabinet Secretary was later to say. Brittan himself has since insisted that he had two reactions to Mogg's suggestion of an immediate 'leak' – the first was enthusiasm, the second was that Downing Street should decide, and indeed do the leaking themselves.

This seems logical: Brittan did not really have the authority to leak correspondence between two other Ministers, one of them a Law Officer. The Prime Minister, however, did.

As soon as Mogg had reached agreement with his Minister, he put in his call to Powell at Number Ten, and was told that Bernard Ingham had already been handed Downing Street's single copy of the letter; any leaking should be handled through him. What was said in this conversation has never been publicly revealed, but the available sources are specific on its nature.

Since the matter was now in the hands of the Downing Street Press Secretary, Mogg called in Ingham's 'opposite number' at the DTI, the Chief Press Officer, Colette Bowe.

She had only returned from holiday that same morning and must therefore have been quite ignorant of that weekend's events.

Bowe's job, like that of her fellow spokesmen, involved identifying zealously with the interests of 'her' Minister. She was a cut above the former journalists who make up the corps of Whitehall information officers. Like John Ledlie, her counterpart in Heseltine's ministry, she was a career civil servant, and a very successful one. Indeed, 39-year-old Bowe, a brilliant graduate from working-class Liverpool, had previously been in charge of shipbuilding. She had also been seconded to Heseltine's Merseyside task force. She thought the world of him, colleagues say.

But loyalty to Brittan came first. Indeed, part of the 'politicisation' of the civil service which has taken place under Mrs Thatcher has been to emphasise the importance of zeal rather than scrupulous objectivity. All the civil servants in the Westland affair felt this pressure. But Bowe faced another pressure: all information officers had to attend meetings every Monday in the Cabinet Office basement, chaired by Ingham, to 'coordinate policy'. Ingham regarded himself, with only limited justification, as her boss too.

Ingham spoke to Bowe on the phone.

'What do I do with this?' she said.

Ingham told her that he did not want the leak to come from Downing Street. He told her instead to give the contents of Mayhew's letter to Chris Moncrieff at the Press Association. This was an efficient way of ensuring that a story would appear on every Fleet Street teleprinter before that afternoon's press conference at Westland.

Mrs Thatcher herself was later to say that there had been a 'misunderstanding' between officials at Downing Street and the DTI. But there is nothing in these exchanges to suggest that the understanding on both sides was anything but extremely clear: Ingham, senior in rank and experience, was giving Bowe instructions that she, and not Downing Street, should feed the Mayhew letter to the press.

What Bowe had in front of her was the DTI's own copy of the letter, on which Mogg had marked the words 'material inaccuracies' as the verbatim phrase to leak to the press. It was scarcely a fair summary of all Mayhew's qualifications, and Law Officers' confidential legal advice was not normally the stuff even of 'background briefings', never mind flagrant verbatim leaks.

Bowe, despite the pressure she was under, displayed some sense of propriety. She mutinied. Her friends say she refused three times to do it. The Cabinet Secretary puts it differently: 'I think there were misgivings, but no refusal.' She 'shared her burden' with Mogg in the private office, Armstrong says, but was still sufficiently alarmed to decide that she should refer to her superiors in matters of professional duty – the Principal Personnel Officer, and her Permanent Secretary, Sir Brian Hayes. Neither, however, was in the building.

It was the same situation Clive Ponting had described at his Old Bailey trial. A civil servant was being asked to behave improperly at ministerial behest. What should she do? Sir Robert Armstrong, her ultimate boss, has no answer: he was later to make clear that, in his view, civil servants have no right to appeal to any independent outsider. Colette Bowe could either lose her job – or keep silent and obey.

Chris Moncrieff, veteran lobby correspondent of the Press Association news agency, takes up the story:

I was in the PA room at the Commons Press Gallery. I'd been on to the DTI earlier in the morning, because I'd put in a request to speak to Brittan; I'd pointed out that Heseltine was getting all the exposure and I hoped for material in response, from him.

At 2.15 pm a message came through from the DTI that I was to ring them. I called, thinking it was about the Brittan request: 'No, this is something more pressing than that.' The letter was paraphrased, with just two words given in quotes – 'material inaccuracies'. I think it was understood that this was un-attributable as usual, but it was also something special. I mean, you could tell the nature of what you were getting was rather more important than the stuff Bernard gives you upstairs. It was made clear the information didn't need any checking. So I went off and put it on the tapes straightaway.

The Commons Defence Committee were later to subject this sequence of events to the closest scrutiny. In the course of their inquiries they rendered the Cabinet Secretary, in whose Downing Street domain the key decisions were taken that lunchtime, extremely uncomfortable:

> 'How would you have reacted if it had been you in the PM's office at the time? Would you have rejected what the DTI said as an impudent suggestion?'
> 'I hope I would have heard alarm bells ringing... I could have rejected it... I could have consulted Nigel Wicks, the Principal Private Secretary... I could have spoken to the Prime Minister.'
> 'Was it not some inter-departmental struggle?'
> 'It was in the background...'
> 'Was it not improper?'
> 'It would have been much better not to have disclosed the information in that way.'

Pressed further, the hapless Sir Robert said:

> 'There is a clear rule one does not disclose the advice of the Law Officer and therefore it was very regrettable... It should not have been done... I wished they had had that consideration in their minds... some of them I think, did not.'

John Gilbert, the Labour vice-chairman, suggested there were two possible explanations:

> 'The officials at Number Ten either thought they had general authority from the Prime Minister in advance about this issue; or they knew they had no general authority, but thought their conduct would not attract censure.'

The Cabinet Secretary's public view was that he would not care to choose between these alternatives.

Whichever was right, the result was to enrage the Solicitor-General. At the same time as the Fleet Street teleprinters were clattering, Heseltine sent round a defensive reply to the private letter he had received from Mayhew. Before Mayhew could respond to this, however, he was shocked to read his own private words in the headlines of the evening paper.

His actions had the promptness of a very angry man. His confidential correspondence had been leaked behind his back; he had been made a political catspaw; and it was quite likely that he and his legal office would be sullied by suspicions that he had leaked his own letter on behalf of the Thatcher faction.

He dashed off a letter to Heseltine himself:

I want to express my dismay that a letter containing confidential legal advice from a Law Officer to one of his colleagues should have been leaked, and leaked, moreover, in a highly selective way. Quite apart from the breach of confidentiality that is involved, the rule is very clearly established that even the fact that the Law Officers have tendered advice in a particular case may not be disclosed without their consent, let alone the contents of their advice. It is plain that in this instance, this important rule was immediately and flagrantly violated.

He added, cautiously, but helpfully to Heseltine's position:

The additional evidential material on which you rely, and in particular the conversations with your European colleagues to which you referred, is identified to me in your letter in terms too general for me to be able personally to assess whether the accuracy test is fulfilled. I quite understand why this may be unavoidable, particularly in the case of the conversations with your European colleagues, but it means that the judgment as to whether that test is satisfied must remain your own responsibility.

Mayhew had, in effect, withdrawn his legal request for a correction. Heseltine, far from retracting, issued a public repeat of his original statement to the European Consortium, and stood by his words.

As a 'dirty trick', the leak of the Solicitor-General's letter fell into the category of unscrupulous – but clumsy – tactics. It was obvious to all that it was a 'planted' story. It was also clear that the full text of the letter was less than sensational, or it would have been leaked verbatim. The Heseltine camp later theorised that it was precisely because Mayhew's letter was so disappointing that it was leaked in the way it was.

The later excuse – that the Government had a bounden legal duty to let Westland know the position before its 4 pm press conference – is hard to take seriously. Cuckney was so little excited by the content of the leak (already 'confidentially' signalled to him the previous day) that when Michell of the DTI called his office to say, 'The news is coming out,' Cuckney could not later recall whether his secretary had mentioned it to him or not.

At 2.50 pm, the story on the PA tapes was 'faxed' over from Carlton Gardens to the meeting at Lazards of the pre-press conference War Council. One of those present says:

> We discussed whether to use it. Someone, it might have been Gordon Reece, or one of the other PR men, said, 'No, it's a cheap point. Let others raise it.' We left it to the journalists at the press conference to bring up if they wanted. We said nothing.

While the saga of the Mayhew letter was unfolding, the main Westland battle was pounding away on the commercial front. The European Consortium was threatening legal action and demanding that the vote due at the crucial shareholders' meeting on 14 January be postponed. Cuckney had given ground, and had at last agreed to circulate the European proposals, coming from what he described as 'this uninvited guest barging its way into your home'.

Sikorsky had consequently been obliged to improve their offer – something that, as Heseltine repeatedly pointed out, they would never have done if the whole deal had been left to Cuckney. The value of their cash contribution was going up from £30 million to £40 million and they had dropped their proposed right to aquire as much as 40 per cent of the stock if they wished, at the expense of existing shareholders. The Europeans in their turn were preparing a better offer.

Sir Raymond Lygo now persuaded his chairman at British Aerospace to ring Cuckney and try to meet the suspicions voiced by Admiral Treacher about the ultimate intentions of the French: 'I suggested to Pearce they would suspect [the new offer] was merely . . . some kind of red herring . . . so we should call Cuckney and actually assure him we had examined the work-sharing scheme, it was genuine.'

Pearce's phone-call did not get far. 'Cuckney's first question to me was, "Is this a takeover bid?" to which my answer was "No".'

Cuckney called his 4 pm press conference to repeat that he intended to recommend the new Sikorsky offer – just like the old one – to the Westland shareholders.

The European team now arrived at Carlton Gardens, to outline their own new offer to an unwelcoming Westland Board. As the gangs of camera crews clustered around the doors, another acrimonious meeting began.

The Westland men hoped that the Europeans would feel disconcerted by a copy of the afternoon *Standard*, left pointedly where they could see its headline story about the Solicitor-General's letter. There was only one man likely to have thought of such a ploy, and indeed Sir Gordon Reece was present at the meeting.

The cash offers were virtually identical by this time, but Cuckney continued to turn his back on the Europeans, relying on Westland's claim that they were merely offering unglamorous bits of out-of-date sub-contracting to fill the factory floor.

Teti of Agusta says:

> We were mystified. Our offer was better than UT, therefore we couldn't understand why we were rejected. We didn't feel angry. In industry, anger does not exist. We simply noted the facts and began to think about the next step we should take. Our reaction was very *English*.

Lygo's own conclusion was typically forthright:

> It seemed to me that no matter what we were able to offer, it would not be acceptable to the Westland Board... Although a commercial excuse was being made about the unacceptability of the Euro-offer, I actually suggested to Sir John it was in fact a cultural problem.

On this note, the meeting broke up, and the European team went out to see the press. The Westland Board did not want to be button-holed by journalists, and it was Reece who offered them a solution. 'I know a back door,' he said. 'I always go out that way, which is why nobody realises I come to these meetings. Follow me.'

Leaving Cuckney to head for the main door with a prepared statement, the rest of the Board obediently followed. What Reece did not realise, however, was that, by 11 pm his favourite exit was automatically wired to the burglar alarm. As he opened it, bells rang, and searchlights came on.

The camera crews arrived, attracted by the hullabaloo, and pounced on a sheepish Lord Fanshawe. Sir Gordon pulled his long coat with the fur collar around him, and flitted away, once more unrecognised, into the winter darkness.

It had been an eventful Monday.

Every morning at Downing Street Mrs Thatcher goes through the contents of the papers with Bernard Ingham. Their main feature on the Tuesday was a number of 'splashes' about the amazing leak of Mayhew's letter. The Murdoch-owned *Sun* shrieked, 'You Liar!' at Heseltine. (They had to apologise and retract later after receipt of a writ.) How far did the Prime Minister and her Press Secretary note their joint achievements in the campaign to discredit Heseltine? As Sir Robert Armstrong put it:

> In the course of a discussion of business with members of her staff... which was not recorded and at which a considerable number of other matters were discussed, the Prime Minister was told there had been contacts between her office and the DTI. But not in any detail. People were in and out of the room during this, including Nigel Wicks, her Principal Private Secretary... Events do move very fast in the PM's office... you don't go over events that happened three or four hours ago.

Clearly it was felt there was no need for a long post-mortem.

However, the morning also brought an unwelcome envelope. It was a copy of a letter to Sir Robert Armstrong, who as well as being Cabinet Secretary is also Head of the Civil Service. It was from the Attorney-General.

Sir Michael Havers, who had just returned to his duties, had found his deputy, Patrick Mayhew, in a state of rage. As Havers wrote, the unauthorised leak of a classified letter from one Minister to another was a serious matter. He therefore suggested that Armstrong should set up one of the 'leak inquiries' which were such a regular feature of the Thatcher administration, and had so publicly in the past led to the arrest of civil servants under the Official Secrets Act.

Curiously, Mrs Thatcher did not seem to spring on this suggestion with her usual zeal, although she discussed it with her staff. 'I was told that the Solicitor-General's advice had not been disclosed by *my* office,' she says. 'I did not know about Leon Brittan's own role.'

Mrs Thatcher may indeed not have known precisely how Leon Brittan's departmental discussions had been arranged. Nor, as her subsequent behaviour made quite clear, did she particularly care. She did not institute any inquiry.

Instead, following Havers's complaint, she spoke privately to Brittan about the leak. Although this is something the Prime Minister has failed to disclose, to widespread disbelief, the evidence comes from an authoritative source, who told us:

The Prime Minister knew about the leak. She was pleased it had been done. There was a meeting between Brittan and her after the complaint from Mayhew. Only the two of them were present... Brittan assumed she knew of [the leak's] origins. You must draw your own conclusions.

One of Brittan's friends adds, 'Nobody thought it was a problem. The complaints were out of the public domain and any inquiry was expected to be a formality. Leon wasn't worried at all about it.'

It became clear to a number of people that, so far from being abashed, Brittan had, on the contrary, become bolder still in his campaign to undermine Heseltine before the key Cabinet meeting due on the Thursday.

James Prior of GEC was due to see him 'to explain GEC's position'. Brittan made it clear in a manner that those present saw as heavy-handed that he was 'not at all pleased' by the existence of the Consortium.

Next he egged on his back-bench colleague Patrick Jenkin to attack Heseltine in a radio interview. It was another clumsy move. Jenkin confided in Sir Robin Day over the airwaves, 'I found myself talking to Leon and he raised the issue, and we talked about it, and he said, "Well, it would be very useful if you were to say that."'

Propaganda tends to fall a little flat when its true purpose is revealed so candidly.

The next day, Wednesday 8 January, only twenty-four hours before the fateful Cabinet, a new initiative on the leak inquiry was blunted.

The Attorney-General 'had some conversation with' Armstrong (the words are the Cabinet Secretary's) about the progress of his complaint to the Prime Minister and Sir Robert. Mayhew had been serious about the leak, he said. But once again, matters progressed no further. Armstrong told the Defence Committee later that it had been a taxing week. He found himself to be busy and distracted, unable to apply his mind to the matter...

Brittan renewed his war of attrition against Heseltine, supported now by another colleague and friend, Sir Geoffrey Howe, the Foreign Secretary. His department played its part by instructing the British ambassador in Rome to ask the Italian premier, Bettino Craxi, to desist from sending messages of support to the European Consortium. It was an unusual attitude to diplomacy; if the Italians still believed that Heseltine spoke for a united British Government, they must have been rudely disabused.

Brittan's contribution on that Wednesday was an attempt to copy tactics first adopted by Heseltine, who had used the commercial influence of his own department, Defence, to try and damage Sikorsky. Brittan, for his part, set out quietly to use the powers of the DTI to do down the European Consortium. It was an example of rough play, out of character for Brittan, which he would only have undertaken in the conviction that Mrs Thatcher was behind him.

The result was what Sir Austin Pearce of British Aerospace called 'rather a nasty day for us'.

It began after BAe's Chief Executive, Raymond Lygo, had drawn up a new scheme for Westland, offering the company some of BAe's own high-quality 'tin-bashing' as part of the package: 'We offered 100 man-years, including design, software, engineering, various packages, both from the dynamics side and the aircraft side ... it was an offer made genuinely, if very late in the day.'

Pearce adds, 'It was very marginal for us commercially, a way of helping the European Consortium. The answer was, "No, we are not interested."'

Admiral Lygo appears to have become irritable once again:

> I remember saying, of course which is the better offer is a matter of opinion ... I pointed out to Admiral Treacher you'd have to make and sell 200 Black Hawks before you recover your start-up costs. I calculated there and then ... it would be 1992 before you start to recover your costs.

The Westland affair by now had been a major public drama for weeks, with each new development eagerly reported. That morning's papers were full of the triumphant visit by Bill Paul of Sikorsky to the workers at the Yeovil plant, who had voted overwhelmingly for the devil they knew, in the shape of Sikorsky, rather than the perfidious French. There were whispers that Heseltine might have to resign – though in fact his impulse to go had at this point largely evaporated.

The Consortium, however, was also gathering allies every day. Lygo, urged on by both Agusta and Lord Weinstock of GEC to stress the *British* nature of the deal, had taken the floor at the European press conference reported in that morning's papers, and stoutly denounced Cuckney for 'terrorising shareholders' with unreal threats of receivership if the Sikorsky bid got too few votes.

To the consternation of the DTI the EEC Industry Commissioner, Herr Karl-Heinz Narjes, had publicly backed the Consortium, and so had the European Defence Ministers whom Heseltine had so energetically cultivated.

More and more attention was focussing on the Westland electorate. Could the shareholders themselves either be wooed or suborned into second-guessing the board which Cuckney so clearly dominated? BAe decided to call a board meeting of its own that night, and decide whether to test this proposition by plunging into the stock market.

Lygo first had another fish to fry – one of much greater significance to him than the affairs of Westland. He went to the DTI to have talks with the Junior Minister Geoffrey Pattie on BAe's major proposition for a new development of the European airbus, which was so successfully competing with the giant US firm of Boeing. BAe wanted another huge sum – more than £300 million – of DTI 'launch aid'.

When Lygo's chauffeur-driven Daimler pulled up at the Industry Department building at 5 pm, he found an ominous-looking reception committee had been prepared. Pattie said that Leon Brittan wanted to see him, and shepherded him upstairs to the Secretary of State's office. Lygo, unbriefed and unaccompanied, walked in and found himself facing a long table.

Brittan was sitting at the head of it on the left, and on the right were clustered three officials, Alastair McDonald, John Michell, the assiduous pro-Sikorsky briefer, and John Mogg, Brittan's Private Secretary. Lygo knew them all well. Pattie slipped across to sit in the middle of the table on the far side, and Brittan gestured the admiral into a chair facing the Junior Minister.

Brittan then proceeded to deliver Lygo a stern lecture. The DTI, he said, was BAe's sponsoring department, and, as he had pointed out before, BAe should have consulted him before joining the European Consortium. Had Lygo properly considered that the 'anti-American sentiment' of the European campaign might harm US sales of his Airbus, and 'fuel protectionist sentiment in the US'?

The DTI, he said, had been involved in difficult talks in the recent past about steel imports; now Lygo was taking the lead in anti-American suggestions that the Sikorsky deal would deprive Westland of independent design capacity.

Mogg's notes of the meeting – a sanitised Whitehall version of a brief remarkably similar to the one Michell had been ordered to deploy with Fleet Street a week earlier – still capture the flavour of an officially neutral 'line' tinged with unmistakable threats:

It might have been helpful if BAe had spoken to him initially. However, having not done so, and BAe having taken a commercial decision to participate in the Consortium, the Secretary of State took no view on that position. Nonetheless, he hoped the way in which the negotiations were conducted would not damage BAe's wider commercial interests, especially in the US...

There is no doubt the impression Lygo received of what was being suggested – especially given repeated mentions of the Airbus which depended so heavily on Government support. One can turn to the French at Aerospatiale for the bluntest translation. Henri-Jean Dugage, the 'little admiral' who handled the Westland negotiations, says, 'The Industry Minister used what amounted to straightforward pressure, threatening to pull BAe out of the Airbus programme if it worked with Aerospatiale [in the Consortium].'

Lygo replied that he was not acting against Government policy. The NADs agreement was still on the table. Brittan interrupted: it was not on the table, he said. It had fallen. He could show him the Cabinet Committee minutes to prove it. Lygo said he would ask Whitmore at the MoD if what Brittan said was true. (Brittan was splitting hairs here. Although the NADs agreement had not been signed by the Government, if the Europeans won the day on their own merits it might then be endorsed as a matter of practical politics. On the other hand, as Heseltine was probably careful not to over-emphasise, it might not. Either way, it was still on or near 'the table'.)

Lygo went on:

This high-profile role was only adopted by us twenty-four hours ago. Our Board agreed before yesterday's press conference that it would be nonsense for foreigners, not all of whom speak good English, to take the press conference. I went out of my way there to make a lengthy statement to one of the US correspondents that the debate shouldn't be trivialised as anti-American. I said, 'It is not in the interests of the US to have a weak defence industry in Europe. Quite the reverse.'

Brittan, however, made it clear that he had been reading the morning's press coverage, and listening to Lygo on the *Today* programme. He did not like what he had heard of his attitude.

Lygo, unabashed, responded:

Damage to our US business would concern me greatly. I chair our US subsidiary which is very concerned about this. It is United Technologies themselves who are actually our US agents for weapons, and they are now claiming there may be a threat to US Army sales of our Rapier missile. We got the words in the NAD agreement amended to avoid implying it was protectionist... I am married to an American! I have spent many happy years in the US and served in the US Navy. I suspect that is a greater involvement in the US than anyone else in this room has. The last person you can accuse of anti-Americanism is me...

Brittan appears to have got the impression that he had bitten off rather more than he could chew. 'This conversation is going further than I intended,' he said.

Lygo asserted that 'someone had to take the lead' in the Consortium. Aerospatiale and MBB were BAe's regular collaborative partners and MoD was their biggest customer. 'I would have been regarded as letting down the Europeans otherwise.'

Brittan looked at him fixedly at this point, Lygo says, and said meaningfully, 'The DTI is your sponsoring department.' He went on, 'It is not in the national interest that the present uncertainty about Westland should drag on.' The message could scarcely have been clearer.

Lygo responded as spiritedly as he could. 'I find your reference to the national interest confusing. We have been told by another great department of state that what we are doing *is* in the national interest.' He also turned to the little phalanx of civil servants and said angrily, 'I hope you're writing all this down!'

The twenty-minute conversation reached a climax. Brittan – 'waving his finger at Lygo', according to one witness – said, 'I think you should withdraw.' What did he mean? This was the only section of the conversation which Brittan made any serious attempt to dispute, and it was to be put under a number of microscopes in the following few days.

The unmistakable impression given to the BAe board, when Lygo reported back to them, was that they were being asked to withdraw from the Consortium altogether.

Brittan, knowing that he was not allowed by the 'even-handed' image which he was under orders to promote, to take sides openly, now claims he meant that Lygo should personally withdraw from the prominent role of Consortium spokesman. Unfortunately, he did not think it politic to have Mogg record this episode on the official minute. He later volunteered, 'I can understand how Lygo could have misunderstood what I said.'

Lygo stormed out, saying he would report instantly to a board meeting that night. He was angry, and perhaps alarmed for his company's sake by what he took to be the nakedness of Brittan's threats. They certainly indicated that the Government's talk about leaving the decision on Westland to 'market forces' was open to question; BAe had been privatised in order to take what commercial decisions it wished. The DTI was scarcely more of a shareholder in BAe than it was in Westland. Yet, given the chance to exert behind-the-scenes pressure, Brittan, it seemed to him, was treating its Managing Director like a schoolboy.

Lygo stormed out of his Daimler and into BAe's headquarters in Pall Mall. He told the Board – which was still in session – what had happened, and said, 'I would like to be accorded the protection of the Board, since the matter in which I have been nominated to be spokesman has become so personalised. I am deeply unhappy with this situation.'

Back in Whitehall, Clive Whitmore's phone rang. It was Brian Hayes, Permanent Secretary at the DTI: 'You'd better know, there's been an almighty blowup with Lygo,' he said. Hayes reported that Lygo was now at some kind of emergency board meeting as a result. Richard Mottram was hastily sent off to look for Michael Heseltine, who was at the Commons, and Whitmore picked up his own phone.

Lygo answered it at BAe headquarters where he was in his office, writing out a complete note of all he could remember of the session in Brittan's office.

'Ray, what is going on? Have you called an emergency board meeting?'

'No, you've got the wrong end of the stick. The meeting was to decide whether to buy Westland shares. I wanted them to, but they won't. Can you confirm that the NADs agreement will be ratified?'

Whitemore said it was likely. His understanding was that the Cabinet Committee had decided that if the Consortium won, they would decide then whether to endorse it. The agreement had not been ratified as such, but it probably would be in such an event.

Lygo told Whitmore precisely what had happened. Eventually, late that evening, Mottram found Heseltine. When he heard that Lygo had been 'got at', he, in turn, became angry.

He tried to ring Mrs Thatcher on the spot, but could not raise her. Instead he rang up the Chief Whip, John Wakeham. 'There's nothing neutral about this kind of behaviour,' he said. 'It's absurd! I want you to make it clear that I will not put up with it. You tell them to lay off!'

The following morning, Heseltine at last began to understand at Cabinet what the events of the previous week had signified. Mrs Thatcher produced her document, ordering all Ministers to speak on Westland only after receiving Cabinet Office clearance. The old arguments went back and forwards. In her mind was the possibility that Heseltine would be forced to write a resignation letter. But, instead, he dramatically pushed back his chair and walked out.

The truth, and it was a truth that was to dawn on his friends first, was that if he had wished to beat her on the Westland issue, his resignation was an impulsive mistake. No matter what damage she suffered in the process, Margaret Thatcher was not going to let him defeat her now. Thanks largely to the manoeuvres of John Cuckney – and it was perhaps his cleverest achievement – her self-esteem was bound up with the fate of his helicopter company.

But Cuckney had not won the game. Two things happened with Heseltine's forced resignation which were to launch the Westland affair into new dimensions of deception and intrigue.

In the City, one person had been covertly buying shares in very large numbers indeed. At the same time as Heseltine was walking out of the Cabinet, it was revealed that this individual already personally controlled 11 per cent of the Westland stock. The blunt tycoon Alan Bristow had been in the wings for six months. But he had not been sleeping. He had been waiting.

The second thing that happened was what the more timorous in the Thatcher circle had always feared. Forced out, Michael Heseltine started spilling the beans.

Chapter Twelve

DROPPING THE PILOT

'Truth is often stranger than fiction'

– Margaret Thatcher, January 1986

It was, pronounced *The Times*, a very good resignation; dramatic, stylish, and statesmanlike. There must have been other more faint-hearted Ministers, said the paper, who envied the manner of Michael Heseltine's going.

If he himself had any second thoughts, he scarcely had time to consider them. His hurried lunch over, he drove back to the Ministry, sat down at his desk, loosened his tie and began writing out the longest resignation statement a Minister has ever given. The events were clear in his head, but he was helped by a detailed aide-memoire which his civil servants had kept up to date. By 4 pm he was ready.

He called in the press, and began to read out a 2,500-word account of his running battle with the Prime Minister and her Secretary for Trade and Industry, revealing in the course of it a picture of Cabinet back-biting and intrigue which few outside Whitehall had ever suspected and none had ever heard direct from ministerial lips.

There was no question that he had his audience hanging on his words; since he had never lacked a nice sense of timing, he made full use of it to enliven the occasion. Asked at one point whether he thought he had been 'set up' at the Cabinet meeting, and that the Prime Minister had anticipated his resignation, he replied, 'It's a good question.' Then, after a pause, 'And that's a good answer.'

He gave as his main reason for resigning his refusal to be silenced over an issue which he believed had profound implications for 'defence procurement and Britain's future as a technologically advanced country'. The Prime Minister, he said, had consistently refused to have the matter discussed, and had sought to prevent him raising it. Meetings with her had been 'ill-tempered'.

After an hour on the platform, Heseltine ended his account with this flourish:

> To be Secretary of State for Defence in a Tory Government is one of the highest distinctions one can achieve. To serve as a member of a Tory Cabinet within the constitutional understandings and practices of a system under which the Prime Minister is *Primus inter pares* is a memory I will always treasure.
>
> But if the basis of trust between the Prime Minister and her Defence Secretary no longer exists, there is no place for me with honour in such a Cabinet.

Heseltine was to develop this line over the next few days into what he called 'an issue of fundamental constitutional principle' and an 'outrage' against the principles of Cabinet government. But it never sounded entirely convincing. He was better on the solid ground of his war over Westland.

His mood over the next few days, however, did not tend towards restraint. Free for the first time from ministerial restrictions, he threw himself into a seemingly endless series of press conferences, interviews and television appearances.

In public, he was grave and statesmanlike, in private euphoric about the prospect of winning outside Cabinet the battle he had lost inside. On the day after his resignation, he gave a press conference in which he again urged the virtues of the European Consortium. Afterwards, he was told that another block of shares had been pledged to the Consortium; United Scientific Holdings, whose former Chairman, Peter Levene, now headed the MoD's Procurement Executive, had decided to vote its stake in favour of the Europeans.

Punching the palm of his hand, Heseltine happily misquoted the Gettysburg address and talked of 'a battle fought not far from here which will change the fate of our people'.

At lunch that day, he ran over his many rows with the Prime Minister, and concluded wrily, 'There comes a time when a man has to do what a man has to do.' He supposed he would never hold office under Mrs Thatcher again.

Meanwhile his rivals were still trying to absorb the implications of the resignation. The Westland team met at 8.15 the next day to assess the damage. Poring over the newspapers, counting the headlines, Cuckney turned to Reece: 'Gordon, what's your view of the press this morning?'

151

'Tidal, Chairman, tidal!' came the reply.

They decided to ascertain what attitudes were likely to be at the MoD under their new Defence Secretary, George Younger, and whether the tidal wave had thrown the DTI off course. Cuckney therefore wrote to Clive Whitmore asking for clarification of the MoD's Sea King order, and to Brian Hayes at the DTI asking whether he believed the NADs agreement still stood.

The DTI, however, had other things on its mind. John Mogg, in Brittan's private office, had now, two days after the event, compiled a minute of the Lygo meeting. This was, it appears, rather more than a routine secretarial chore. Mogg cleared his final version of the minute with everyone who had attended the meeting, and read it over the telephone to Brittan himself – a highly unusual procedure indicating the importance of having a version of events which could be publicly defended against the Lygo attack. Brittan says the changes he suggested to Mogg's record were 'not substantial'. It is hard to be certain what this implies.

The minute's tone, nevertheless, was very different from the one reported by Lygo. It spoke of Brittan having 'no view' on British Aerospace's decision to take part in the Consortium, but warning about the threat to BAe's 'wider commercial interests' in the US. Lygo was said to have 'understood the Secretary of State's concern' and to have expressed the hope that he was 'capable of managing this delicate balancing act'.

Finally, Brittan had summed up by saying that 'it was not in the national interest that the present uncertainty involving Westland should drag on'. Lygo responded that it was a question of 'what was the national interest'.

Nowhere did the minute carry any mention of pressure being applied by the Secretary of State for BAe to withdraw from the Consortium, or even to withdraw from the public campaign. All in all, it had been, by Mogg's account, a perfectly amicable discussion.

It was not a version that would remain unchallenged.

The Government's defences were under assault elsewhere as well – this time from inside. On the same day – 10 January – Sir Michael Havers went back to Sir Robert Armstrong and told him firmly that he wanted an inquiry into the leak of the Solicitor-General's letter. The allegations made by Heseltine had to be answered, and he could see no other way to do it.

A request of this nature from the Attorney-General was hard to resist. But at least as important was a distinctly mutinous attitude within the DTI itself. Colette Bowe was said to be still angry at the way in which she had been leant on, and to be insisting that responsibility be pinned where it belonged. Armstrong later told the Defence Committee that he 'concurred' with Havers's view. In fact, as he admitted privately, 'unrest at the DTI' was equally serious.

He must, however, have pondered on the merits of holding an inquiry into a matter which could have been resolved by one telephone call, or one discreet conversation. There was no need to search far and wide for the leaker. Unlike, say, the Ponting case, this was clearly an 'authorised' leak – one of those which, as Armstrong himself was to admit later, did not qualify as a leak at all. The inquiry would be, as the Liberal leader David Steel was to remark, a case of 'wasting police time'.

Throughout the following week, the leak inquiry would be a time-bomb, ticking steadily away. But in the meantime Downing Street had launched a full-scale counter-attack against the Heseltine line.

Briefings to the press gave a point-by-point rebuttal of his allegations. But, as always, there was less mileage to be made from disentangling the threads of the argument than from launching it in the first place.

Several Ministers, including Howe, Biffen and Ridley, disputed Heseltine's version and called it 'an exaggerated and misleading picture', but amongst backbenchers there was a growing feeling that his account of Mrs Thatcher's style of leadership was accurate – and damaging for the Party.

This impression was fed by Heseltine, who accused Mrs Thatcher of conducting a campaign of 'whispers from Number Ten', and Brittan of ordering British Aerospace to withdraw from the Consortium. He even took literally to the air, conducting a seminar on the affair from a French helicopter provided by Channel Four News to fly him from his Oxfordshire home to London. (Gordon Reece, in one of his few failures of influence, could not persuade Sir John Cuckney to do the same.)

This was the stuff of the next day's headlines. Brittan's denials rated at best a couple of lines.

In Downing Street the week began with a council of Mrs Thatcher's closest advisers to prepare her for what was likely to be the crucial battle of wills inside and outside the House of Commons between her and her ex-Defence Secretary. A television poll over the weekend had shown that most people thought Heseltine was right to have resigned, and believed he would make the most suitable successor to Mrs Thatcher as leader. More worryingly, a lengthy analysis in the *Financial Times* concluded that, 'Even if Mr Heseltine's allegations against Mrs Thatcher are seriously overstated, the onus of proof is unavoidably on her.'

The word later given out to the lobby correspondents was that Heseltine was to be 'crushed'. The Government machine, it was said, was fully mobilised against him.

First, however, the Prime Minister had to give her response to Sir Robert Armstrong's minute advising her that there should be an inquiry into the leak of the Mayhew letter. It was not a piece of advice that Mrs Thatcher could resist, and, reluctant as she must have felt, she assented to it. 'I readily gave my authority,' she said later.

The resulting report would go to the Attorney-General, to the Director of Public Prosecutions, and to the Prime Minister. Armstrong consulted Havers about whether the police should be called in, but it was decided that an internal inquiry would be more suitable, with the police to be consulted only if charges seemed likely.

That was never a strong probability. After consulting officials at Number Ten and the DTI (almost certainly Ingham and Hayes), Armstrong realised he would have to interrogate Colette Bowe first, since she was the instrument of the leak.

Since, however, she was also known to have disapproved strongly of the action she had been forced to take, and was determined not to be a scapegoat, Armstrong and Havers agreed that she should be offered immunity from prosecution. As Armstrong explained:

I believed I should be addressing the person who had actually passed the information. It was evident that a truthful answer could be an incriminating answer and it seemed, therefore, likely to me that the person concerned might wish to know what the position would be in the event of a truthful answer being given...
I therefore discussed the matter with [the Attorney-General] on, as you might say, a contingency basis, having reason to believe that I should be asked what the position was. Sure enough, I was asked what the position was.

The granting of immunity in such a case was, as Armstrong conceded, highly unusual. Indeed, he himself could only recall the affair of Anthony Blunt, Keeper of the Queen's Pictures and Russian 'mole', which was hardly comparable.

The decision not to call in the police but to have an internal inquiry – described, again by Armstrong, as 'perfectly normal' – was also unusual. In the case of Clive Ponting the MoD police were called in right away since charges under the Official Secrets Act might have – and did – result.

In fact, of course, nothing about this leak inquiry was normal. It was a charade, not least because Armstrong was not authorised to interview the Ministers who most probably bore responsibility for authorising the leak in the first place. If that *had* been permitted, the inquiry would have been rapidly short-circuited, for, as Armstrong himself pointed out later, a leak that is authorised by a Minister is no leak at all. No leak – no inquiry.

Over the next few days, Armstrong conducted five interviews – with Colette Bowe, John Mogg and John Michell at the DTI, and with Bernard Ingham and Charles Powell at Number Ten. Accompanied only by one other Cabinet Office colleague, he spent around three-quarters of an hour with each, going over the sequence of events. No lawyers were involved. The atmosphere was different in the two departments. The DTI officials asked for their Permanent Secretary, Brian Hayes, to sit in on their interviews, which took place in his office at the DTI. Powell and Ingham were seen on their own, back at Number Ten.

Colette Bowe was then telephoned back by Armstrong. Only one discrepancy had arisen. But it was to prove a fundamental one when Armstrong finally compiled his report.

At the same time as Armstrong was making the first approaches to his inquiry witnesses, Leon Brittan was sitting in his room at the House of Commons, putting the final touches to a statement which he had not wanted to make.

He had tried to persuade the Prime Minister that it was she who should be addressing the House on the Westland row, but she had responded firmly that since most of the questions of the moment revolved around Brittan's meeting with Lygo – something she knew nothing about – he would have to do the talking. This was one mess she happened not to be in.

At 3 pm, half an hour before he was due in the Chamber, his private office received a call from Downing Street. Mrs Thatcher wanted Brittan to know that she had just received a letter from Sir Austin Pearce at British Aerospace containing his version of the Lygo meeting. It gave broad support to Lygo and would be an embarrassment at this stage. But it was marked 'Private and Confidential', so Brittan should use this as a reason not to refer to it in his speech.

He should perhaps have realised that the letter, or at least its existence, had been leaked elsewhere.

Brittan had drafted his statement and taken it over to his somewhat soulless office in the upper ministerial corridor behind the Speaker's

155

Chair to give it the necessary finishing touches, when Gerald Malone, his Parliamentary Private Secretary, popped into the room to warn him there was word about of a letter from BAe. Brittan told Malone that he had already decided to say nothing about it.

The House was in an edgy state. Brittan was not the only MP to think that Mrs Thatcher and not he should be at the despatch box, and the Opposition was making its views known before Brittan had even stood up.

His statement was a dry résumé of the history of the Westland affair, and an account of the Lygo meeting that drew word for word on the careful Mogg minute: 'It is untrue that in the course of the meeting I made any suggestions to Sir Raymond that British Aerospace should withdraw from the Consortium, or that participation was contrary to the national interest.'

He said it was Lygo himself who had raised the concern expressed by BAe's American subsidiary about the possible backlash in the United States.

He was immediately attacked by Labour's Trade and Industry spokesman, John Smith, who is also a lawyer and was rapidly proving himself a dangerous foe on the Westland front. Smith pointed out, to Labour cheers, that the very fact of raising the matter with Lygo in the way he had done was tantamount to pressurising him: 'Unless [Brittan] gives a full account of what was said . . . the impression will continue to circulate widely that the Secretary of State will say one thing to Parliament while doing another thing in practice.'

Brittan had responded at length to this point, and had sat down, when MPs noticed that Michael Heseltine was on his feet. In a low, almost inaudible tone, he asked, 'Has the Government received any letter from British Aerospace giving their views on the matter?'

It was a loaded question. Heseltine was well aware that a letter had been sent. His sources at British Aerospace had told him that Pearce had written one, though it had not been completed and despatched until the weekend.

There was a pause, then Brittan replied, 'I have not received any such letter.'

It was a clever reply, but not a sensible one. Brittan could easily have responded that he was unable to answer, or even to admit that the letter was 'Private and Confidential', so could not be disclosed. Instead he chose to spot a legal loophole in the question and exploit it.

As other MPs were prompted to repeat the question in different forms (including, ironically, Heseltine's Belgrano tormentor Tam Dalyell), Brittan took pleasure in evading the issue by varying his response to every question. Perhaps his most devious reply was given to Dennis Skinner, Labour MP for Bolsover, who asked him specifically whether the Government had received a letter from the *Chairman* of BAe: 'It is [your] job to answer for the whole of the Government.'

Brittan responded, 'I am not aware of any letter from Sir Raymond Lygo to anyone else either.'

Listening grimly beside him on the front bench was the Prime Minister. There was no evidence that she was willing to lend her Trade Secretary any support. She may have realised, as others did, that he was not doing himself or the Government much good that afternoon. While the debate continued, she ordered Pearce to be contacted. With his clearance, the existence of the letter was admitted from Downing Street.

At seven o'clock that evening Brittan's PPS, Gerald Malone, watched the treatment of his speech on Channel Four's news programme. Malone realised that he had not been as straightforward as he might have been, and told him, 'Leon, you've got to go back and retract.'

As word spread through the House that Brittan would be returning to the despatch box, MPs streamed back into the Chamber. At 10.30 pm Brittan, tense and white-faced, rose again to his feet. He said that he had been unable to acknowledge receipt of the letter because it had been marked 'strictly Private and Confidential'. But now Sir Austin Pearce had agreed that its existence could be acknowledged. He went on, 'I therefore wished to come and explain this sequence of events immediately. If it is thought that I have in any way misled the House I apologise unreservedly.'

For a Minister to apologise to the House is a rare event which has, in the past, been considered a resignation issue. As question after question followed from the Opposition benches, repeated cries of 'Resign! Resign!' added to the noise in the Chamber. One reporter counted the number of separate occasions on which Brittan was compelled to repeat his apology as six.

But it was John Smith again who made the most effective point:

Throughout the whole performance this afternoon the Prime Minister sat there, and she had more knowledge than any other MP ... In that circumstance, why did [she] not even lean across to Mr Brittan, within inches of her, and correct him if he was misleading the House?

Next day, as the newspaper headlines reported the dimensions of what they saw as a major political crisis, the question was repeated again and again.

To some, it appeared that the Prime Minister was preparing to drop the pilot from the Westland ship.

In the course of his interrogation in the House, Brittan had fielded a request for an inquiry into the Mayhew leak from Michael Foot, the former Labour Leader. He had told him firmly that it was 'inconceivable that anyone asking such questions when his party was in power' would get a response.

Next day, however, Mrs Thatcher announced the setting up of the confidential inquiry and Armstrong's interviews began. Colette Bowe was the first witness he saw. By the time he had seen the other four officials, he had formed a clearer view of what had happened. But there was a distinct clash over *how* it had happened: the versions given to him by Ingham and Charles Powell at Number Ten did not tally with what Bowe had testified.

It was for this reason that, as he later told the Defence Committee, he had to call Colette Bowe again, and check Ingham's evidence back with her. There was still a discrepancy. The compromise he eventually reached was the one eventually reported to the House by Mrs Thatcher, that there had been a 'misunderstanding' between them over the authorisation for the leak. Ingham maintained that when he talked to her he was 'reluctantly' accepting a leak which had already been proposed by the DTI. Colette Bowe said that it was Ingham who insisted that the leak must come from the DTI and not from Number Ten, and had proposed the method by which it should be done. So far as she knew, Mogg had already cleared it with Number Ten.

While these events occurred in private, the public furore took a different course.

The publication on Wednesday 15 January of Sir Austin Pearce's letter did little to damp down the controversy. Indeed, it fuelled it.

'Who Told That Chopper Whopper?' asked the *Sun*. 'I know a stink when I smell it,' said Neil Kinnock.

Again, the drama was played out on the floor of the House as both Mrs Thatcher and Leon Brittan defended their positions in the teeth of baying from the Opposition benches.

Michael Heseltine also weighed in with a speech which contained the first revelations about the Foreign Office role in asking the Italian Government to tone down their support for the European Consortium. His intervention was duly rewarded in the next day's headlines.

The Pearce letter supported Lygo's account of his meeting, and even took it slightly further by saying specifically that Brittan had told Lygo that BAe's leadership role in the Consortium was 'not in the national interest' and that the company 'should withdraw'. He went on:

> I have no doubt that Sir Raymond's account of the events so fresh in his memory and recounted to the Board so soon after the event with the assistance of notes made immediately after that meeting was substantially correct, and are borne out by much other information that is coming to light... Whatever the words used were meant to convey, the message was perfectly clear.

Brittan's version, as drawn up by John Mogg, and published at the same time, made no mention of the Consortium leadership, but said merely that, 'it was not in the national interest that the present uncertainty involving Westland should drag on.'

There was no doubt which account the House of Commons preferred. As Kinnock pointed out, 'Can anyone inside or outside this House imagine a single plausible reason why Sir Raymond Lygo should fabricate those details?'

Mrs Thatcher, however, stressed that it was not just one man's word against another. Brittan's version, she said, was that taken down by the Department of Trade. She then went on to give her first full and detailed account of the Westland affair as she had seen it.

The picture that emerged was of a patient and long-suffering Prime Minister, anxious only to do her best by the Board and shareholders of Westland, constantly harrassed by her intransigent Defence Secretary. She claimed that a majority of Ministers had backed the decision to scrap the NADs agreement, and that the subsequent decision to maintain Cabinet unity had been supported by all except Heseltine: 'He then left the Cabinet.'

Heseltine, she said, 'acknowledged the advantage of collective responsibility without being prepared to accept the discipline it required... the Government heard his decision to resign with great regret.'

But whereas on Monday the House had wanted to hear the Prime Minister, today it was her Trade Secretary who was the main target of interest.

Brittan had, if anything, put more effort into his response to the Pearce letter than he had into his original statement. The experience of having to apologise to the House had had a devastating effect, and his friends said that the campaign of 'character assassination' mounted against him had brought him to the edge of despair. Despite it all, however, he had not so far considered resignation.

What had undoubtedly hurt was the sense that he had been plunged into a campaign of dirty tricks against his will. When he most needed public support, there was clear evidence that Mrs Thatcher was being advised, probably, he suspected, by Ingham, to distance herself from him in case he was 'too badly holed below the waterline to be saved'.

As he sat waiting his turn in the Westland debate, his hands were shaking, and at one point colleagues on the front bench had to help him sort out his papers.

But once he was on his feet his confidence returned. The main thrust of his defence was that his version of events was supported by all the other officials who had been at the Lygo meeting. Three senior civil servants who had served the government of both parties and the Minister of State and himself all confirmed their recollection. Anyone who challenged what he had given as the accurate account of what occurred on that occasion and suggested that he was telling a lie was saying the same about not one person but five people, including three distinguished civil servants.

Time was pressing as Brittan's statement continued. There had to be a division at ten o'clock, and unless he was allowed to carry on without interruption, it looked as if he would not have time to complete it. In the event, Labour MPs were unable to contain themselves and there were several questions demanding he give further details.

Against a background of Labour barracking, he snapped back, 'I am not going to have my defence dictated by you.'

Time then did run out and a division was called. That was a pity. Brittan told friends he would have given 'a limited explanation' of the Mayhew leak, and planned to hit back at Heseltine by revealing his Christmas Eve telephone calls to Cuckney. That would, he thought, show the kind of pressure which Heseltine was prepared to exert to achieve his ends.

In the event neither point emerged. Brittan sat down to Tory cheers, and afterwards, in the Prime Minister's room, received the final accolade: 'You were superb, Leon,' she told him. 'No one could have done it better.'

With a large gin and tonic in his hand, and surrounded by friends – including Whitelaw and Wakeham – he was at last able to relax.

Both Mrs Thatcher and Leon Brittan had made much of the fact that Lygo's own notes of the meeting, referred to by Pearce, had not been released, implying that perhaps his version did not square exactly with what his Chairman had said.

But at midnight, barely an hour after the vote, Lygo's notes were published, in time to wipe any suggestion of a Brittan triumph off the next morning's front-page headlines.

Lygo was able to report on what Mogg, in his civil servant's hand, could not, which was the atmosphere in which the meeting had taken place. 'It was not a pleasant experience,' he said. That, and Lygo's robust tone, his reference to his American sympathies and his American wife, seemed to rebut much of Brittan's account.

But when, on Thursday morning, the text was pored over at the DTI, there was a feeling that, just possibly, the two accounts could be squared.

Pearce had, in fact, by telescoping his account of Brittan's remarks, significantly hardened them. This was what Lygo said:

> He [Brittan] went on to say that, when we first became members of the Consortium, we had kept a fairly low profile, but now we appeared to be coming up-front and taking the lead, and he thought this was not in our best interest...
> He said that he thought this continuing campaign was against the national interest, he believed we should have stayed in the background and he would like us to withdraw.

Perhaps, with a little mediation, the two sides could yet be brought together. An emissary was sought and found.

On Thursday 16 January three crucial meetings took place in London, all secret and separate, but all intimately bound up with the Westland affair.

Two were in Mayfair, in Claridge's Hotel and in nearby Brown's Hotel, and one was in Whitehall, in Sir Brian Hayes's Victoria Street office. There Sir Robert Armstrong had now reached his third witness, John Mogg, and was listening to his account of the lunchtime telephone call to Brittan which had resulted in the Mayhew leak.

In the suite at Claridge's four businessmen were gathering. Commanding powerful City interests, they represented what Mrs Thatcher might have called 'the free market'. As Sir John Nott coolly told his Lazards clients at Westland, 'Never mind who speaks up for us in the debates; all that matters is how the shareholders vote.' That was the subject of discussion between the four: Cuckney himself; the President of Sikorsky, Hubert Faure; Lord Hanson's chief executive, Gordon White; and the helicopter tycoon, Alan Bristow. What was to be offered to Bristow in and around that meeting was eventually to detonate perhaps the most explosive incident in the whole affair...

But for the moment, the future of Leon Brittan was in the air at the third secret meeting. It was at 9 pm over sandwiches at Brown's Hotel, when Michael Marshall, MP for Arundel and 'parliamentary adviser' to British Aerospace, went into the final huddle with Sir Raymond Lygo, BAe's chief executive, and Gerald Malone, Leon Brittan's Parliamentary Private Secretary.

Since Marshall was on Sir Raymond Lygo's payroll, he had felt a particular sense of responsibility. After Brittan's debate he had sought him out and asked, 'How can this have happened?' Brittan had answered, 'Maybe I said *he* should withdraw, but not British Aerospace.'

'Well, why on earth didn't you say so?'

'I'm in enough trouble as it is,' was the candid answer.

Marshall had set out to mediate. That afternoon, as Mrs Thatcher publicly backpedalled from any suggestion that Lygo's word was doubted, Marshall stood up and suggested to the Prime Minister that there might have been 'a case of genuine misunderstanding'.

'Yes,' said a grateful Mrs Thatcher. 'That is correct.'

Lygo, contacted by Marshall, immediately accepted a meeting with Gerald Malone. As cynics were quick to point out, BAe was trying to get more than £300 million launch aid from the DTI at the time, and it ill behoved them to have reached this pitch of dissension.

Lygo was uncomfortable and prickly. When Malone opened by saying, 'This meeting is called at BAe's request,', he snapped, 'If that's the case, it's over. We have nothing to discuss.' He was soothed, and must have accepted that his Chairman's letter was harder than intended. In three hours a draft was agreed of a public letter. After approval by Sir Austin Pearce and Brittan himself, it would say – not for the first time or the last in the Westland affair – that the row had been entirely over a 'misunderstanding'. Lygo would accept Brittan's assurance that he had not said BAe's campaign was 'against the national interest' and had never suggested they should withdraw from the Consortium.

There was an air of gritted teeth about the letter, which appeared to represent a hefty climb-down when published. Lygo was later to tell the Defence Committee that his recollection of the meeting was perfectly clear, quoting again his view that 'whatever the words used were meant to convey, the message was clear'.

But for the time being the letter was good enough for Brittan, who announced that he was 'most grateful': 'I believe the misunderstanding between us has now been cleared up.'

Malone's peace moves on behalf of Brittan chimed in with the mood amongst Tory backbenchers in the House that evening. They were, in the words of one, 'shell-shocked' by the pace of events. Their weekly meeting lasted precisely eleven minutes, not because there was nothing to discuss, but because there was too much.

The main feeling was to retreat and consolidate. As one Tory veteran said, 'We've had a look over the precipice and decided to march away from it.'

A rescue operation was mounted by Nicholas Ridley, who accused Heseltine of being 'out on a limb, screaming from the rooftops', and by Norman Lamont, who admitted that he had considered resigning himself from his post as Junior Minister at the MoD, but had decided that the matter was hardly a constitutional crisis.

Others held back. There was a distinct feeling that the main question had still not been addressed, and that the Mayhew leak was likely to pose far harder questions for Brittan and Thatcher to answer. 'We're not out of the woods yet,' reflected one Tory MP.

Westland's meeting of shareholders held in the Albert Hall turned out to be a damp squib. Fewer than five hundred turned up, and the predictions of a stalemate were borne out: Sikorsky polled only 65 per cent of the votes – well short of the 75 per cent required for victory. Both parties retired to consolidate. There were appeals for an armistice, but the war was by no means over.

The narrowly-rescued Leon Brittan went back on the offensive, and on Sunday chose the ITV programme *Weekend World* to accuse Heseltine of 'persistently, repeatedly and deliberately flouting Cabinet decisions'. A report in that day's *Observer* which claimed that he had 'leaned' on James Prior, Chairman of GEC, in the same way as Lygo, was dismissed as 'the dirty tricks department scraping the bottom of the barrel'.

Mrs Thatcher was delighted. She told him his interview had been 'a very good performance'. He and his supporters repaired to the Pontevecchio restaurant in Fulham to celebrate with a Sunday lunch.

Elation lasted until Wednesday.

That was the day Sir Robert Armstrong delivered a slim sheaf of documents 'in confidence' to the Prime Minister. It was the result of his inquiry into the Mayhew leak. One copy was given to Sir Michael Havers, the Attorney-General, but none to the officials who were the object of the inquiry.

In view of the findings, Armstrong suggested that the next step might be for the Prime Minister to interview the Minister most directly concerned – the Secretary for Trade and Industry. As he explained later, 'The normal rule with leak investigations is that if the question arises of the investigator interviewing Ministers, the Prime Minister's authority is sought.'

It was, he said, a rule laid down 'by successive Prime Ministers'.

Mrs Thatcher agreed, and Brittan was summoned to Downing

Street to listen to the results of an inquiry which would determine his political future.

The meeting that afternoon in Downing Street was undoubtedly the most bizarre of the many and varied encounters that had taken place since the beginning of the Westland affair. Sitting with Sir Robert Armstrong as he read through his report on the Mayhew leak were two people who were only too well aware of the events that had led to it.

Mrs Thatcher had herself proposed the Mayhew intervention in the first place; she had been well aware of and had approved in principle the idea that his findings should be released; she had been pleased when the phrase 'material inaccuracies' was published; she had been informed in outline at least about the process whereby it had been done.

Leon Brittan, for his part, had asked Mayhew to take Mrs Thatcher's instructions about the letter; he had been aware that its purpose was to expose any inaccuracies in Heseltine's own letter; he had sanctioned the leak in the belief that its publication had the approval in principle of the Prime Minister; he had asked for Downing Street's authority to be given before the leak was made; so far as he knew that had been obtained.

The discussion therefore must have taken on the air of a charade. Armstrong was telling neither of the two Ministers he addressed anything of substance that they did not already know.

It would otherwise be hard to account for the fact that when Brittan left Downing Street later that afternoon to return to his office, he was by no means downcast. He told his aides, 'It's manageable.'

The only question now was how the report should be presented. Mrs Thatcher had never originally planned to make it public, and had said so to the Commons the previous week. What changed her mind can scarcely have been the novelty of the information; it is more likely that she feared the consequences if she tried to order Sir Robert Armstrong, Sir Michael Havers and the aggrieved Sir Patrick Mayhew to suppress the facts. Clearly Mrs Thatcher would have to make a statement. But it would have to be managed in such a way that it preserved the career of her Trade Secretary and her own reputation.

Events, however, were now becoming *un*manageable. Tam Dalyell, so often the scourge of the Thatcher Government, had been indicating that he knew the name of the official who had actually leaked the letter. That afternoon he named Colette Bowe in the House of Commons.

Two other Labour MPs, Brian Sedgemore and Dale Campbell-Savours, weighed in with their own information, including an alleged extract from the 17 October minute which the Speaker promised to investigate. And a report began to circulate that an unnamed law officer had threatened to resign unless there was a prosecution under the Official Secrets Act.

Suddenly the affair was ablaze again, with rumours of an impending resignation spreading through the corridors of the House. There were demands for an immediate statement from Mrs Thatcher, and the attacks on her own role increased.

Brittan said that he was not prepared to see any officials in his Department taking the blame, which indicated that responsibility lay higher up. Suspicion of this prompted the SDP leader Dr David Owen to comment, 'The affair is a spider's web and as each strand of the web is unravelled, we get closer to the spider's nest, which is Number Ten and the spider herself is the Prime Minister.'

Undaunted by insults or intricate metaphors, Mrs Thatcher said there would be no resignations. It was said she intended to come out with 'all guns blazing' the next day when she planned a 'robust' statement for the House.

The other lady in the affair, Colette Bowe, said little. But what she did say was intriguing: 'If you have any questions about leaks, you should refer them to Ten Downing Street,' she told reporters.

That evening Ten Downing Street stonewalled on questions and worked late. Mrs Thatcher's statement would not only have to be robust, it would need to tread the most delicate path through the damning evidence presented by Armstrong's report.

Brittan began from a simple position: he had been acting under the authority of his Prime Minister. In those circumstances, he was ready for her to reveal that he had sanctioned the leak, but he was insistent that she should acknowledge her own role.

One must infer that Mrs Thatcher could not do so – at least not in quite those terms. She could, however, claim that her officials had acted without her knowledge.

The fact that this involved doing what Brittan had been at pains to avoid in the course of the day – passing the blame on to officials – did not in the end weigh as heavily as the need to protect the office of the Prime Minister.

It was, by all accounts, a long and agonised discussion which carried on the following morning, right up to that day's Cabinet meeting. By the time she went in, Mrs Thatcher had her story straight. 'The truth must be told,' said her deputy, Lord Whitelaw, in the course of talks, 'and it must be told in full.'

But a different decision had already been taken. The whole truth was, in fact, to be delicately skirted.

As a result, perhaps, there was nothing noticeably robust about the statement Mrs Thatcher gave that afternoon in the House of Commons. MPs, used to varying degrees of Thatcher stridency, were taken aback by the low monotone she employed to race through her account of the leaking of the Mayhew letter.

It was heard in near silence until towards the end when it began to arouse a combination of hilarity and derision. Most of her back-benchers listened in embarrassed silence. The House, as the *Guardian* reported next day, was 'tossed on an ocean of sheer disbelief'.

The sequence of events as recounted by the Prime Minister was, indeed, incredible, for it required MPs to believe that she had never herself asked a single pertinent question about a scandalous action which directly affected her Government.

She claimed that she had been given the 'full facts' only on Wednesday, sixteen days after the leak and at the end of Armstrong's inquiry. She admitted that officials in her own office had been involved, but she herself had not been consulted. The urgency of the affair had been caused by the overriding necessity to get Mayhew's views publicised before Cuckney's 4 pm press conference.

It was, she said, Brittan who had approved the leak, and officials at the DTI and Downing Street who had arranged it:

> They did not seek my agreement. They considered – and they were right – that I should agree with my Rt. Hon. friend the Secretary of State for Trade and Industry, that the [Mayhew letter] should become public knowledge as soon as possible and before Sir John Cuckney's press conference.
>
> It was accepted that the Department of Trade and Industry should disclose that fact and that, in view of the urgency of the matter, the disclosure should be made by means of a telephone communication to the Press Association.
>
> I should have said that a different way must be found of making the relevant facts known...
>
> ... insofar as what my office said to the Department was based on the belief that I should have taken that view, [of the need for 'public knowledge' of the letter] had I been consulted, they were right.

To accept Mrs Thatcher's full explanation it was necessary to believe that both she and Bernard Ingham had behaved entirely out of character; that she had never thought to ask a man in her own office, and with whom she worked in conditions of great intimacy, how a leak of major political significance had been effected; and that he, who knew more about the art of leaking than any other man in the country, had never told her what had happened.

It showed a Prime Minister apparently unable to control her own officials, but approving of the use of smear tactics against a fellow-Minister.

'What I minded most of all was the aura of seedy incompetence it exposed,' said one Tory backbencher. Another senior Tory was more outspoken. 'It was a pack of lies,' he said.

The statement brought Opposition Leader Neil Kinnock's most powerful assault on the integrity of the Prime Minister. Her explanation, he said, had been given, not through frankness but because of 'heavy and inerasable guilt': 'The stain will stay with you for as long as you endure in politics.'

But perhaps the most effective interjection came from one of her own backbenchers, Alexander Fletcher, a former Minister, who asked, 'Are you satisfied that the statement you have made this afternoon has enhanced the integrity of the Government?'

It was an unanswerable question, and Mrs Thatcher did not seek, directly, to answer it. Shortly afterwards, the Opposition claimed an emergency Commons debate to be held the following Monday.

Almost forgotten in the course of question and answer was the man who had been named as the instigator of the leak. Leon Brittan was now more exposed than he had ever been. Although he had approved the wording of Mrs Thatcher's statement beforehand, hearing it read out was different. The manner in which it was delivered, the tone of voice, the implication of guilty conduct, and the distancing of the Prime Minister from the act itself, all placed him, as a Minister, under acute pressure.

That evening, 180 members of the Tory Party's powerful 1922 Backbench Committee crowded into one of the Commons Committee rooms to debate the matter. They declared full backing for Mrs Thatcher after rousing calls for unity from a former Minister, Norman St John Stevas.

But speaker after speaker called for the head of Leon Brittan. He should, they said, 'do the decent thing' and resign. Failing that he should be sacked. MPs who were present calculated that that view was held by four out of five present.

Although no vote is taken, the mood of the 1922 Committee on occasions like this is crucial and often decisive. Their sombre view of Brittan's future was conveyed to Mrs Thatcher by the Chief Whip, John Wakeham, after he had been briefed by the 1922 Chairman, Sir Cranley Onslow, and by her PPS, Michael Alison.

Waiting in his bleak upstairs room, Brittan heard the news from his own PPS, Gerald Malone, who reported a sense of prejudice against Brittan which went beyond the statement itself. Brittan had not done much to win favour amongst his own backbenchers, and Malone had also noted that the Whips were not performing what might on other occasions have been their function – rallying the troops, squeezing elbows, making calming speeches, spreading support for a beleaguered minister.

Brittan, it appeared, was isolated. He left the House after calling an early morning meeting at the DTI.

At 8.30 next morning, Brittan chaired a meeting of his advisers, attended by junior ministers, his PPS and department officials. The subject of discussion: his own future.

Brittan had studied the newspapers that morning and had concluded that, despite Mrs Thatcher's public support for him, Bernard Ingham was briefing the lobby the other way. The message given out was that the Prime Minister had not asked him to resign – it was entirely a matter for him to decide.

For Brittan the implication was clear: he was expected to do the decent thing and go. A message from the Prime Minister's Press Secretary is always taken as expressing the view of the Prime Minister herself.

Nevertheless Brittan went round the table and canvassed opinion, rather as he might have done at a departmental conference. Views for and against were sought, and dispassionately summarised. It was, according to one of those present, a virtuoso performance from a man who was contemplating the end of his ministerial career.

Sir Brian Hayes and the officials were against him going. They argued that, despite the heat engendered in the House, nothing fundamental had changed. Just as in the Lygo case, something was likely to turn up to change the situation.

The politicians were less certain. They had talked to Tory MPs and knew what their mood was. They thought the prospects for survival were bleak.

That morning, Brittan's friend and mentor Geoffrey Howe called to urge him to stay. Brittan telephoned Whitelaw, who said the same. He did not, however, place a call to Number Ten.

Later that morning, he and Malone went over to Brittan's ministerial room in the Commons, to see the doyen of backbench Tories, the Chairman of the 1922 Committee, Sir Cranley Onslow. His view would be crucial. Irrespective of what had happened the previous evening, Onslow was in a position to give Brittan the considered judgment of the parliamentary Party.

Oddly enough, Sir Cranley also had a connection with the Westland dispute. He had been for many years 'parliamentary adviser' – or lobbyist as his employer put it – for Bristow Helicopters. Bristow, now retired from the helicopter firm, was loudly backing the Europeans. A more finicky parliament than Westminster might have concluded that Onslow had a conflict of interest, as did Michael Marshall, sitting on the Defence Committee and working for British Aerospace. But it was no secret to his colleagues, and this morning Onslow was wearing another hat. He had a habit of speaking his mind, and on this occasion he had no comfort to offer. The mood of the Party seemed to be that Brittan should go, and he was not going to argue against that.

Alone, Brittan then called on the Chief Whip, John Wakeham, after which he concluded that he would certainly have to resign. He told his PPS that he would not now change his mind, and rang Downing Street.

By this time, Mrs Thatcher was on her way to a long-standing lunch engagement with a conference of provincial newspaper executives – a somewhat humdrum annual event – so missed Brittan's call.

She arrived looking tired and under strain, accompanied both by her husband Denis and by Bernard Ingham. Her hair, usually immaculate, was awry, her dress crumpled, her famous self-possession lacking. 'For the first time, I thought she looked like an old lady,' said one of those present.

She was also on her guard. That morning the *Scotsman* newspaper had published details of the Solicitor-General's second letter to Heseltine, in which he had protested about the leaking of his first one. Copies had been sent to Downing Street and other Ministers. It showed just how strongly Mayhew had felt.

Mrs Thatcher made no reference to the affair in the course of a low-key speech. But immediately afterwards she was plied with questions. Asked about Brittan's future, she said, 'I see no reason why Leon shouldn't be there on Monday beside me. He's not going to resign.'

To a hostile question about Ingham, she replied, 'Don't attack Bernard. One could not have a better friend than him.'

Finally, a journalist from the *Scotsman* brought up the matter of Mayhew's second letter – and Mrs Thatcher finally wilted. 'Oh, don't go on,' she asked him.

And then, when he persisted: 'Don't go on. Don't go on...'

After lunch, the Prime Minister returned to the House of Commons for routine business, and was told that Brittan wished to see her. For the next half hour, in her room at the House, she attempted to persuade him that he should stay. She told Brittan that she had received many messages of support for him, and wanted him to continue on the Front Bench.

There seemed no doubt that she was genuine. In contrast to what he thought had come from her Press Secretary the previous evening, she made it plain that she was not pressing Brittan to stand down – exactly the reverse. Not for the first time there seemed to be a distinct lack of liaison between the Prime Minister and her officials.

Brittan, nevertheless, had made his mind up. He had been told that the Commons did not take kindly to ministers who have to be dragged into resignation, and he realised that it would be for him to wind up the emergency debate on Westland planned for Monday. The chances of a massacre were very great.

His letter to the Prime Minister that afternoon reflected his disappointment:

> My Dear Prime Minister,
> Since your statement in the House yesterday, it has become clear to me that I no longer command the full confidence of my colleagues.
>
> In these circumstances, my continued membership of your Government would be a source of weakness rather than strength, and, as I have explained to you, it is for this reason that I have tendered my resignation.
>
> It has been an honour and a privilege to serve in your Government...

To which Mrs Thatcher responded:

> My Dear Leon,
> I am very sorry that despite all the arguments I could use I was unable to dissuade you this afternoon from resigning... It was my wish that you should remain as a member of the Cabinet. But I have respect for your decision...
>
> We shall all miss you. You have been a steadfast exponent of Government policy and I have admired the dedication and loyalty with which you have carried out your duties. I hope that it will not be long before you return to high office to continue your ministerial career.

It was two hours before confirmation of Brittan's resignation was given to the Press Association. By that time he was on his way north to his Richmond constituency and his first weekend as a backbench MP.

Next day the *Daily Telegraph* pronounced it the worst crisis in Mrs Thatcher's six and a half years as Prime Minister.

It was the sunniest January weekend of the century. True to their instincts, the popular newspapers photographed bikini-clad beauties basking in the unseasonal warmth, leaving the 'heavy' Sundays to dissect the Westland saga.

With the sun came a collective release of the national breath, as if a great battle had been fought. As the smoke cleared there seemed to be far fewer bodies on the ground than had at one time been feared.

True, there was one more act to come, and there was no lack of speculation about how the Prime Minister would play it. But it was hard to see how it could equal the nervous tension of the previous ones.

Mrs Thatcher appeared on the ITV programme *Face the Press* – booked weeks before – but refused to be drawn on what she intended to disclose in the course of Monday's emergency debate. The most she would say, enigmatically, was, 'Truth is often stranger than fiction.'

She chose instead to blame her former Defence Secretary for the débâcle, accusing Heseltine repeatedly of having refused to abide by collective responsibility: 'It was the kind of period we hope never to live through again, when one member of a team isn't quite working as a member of a team,' she said.

Should she have sacked him earlier? Possibly, but then she would have been accused of being a 'bossy-boots'.

Throughout the day Ministers and senior members of the Party showed signs of uniting behind their leader and turning against Heseltine as they sought a scapegoat for the wounds inflicted on the Government. Douglas Hurd, Home Secretary, said, 'The worst thing for the country now would be a lurch into some kind of discussion of the leadership'.

This did not prevent an active debate about the succession – if not immediately, then perhaps before the autumn – but most Party analysts concluded that it was best, for the moment, to 'cling to nurse, for fear of finding something worse'.

Mrs Thatcher spent the rest of Sunday working on her speech, and then summoned Whitelaw and Wakeham to advise her.

One useful piece of assistance was offered by Cuckney, who assured Sir Robert Armstrong that the leaked letter, coming as it did before his Monday press conference, had indeed been useful to the Board. Although they had not made any public use of it, they had welcomed the gesture.

171

Since the debate was an emergency one, held at the request of the Opposition, it was opened by the Leader of the Labour Party, Neil Kinnock. His handling of the affair so far had been skilled, and he had made some memorable interventions. But on this occasion, with the Tory back benches poised to exploit any weakness, he began on a note of high rhetoric which was clearly going to require some sustaining.

He then made an unfortunate slip of the tongue by saying that the Government had always been partisan about 'Heseltine' – instead of 'Westland'.

The mistake brought gales of laughter from the Tories. Kinnock reprimanded them for being cavalier towards 'dishonesty' – a forbidden word in the House. Immediately the MPs on the benches opposite him were on their feet demanding a retraction. Kinnock attempted to fend them off, but finally had to withdraw. Faced by constant heckling, his speech never fully regained its momentum.

By the time Mrs Thatcher stood up to reply, the tide was already running her way, and though, towards the end, there were Labour interruptions, she did not allow them to interfere with what she had to say. Her self-confidence had returned, perhaps because she sensed that her backbenchers were now prepared to give her the support they had denied, in similar circumstances, to Leon Brittan.

She came quickly to the main point, which was the Solicitor-General's letter. She admitted that she herself had prompted Mayhew to write it, and had heard directly about his conversation with Brittan.

She conceded that the way the letter had been leaked was regrettable: 'Indeed, with hindsight, it is clear that this was one, and doubtless there were others, of a number of matters which could have been handled better, and that too I regret.'

She said that she had not herself learnt about the leak until 'some hours after it occurred', and had not made any inquiries about how it had happened.

Her lengthy explanation of the leak inquiry showed that it had only been set up on the insistence of the Attorney-General, and after a formal minute to her from the Cabinet Secretary. It had taken six days – from Tuesday 7 January to Monday 13 January – to get under way, and another nine days for Armstrong to report back.

Mrs Thatcher was told 'in general terms' that there had been contacts between Downing Street and the DTI, yet at no time, she claimed, had she asked her own officials or her own Minister, Leon Brittan, what had actually happened.

That silence, and the apparent lack of curiosity on her part, remains the least plausible of her public statements on the affair. And it is not, one may conclude, one that accords with the known evidence.

172

The longest passage in Mrs Thatcher's speech was devoted to an explanation of what the inquiry had concluded about the discussions between Downing Street and the DTI over the leak. It was detailed, but it was flawed.

Mrs Thatcher said that, on being informed that the Trade Secretary had authorised the leak, her officials in Downing Street had 'accepted that the [DTI] should make it and they accepted the means by which it was proposed that the disclosure should be made'. They had *not* consulted the Prime Minister because they did not believe that they were being asked for her authority, merely being informed about the course of action.

The DTI officials, on the other hand, thought they were seeking 'agreement to the disclosure as well as to the method'. And, after talking to Downing Street, they believed that they had received both: 'Though clearly neither side realised it at the time, there was a genuine difference in understanding between officials as to exactly what was being sought and what was being given.'

She said it was 'common ground' between them that the method and timing of the leak had been correct, but was careful this time not to say that she approved of it, and she ended on a strident note which brought cheers from her supporters:

We are not going to be diverted from the tasks we were elected to carry out. We shall gather with renewed strength to extend freedom and ownership; to give power back to the people; to keep our country strong and secure.

The questions that followed were fierce. But now she was back on form she found no difficulty in handling them – on her feet in the House of Commons, the Prime Minister is at her most formidable.

Then, to everyone's fascination, Michael Heseltine rose. He had not, he said, intended to take part in the debate, but he thought that it had been a difficult but very brave thing for the Prime Minister to say that she regretted the leak of the Solicitor-General's letter. And he added, 'As far as the politics are concerned, I believe that what the Prime Minister has said today should bring the politics of the matter to an end.'

It was just the kind of message the Tories wanted to hear, and they roared their approval. Despite Labour derision at the sight of Mrs Thatcher's implacable critic apparently backing down (Michael Foot recalled Winston Churchill's words: 'It's all right to rat, but you can't re-rat'), it was clear that the storm had passed. 'Absolute magic,' was one Tory MP's reaction to his leader's speech.

The papers next day reflected their attitude. As the *Guardian* summed up, 'Mrs Thatcher told her supporters that the nightmare – her nightmare, but their nightmare too – was ended. And they, for the moment at least, were quite desperately ready to believe her.'

As if to harmonise with the new mood, Westland unveiled a revised £80 million package put forward by its favoured partner, Sikorsky. It was a scheme that would this time require a simple majority vote by shareholders. The Westland Board hoped that this would end 'the uncertainty' of the past eight weeks.

In this case, the wish was premature. The City battle for Westland was only now reaching a climax. And for those observing it, the ruthlessness and the scheming of big business interests was beginning to acquire dramatic proportions.

The details that we have pieced together of what actually happened in the course of the financial struggle for Westland suggest that the behaviour of the City of London matches anything that had taken place in the corridors of Whitehall.

Chapter Thirteen

THE FAN CLUB

*'What one has to realise is that one is dealing
with some of the most ruthless individuals in the
business'*

– Lazard director

When Mrs Thatcher told her Cabinet colleagues and the country that
the future of Westland was to be a matter for the company's
shareholders, she could scarcely have anticipated the events that were
to follow.

They were dictated by the City rather than by Whitehall from the
day of Heseltine's forced resignation, 9 January, when Alan Bristow
made his opportunistic foray into the market for Westland shares, at a
personal cost of more than £6 million. The move caught the rejoicing
Westland camp severely unawares just at the moment when they
thought they had seen off their main opponent.

The following morning, when Bristow's 10.5 per cent stake was
disclosed at the regular War Council meeting, participants recall that
there was an atmosphere bordering on panic.

Over the previous ten days Cuckney, helped by Lazard and the
Westland stockbrokers, Rowe & Pitman, had been trying to sweet-
talk the big institutional shareholders into backing Sikorsky/Fiat.
They had been accompanied by Bill Paul, whose smooth, easy style
provided a useful counter to the stiff, clipped approach of Cuckney,
rarely at ease when talking about the vagaries of the world helicopter
market.

Most institutions had reacted positively to Cuckney's argument that
he was trying to rescue a near-insolvent company, not playing politics.
But several wondered why he was so virulently against the
Consortium. They were dismayed when he publicly ruled out any

shareholders' vote on the rival European rescue plan.

Some began to waver in their support; and it was these whom Bristow tapped when he ordered his stockbrokers, Hoare Govett (also brokers for the European Consortium), to offer a price of 109p for a block of Westland shares, some 20p above the prevailing market price.

Bristow's unexpected intervention had not been the only bad news to consider on Friday 10 January. Peter Wilmot Sitwell, senior partner at Rowe & Pitman, reported that Westland's single largest institutional shareholder, Robert Fleming Investment Management, holding a 9.1 per cent stake, had indicated that it was considering voting for the Europeans. Fleming's change of heart followed meetings with Sir Austin Pearce and Sir Raymond Lygo of British Aerospace.

Almost as serious was the desertion of another important shareholder, United Scientific Holdings, the UK defence contractor holding just under 5 per cent. USH's former boss was Peter Levene, who had originally bought the stake. And Levene was now installed at the MoD, as Heseltine's procurement chief. The former Permanent Secretary at the MoD, Sir Frank Cooper, had also been awarded the vacant chairmanshp of USH, in something of a game of musical chairs.

By paying a premium, Bristow had flashed a message to the rest of the market; Westland shares, previously consigned to the institutional out-tray, had suddenly become valuable pieces of paper to be horse-traded between the rival camps.

This was doubly disturbing for Cuckney and Paul. It meant that they could no longer rely on the institutions, always vulnerable to offers of cash and short-term return. But above all, Bristow's new stake of 10.5 per cent in Westland gave him a potentially decisive influence on the outcome of the shareholders' vote, the following Tuesday, on the Sikorsky/Fiat rescue.

Some quick sums were done. If Fleming combined with Bristow and USH, the Europeans could speak for almost 25 per cent of Westland's shares, enough to block Sikorsky. No wonder the Westland camp recalls that day as 'Black Friday'.

The magic figure of 75 per cent had never appeared to be a problem back in December when Cuckney and his advisers had hammered out the final details of the rescue plan. It arose because of the particular rescue scheme chosen for Westland, one which was almost a carbon copy of the successful rescue of John Brown Engineering carried out by Cuckney and Lazard the previous summer.

Westland's financial problem was that it had huge outstanding debts and liabilities and very little security in the form of capital, a mismatch that could only be corrected if the company's balance sheet was rebuilt.

Put crudely, this was to be achieved in three stages: the banks, as major creditors, would agree to convert their debt into shares; Sikorsky and Fiat, the new partners, would put cash into the company in return for shares; and finally, the long-suffering shareholders would also put up money in return for new shares. In this way, a new recapitalised Westland would emerge.

With hindsight, the hitch about this capital reconstruction lay in the deal struck with the banks. Because banks do not like owning shares in companies, the tradition in such rescues is to offer them more favourable treatment as shareholders. Hence, the Westland plan was to allow the banks to hold *preference* shares which gave them first call on future dividend income.

There was nothing unusual about this arrangement for preferential treatment of the banks as creditors. But under the company's articles of association, it required a 75 per cent majority approval by shareholders in the form of what are known as special resolutions. In previous capital reconstructions in Britain, this was a formality. Who could possibly object to a rescue designed to stave off bankruptcy and to save something for shareholders? What no one could have envisaged was that shareholders in a technically insolvent company, with massive liabilities, would have the luxury of two rival rescue plans.

Bristow's share-buying and Fleming's suggestion of selling out underlined the fact that Westland had been caught in the throes of a contested capital reconstruction, a phenomenon which all parties admit had never been seen before in the City of London and one for which there were simply no rules.

The moment this was recognised, the aim of all parties in the Westland affair was to grab as many shares as possible in order either to block or to push through their respective rescue plans. This was to lead to extraordinary manoeuvering by both sides, which began and ended with mystery buyers baffling the small shareholders and leaving the regulatory authorities floundering.

Cuckney had other pressing engagements on 9 January; at 9.15 am he took his seat at a full board meeting of Midland bank, where he was a director.

Meanwhile, the remaining general staff of the Westland-Sikorsky War Council brooded on ways both to get the threatened shares back into safe hands and to block any more purchases. There were two ideas, the first obvious, the second perhaps less so...

The obvious one was immediately seized on by Sikorsky. Bill Paul was unusually nervous. Gone was the reassuring smile of confidence; one of his advisers recalls that he was 'in a frightful pickle', worrying about the shareholders' meeting whose outcome had now become so uncertain. He wanted to buy shares on Sikorsky's own behalf as the best way of settling the vote beyond doubt. The problem was that it was far from clear whether Sikorsky, as a major player in the rescue plan, was allowed to buy shares in Westland. Since no one had ever envisaged that this would be necessary, nobody had checked to find out.

Paul, flanked by his merchant bank advisers, Morgan Grenfell, and his own brokers, Cazenove, was asked by Sitwell what he wished to do.

'Buy,' came the response, and that morning Rowe & Pitman scooped up 500,000 shares.

After lunch, the picture suddenly changed. Having double-checked, Morgan Grenfell discovered that there were indeed doubts about whether Sikorsky could buy in the market.

'Sell,' came back the order from Sikorsky to Rowe & Pitman.

The problem was how to find safe buyers, but also to find someone prepared to take the stock at something near the premium price paid by Sikorsky. It proved impossible; Westland shares were still regarded as too dodgy. In the end, having twisted numerous arms, Rowe & Pitman offloaded the shares to eight institutions, at an immediate loss of almost £250,000.

The second plan was for Sikorsky to offer to buy out either Bristow's stake or Fleming's existing 9 per cent block of shares.

But some outsider would have to hand over a premium price for them, and hold them in safe hands. Who was willing to step in to help? Who could be relied upon to stay absolutely loyal in the battle to follow?

That Friday, someone in the Westland War Council earned his money a hundredfold by coming up with a name. It was that of a very rich peer, with extensive US interests, a need for goodwill in his current large takeover bid and a reputation for backing Mrs Thatcher against all comers. It was decided that this man should be approached.

Fleming would probably sell out to someone – at a price. But would Bristow? Cuckney made time to see him at 5.30 pm that Friday afternoon. According to the Chairman of Westland, although Bristow did see that he was 'financially exposed', he also had another ambition. He himself wanted to become Chairman and Chief Executive of the new Westland. Control of Westland Helicopters had been his original idea when he had mounted his own takeover bid the previous April.

This ambition was going to make matters very tricky. Cuckney must have temporised, and suggested that it was a matter for Sikorsky's own president, Hubert Faure. There must also have been in his mind the slight hope that Bristow would still be tempted to back off by the smell of hard cash.

That weekend the stockbroker Wilmot Sitwell went off shooting. A pleasant outing was clouded only by the prospect of haggling over Westland shares. In the subsequent dealings, he was technically not acting for Cuckney – he was acting for Sikorsky. On Sunday morning, he phoned John Emley, head of UK equity investment at Robert Fleming.

Emley gave him a long speech about how he had come round to backing the Europeans. 'Cut the cackle,' said Sitwell, 'what price would you be prepared to accept for your shares?'

The answer was somewhere near 125p, substantially higher than the 109p paid by Bristow three days before. Sitwell did not make a firm offer.

Instead, he tried to sound out Bristow himself. But, without a home phone number, he took a long-shot and phoned Christopher Eugster, a senior director of Kleinwort Benson, the merchant bank which had advised Bristow during his takeover bid the previous summer.

Eugster, who had not been impressed by Bristow's gung-ho style during that affair, was irritated to receive a call which appeared to suggest a link he had firmly severed. Sitwell's inquiry therefore met with a rather abusive response and a demand that the man from Kleinwort kindly be allowed to get on with his lunch.

At 4 pm Sitwell tried a different tack, phoning Richard Westmacott, senior partner at Bristow's own brokers, Hoare Govett. The cat-and-mouse conversation that followed ended with Sitwell offering something well above 110p, but not above 130p. Westmacott replied that he would phone back, but it was unlikely that Bristow would sell.

Sitwell had now finished testing the water. At 5 pm, following a stiff drink, he phoned his potential buyer. He was informed however that his Lordship was having an afternoon snooze and could not be disturbed. Never having met the mystery peer before, Sitwell decided not to push his luck but to try later.

The man he was ringing, whose name had been brought up forty-eight hours earlier at Carlton Gardens, was James, Lord Hanson – the 'predatory peer'. He had twice the previous year declined to interest himself in Westland, when approached for backing first by Bristow, and then by Sir Basil Blackwell, the doomed Westland chairman. His company rarely held passive investments in other firms; either Hanson

Trust took them over, or he was not interested.

Of all the Westland 'fan-club', Hanson was the one who might most easily have stepped from the pages of a thriller about Power and Money. Described by observers as 'rich, arrogant and pleasure-loving', he was one of the Yorkshire Tory rich; his start in business had come from a £3 million cheque handed over by the post-war Attlee Labour government, when they nationalised his father's haulage firm.

Hanson was the kind of millionaire, like Rupert Murdoch, who was often found on good terms with ruling politicians. Whilst chairing Yorkshire TV, he appeared on Harold Wilson's famous 1976 resignation honours list, as a knight.

Another of his associates was the merchant banker's son and property dealer, David Hart, who was to emerge during the 1984 miner's strike as a self-styled adviser to Mrs Thatcher and backer of anti-union miners' groups.

Mrs Thatcher thought highly of Hanson, whom she promoted to a peerage. He himself was vociferous in her support, and his company has donated £80,000 to the Tory Party during her premiership.

Hanson had built up a huge financial empire. He and his friend and colleague Gordon White had graduated from escorting filmstars in the 1950s to regular appearances in the business columns as captains of industry. They had large interests in the US; their activities ranged from bricks and batteries to gambling clubs, after a series of takeovers and shake-ups which they described as 'liberating the talents of middle-managers', and which their enemies referred to as asset-stripping.

White, also knighted, was chairman of Hanson's US operations, Hanson Industries. He was a mixture of northern grit and Mid-Atlantic flashiness. He had served in the Special Operations Executive during the war, but, at 63, he was still appearing in Fleet Street gossip columns and the *Tatler*, pictured in night clubs in New York and London. He lists his address in *Who's Who* as 'Sleepy Hollow, Bermuda'.

White's charm masked a ruthless streak which served him well in his business dealings in the United States. In January 1986 he had just pulled off a notable coup, winning a $927 million contested takeover battle for SCM, the American typewriter and chemicals group, which included a four-month battle in the US courts.

White was more than keen to help Sikorsky. He now claims it was his idea, not James Hanson's, to buy Westland shares. 'It was half political,' recalls White, who says that he was alarmed about the anti-Americanism building up in the Westland affair. 'But it was also a good investment with a company like United Technologies [Sikorsky's parent] coming in. That limited the downside risk.'

The two men were currently locked in a £2.7 billion contested takeover bid with United Biscuits for the giant Imperial group, best known for making Courage beer and John Player cigarettes. United's bid looked like being referred to the Government's Monopolies Commission; if Hanson Trust escaped the same fate – as it was to do – it could almost rank alongside such titans as GEC or ICI.

When Sitwell finally got through to Lord Hanson that Sunday afternoon, he found himself on the receiving end of a long lecture. Hanson appeared remarkably well-informed and very passionate about the Westland affair. He indicated that he was indeed a likely buyer either of Fleming's share stake or of Bristow's.

At 6 pm Sitwell called Bristow's stockbroker, Westmacott, who said that Bristow refused to sell. Sitwell phoned Hanson back and said it was Fleming or nothing. Hanson wanted a price. Sitwell resumed his telephoning; Emley of Fleming told him that an offer that would be taken seriously was 125p.

At 7.15 pm, Sitwell rang Hanson for the last time and briefed him. 'Have you gone firm?' asked Hanson, adding only that he would now have to clear the share purchase with his colleagues that night. It looked as though the shares were safe.

Hanson's share buying, for which he paid almost £7 million, remained secret for as long as possible. Under Stock Exchange rules, Hanson Trust was entitled to keep quiet about its stake for seven days. With only two days to go before the shareholders' scheduled meeting in the Connaught Rooms, Covent Garden, it suited everyone to keep the Europeans and Bristow guessing.

But this 9 per cent purchase only solved part of Sikorsky's problem. Bristow was still buying, and several institutions, including the Prudential, were playing coy. A new means had to be thought up, something designed to defer the vote, to give Hanson a chance perhaps to acquire more shares, and – most important – to flush out Bristow.

Cuckney had already floated the idea of postponing the vote during a television interview on the previous Sunday afternoon, before Hanson was enlisted. 'There are two considerations,' he told Channel Four's *Business Programme*; 'one is the likelihood of getting the two special resolutions through, and the other is whether with all the political trauma it would not be wiser to have a cooling-down period.'

The difficulty was justifying a postponement of what had already been billed in the press as a shareholders' meeting not to be missed at any cost. Perversely, the saturation coverage of the Westland affair in the newspapers and on television gave Cuckney and his advisers the escape route they needed.

For several days, Westland had run a hot-line advice service for its own small shareholders, many of whom were baffled by the barrage of paper emanating from the two rival camps. There had been a big response. According to Westland's public relations department, hundreds of callers had pledged their support and their intention to attend the meeting. One woman had sent a lump of coal from Scotland, as a New Year token of good luck. (The package was feared by Westland to be a bomb.)

The justification for adjourning the meeting without a vote originated with one of the members of Westland's legal team from the City solicitors, Slaughter & May. The lawyer pointed out pedantically that if hundreds of shareholders turned up at the Connaught Rooms, it was possible that some would be excluded. If any shareholder entitled to vote was excluded or not fully inside the building (even to the point of having an arm and leg outside), then the meeting could be ruled invalid.

Westland rushed out a press notice saying the following day's 14 January meeting was to be adjourned. A breathless Sir John Treacher explained that the company had been examining all options to accomodate an estimated 2,000 shareholders, such as bussing or sending them by train to the National Exhibition Centre in Birmingham or hiring Wembley Stadium (which, it transpired, was only available on Sunday).

It sounded faintly ludicrous. A more serious note was struck the following day when Cuckney, having successfully moved an adjournment before a handful of disappointed shareholders in the Connaught Rooms, said of the mystery share buyer, 'I look forward – as I am sure many people do – to knowing his identity.'

To some observers, Cuckney was stretching credulity. The man who was at times better informed than Cabinet Ministers during the Westland affair was now apparently ignorant of a major twist in events arranged by Westland's own stockbrokers. Given his absence from the previous Friday's War Council, it is entirely possible that he did not know about Hanson. But it was an unusual lapse in intelligence gathering.

Hanson's stake was only revealed two days later when Hanson himself released an open letter to Cuckney, stressing that the purchases had been made without Cuckney's knowledge. The letter also mentioned the company's helicopter subsidiary Air Hanson, though with only half a dozen helicopters it hardly constituted a grand fleet. Hanson declined to say precisely which way he intended to vote his shares, but the letter ended with the words, 'With very best wishes for your endeavours, sincerely, James.'

As the press digested the news that one outspoken supporter of Mrs Thatcher had already thrown his weight behind Sikorsky, further extraordinary events had already taken place behind the scenes, as the Westland camp made one last attempt to win round its most obstinate opponent, Alan Bristow.

Shortly after the postponement of the Westland meeting, Bristow had some conversation with his long-standing aquaintance, 76-year-old Lord Forte, whose chain of hotels, restaurants and motorway cafés had grown to a £1.2 billion empire. Forte was frequently invited to shoot on Bristow's Surrey estate at Cranleigh. He too was a friend of politicians; he had lent his yacht to Labour Ministers in 1969, and was knighted in 1970 – he described himself, at 5ft 4in, as 'the shortest knight of the year'. In 1982 he was made a peer by Mrs Thatcher, and he remained a wholehearted supporter of the Prime Minister.

In the next couple of days Bristow was brought into contact on his car-phone with a second peer he hardly knew at all, who was also a devotee of Mrs Thatcher.

This was the Prime Minister's appointee as Chairman of British Airways, the self-made, fox-hunting Lord King – the man who had forced through the route allocations he wanted for his airline with the same sort of political lobbying methods that Cuckney had used so effectively to get Westland what it wanted. King says he knows Bristow, but refuses to describe their Westland discussions.

Bristow received the impression that he was being offered a high price – 135p – if he agreed to sell his shares. He also received the impression that he might be awarded a knighthood.

He told friends that it was in connection with these conversations with peers that he came to feel first, that Mrs Thatcher wished to have the Westland problem resolved; second, that 'it would be regarded as a statesmanlike act' if he withdrew; and finally, that a suitable reward for statesmanlike behaviour might be a 'K'.

One of Bristow's close associates says:

He was really upset by this. It was the thought that people who knew him well would believe he came so cheap. He didn't want a knighthood; he was offered one by Harold Wilson, he says, and refused it. He values the Croix de Guerre more that was given him by the French in Indo-China.

Bristow eventually revealed this 'knighthood' incident in public, and was forced by a Commons committee to disclose the names of the peers he said were connected with it. Lord King issued a denial. Mrs Thatcher said that she had never been approached to authorise such an offer in advance. It would, she said, be 'a total abuse of the Honours system'.

Bristow clearly felt he was coming under pressure. But he was exerting some of his own. On the day of the postponed meeting, Bristow lunched with Hubert Faure, President of Sikorsky.

There is some evidence that Sikorsky were considering offering Bristow at least a seat on the Board of Westland, if that was the price of his cooperation. But most City people would have been astonished if Sikorsky could have honoured any such offer; the two big banks, NatWest and Barclays, were unlikely to have forgiven Bristow for the way his original takeover gyrations had jeopardised their loans.

Two days later, on the eve of the crucial shareholders' meeting, and while the political uproar over Leon Brittan and Michael Heseltine was at its height, Bristow found himself in a suite at Claridge's with three other powerful men who were his opponents – the respective heads of Hanson Industries, Sikorsky and Westland. The last ditch had been reached for all concerned.

The accounts of the meeting in room 517 at Claridge's differ substantially and are unlikely ever to be completely resolved. Previously published versions have already attracted writs for libel from two of the parties concerned. Only two facts are beyond dispute; the four people, each playing a key role in the Westland affair, did find themselves in the same room on the eve of a shareholders' meeting to decide the company's future. And, at the end of the day, the upshot was 'No Deal'.

Bristow says that he had arranged a meeting there at 3.30 pm with Hubert Faure, President of Sikorsky, to discuss the merits of the Black Hawk helicopter.

Sir Gordon White of the Hanson Trust says he had independently arranged to meet Cuckney at the same spot, because Cuckney had fixed to see Faure. Claridge's was convenient because it was just a ten-minute walk from Cuckney's usual business base at Thomas Cook, the travel company which he chaired.

Although Bristow describes his meeting with Faure as a technical pow-wow with a fellow helicopter expert, he almost certainly wanted to gauge where the Americans now stood. By now he had spent almost £10 million on share-buying, and his ambition remained to play some role in Westland's management.

In Bristow's version, he walked through the lobby of Claridge's and was stunned to see Cuckney and White together there. He went up to see Faure. At 4 pm Cuckney and White joined them.

'There is one easy solution,' White is alleged to have said, 'sell your shares.'

White himself says, 'It was a pretty strange business because I had never met any of the people in the room before. Bristow was agitated . . . and he demanded that either Sikorsky or Hanson bought his shares. He also wanted a seat on the Westland Board. He said to us, "I lost money on my bid and I want to come out clean."'

Both Cuckney and Faure deny that any offer to buy out Bristow and to offer him a seat on the Board was ever discussed in front of them, though Cuckney supports White's claim that Bristow did demand a Westland directorship. Cuckney says he told Bristow that the Westland Board would not wear it.

Cuckney, who had talked himself hoarse over the previous week and was suffering from a heavy cold, says he then left the room.

Bristow, however, insists that he was made several specific offers by all three of his adversaries. Cuckney is alleged to have said he would buy him out at 135p a share; alternatively he suggested that Bristow could sell his shares now and buy back later. White is said to have offered Bristow a written guarantee of the promise to put him on the Board, while cash 'could be easily arranged'. Faure is then supposed to have said that he would phone Bristow to confirm the proposed deal.

Bristow says he was outraged at these propositions and stormed out of the room. For such a hardened operator it sounds an over-sensitive reaction.

What is not disputed is that when Bristow returned to his London flat he immediately phoned Norman Tebbit, the Chairman of the Conservative Party, to tell him about the various deals he claimed to have been offered, and to seek his advice. Although Bristow knew Tebbit personally from his days at the DTI, it is not immediately obvious what role Bristow thought the Conservative Party was playing in these negotiations.

Tebbit listened and, in Bristow's account, said, 'You must do what you think is in your best commercial interests.' It was, in its open-endedness, very much the politician's response. But when Hubert Faure phoned Bristow from Carlton Gardens later in the evening, Bristow says he told him to get lost. He was not selling, whatever the promised profit.

For all the heady predictions of the Westland Board and its advisers, the first shareholders' meeting which convened in the Royal Albert Hall on 17 January was far from an all-ticket affair. There was enough seating for 4,500 people; in the event barely 500 shareholders showed up.

Cuckney looked haggard that morning; his eyes were bloodshot and his voice was cruelly strained. Pausing occasionally to sip from a glass of water, he recounted the history of his seven-month tenure as

Chairman; the refusal of the Government to bail out the company; the search for an international partner; the entry of Sikorsky and Fiat; and finally what he considered the obstructive attempt by the Europeans to sabotage a sound private-sector solution. His remarks, though typically understated, still betrayed some bitterness about the way politicians had prevented him from carrying out a job he had never sought in the first place.

Two hours of questions followed, with some shareholders of thirty or forty years' standing expressing their anger at the fate of a once proud engineering company. Some concentrated their fire on the recent performance of Westland senior management. Two survivors were sitting alongside Cuckney; Hugh Stewart and Sir John Treacher. They grimaced as several shareholders read out some of the Board's more optimistic profit projections over the past two years.

In one sense everyone was waiting for the heavily built gentleman in the second row of the auditorium to move centre stage. Alan Bristow ambled over to the specially arranged microphones at around lunchtime. His speech began impressively as he spoke of his experience as a helicopter pilot and his assessment of the Black Hawk. The Westland Board, he said, removing his glasses with a flourish, were pursuing a blind love-affair with Sikorsky in pursuit of a product which simply would not sell.

But gradually Bristow began to run out of steam. The passion was there but the arguments were becoming ragged. Several shareholders coughed. Cuckney tried to intervene. 'Let him speak,' shouted a couple of dissident shareholders, as Bristow, anxious to continue, asked for a glass of water.

There was an embarrassing silence as the stewards looked towards the directors' podium for guidance. Cuckney remained motionless; and then there was a burst of laughter as one of Bristow's supporters rushed up to the microphone to offer the great man sustenance.

At 2 pm Cuckney called for the votes to be counted. The shareholders delivered their proxy forms and filed out for lunch. After four hours of announcements that the result was imminent, the final vote was revealed just after 6 pm.

On an 85 per cent poll, the two special resolutions providing for the Sikorsky/Fiat rescue to take effect were defeated, achieving only 65.2 per cent against 34.8 for the Europeans. It was no consolation that the third, ordinary resolution, allowing the company to increase its borrowing powers, easily passed the necessary 50 per cent majority.

Cuckney, looking taut, spoke briefly to an emptying hall. He intended to fight on. The rescue proposals would be amended so that a simple majority only was required. And then came an impassioned attack against the European Consortium.

'I hope they accept the democratic verdict of the ballot box,' he said, calling on the Europeans to do the honourable thing and withdraw. Unless the Consortium dropped its proposed rescue, Westland faced the appalling prospect of stalemate, he warned.

On hearing the news, Michael Heseltine, no longer Secretary of State for Defence, said the result was 'a very considerable achievement' for the Consortium. 'I will be looking now very carefully to see if there is any way in which I can help further.'

But by now the game had moved into a different sector altogether.

Both sides now had around three weeks to devise some way of breaking the stalemate before they crossed swords at the next extraordinary general meeting.

David Horne was working with a handicap far higher than anything he experienced on his beloved golf courses. Even in his moment of apparent triumph, a piece of news sent him scurrying out of the Albert Hall to check with British Aerospace executives that they were still on board. The news was of Admiral Lygo's sudden climb-down over the Leon Brittan meeting.

By the weekend, it was clearer than ever that the British company's leading role in the Consortium had been torpedoed.

The BAe board was disturbed by the public controversy; its share price had fallen sharply in the preceding weeks, and there were suggestions that there was a split within its board. One senior executive commented privately that weekend, 'I am concerned what the Westland affair is doing to the company and to Ray Lygo. There is no question of us going up-front any more.'

Horne had to negotiate with five different partners at once, none of whom now wanted to take a lead. Nevertheless, he decided that the best way to beat Cuckney was to put together an improved European offer which would put Sikorsky/Fiat on the defensive, while at the same time trying to pick up Westland shares in the market to block a rival rescue plan.

Cuckney had a different set of concerns. The defeat at the EGM had been expected, but was still a blow to his pride. Now, more than ever, he was determined to win. So too were the Sikorsky executives who had pledged to fight on before the TV cameras at the Albert Hall. Bill Paul flew home on Concorde to talk tactics. Meanwhile Cuckney decided to reformulate the rescue plan so that it could be passed by a simple majority, using ordinary rather than special resolutions.

The difficulty lay in keeping the banks on his side. Under the new scheme of capital reconstruction, they were no longer likely to enjoy the status of preferred creditors. Several days of negotiations followed which by all accounts were just as tense as those the previous month.

For a moment it looked as if the banks were going to play hard to get. This was not surprising given the result of the shareholders meeting and the obvious support gained by the Europeans. However parlous the financial state of the company, there was obviously some value in what had until very recently seemed a bust company. If there were two rival rescue plans, why not squeeze out the best deal possible?

The same thought occurred to those fund managers who had stuck by the Board and refused to sell at premium prices to Bristow or the Europeans. Very soon Cuckney and his Lazard advisers, Michael Baughan and Marcus Agius, were faced with a fickleness which they had scarcely imagined, even during the frantic share dealing in the run-up to the first shareholders' meeting.

It was this uncertainty which the Westland camp was now determined to end, and which was followed by a series of extraordinary events in the next two weeks. They eventually led to a Stock Exchange investigation and to calls for a Government inquiry.

Sikorsky decided that their previous Stock Exchange advice had been too cautious. They were now prepared to go back into the market and buy on their own behalf – at least until they ran up against a new regulatory obstacle.

At 4.50 pm on Tuesday 22 January, Peter Sitwell was at the offices of Morgan Grenfell merchant bank in Great Winchester Street when a message came through from the secretary of Jim Findlay, the senior investment fund manager at Prudential Assurance, one of the most powerful City institutions and an owner of a 4.4 per cent Westland share stake. 'Call me in the next fifteen minutes,' ran the message, 'otherwise don't bother ringing at all.'

Sitwell in fact was sitting with Peter Cadbury, Sikorsky's adviser at Morgans. Somewhat bemused, he rang Findlay.

'We have been bid for our shares,' said the man from the Pru, 'what price can you offer?'

Sitwell told Cadbury the bad news. Several phone calls later, he called Findlay back and said that Sikorsky were willing to bid more than 125p. 'Is that a firm offer?' asked Findlay, who then instructed Sitwell to put in his highest bid by 6 pm. It came out at 151p, the highest price paid yet, and well above the 135p bid by Hoare Govett, acting for the Consortium.

The confidential Stock Exchange inquiry into share dealing in Westland was later to question the ethics of such an auction. In fact, no rules were broken; it was just what the City would describe as an example of sharp business practice conducted in the interests of the Prudential's investment clients. As one senior Prudential fund manager, referring to the group's traditional reputation for backing boards and looking after the small shareholders, explained, 'Maybe it's not such a bad thing if we lose our virginal image.'

News of the Pru's lost virginity travelled fast. Minutes after the deal was struck, Andrew Cherniavsky, head of UK equity investment at Prolific Unit Trusts, holding 2.3 per cent of Westland, phoned Rowe & Pitman to say he too had been bid for his shares. Again, the price was struck at 151p. Sikorsky, previously wary of buying shares, was now sitting on a 6.7 per cent block.

The entry of Sikorsky – the main protagonist – into the stock market changed the nature of the game. From now on, brokers and fund managers knew that the Americans would pay very fancy prices to win the day, adding a new spiral to the whirlwind share dealing already taking place in the market. It revealed a new determination to win, whatever the cost.

Somebody, somewhere had decided that it was time to play hardball.

Two days after Sikorsky had entered the market, Rowe & Pitman received another unexpected phone call. This time it was not a fickle British institution wanting to sell, but a genuine buyer, all the way from Sydney, Australia.

It was 10 am when David Mortimer, finance director of Thomas Nationwide Transport, Australia's largest transportation group, came on the line. He wanted to buy 2.6 million Westland shares. The figure was significant because it amounted to just under 5 per cent of Westland shares, therefore low enough to remain anonymous under Stock Exchange rules.

There was no explanation for the purchase order, and no explanation sought. Sitwell told friends that the call came out of the blue, but there are others in the Westland camp who now say that the order was less unexpected than it appeared.

The group, with the aptly explosive acronym TNT, jointly controls Ansett, the Australian airline, along with Rupert Murdoch, the newspaper and media magnate. Its UK connection with Murdoch had grown much closer in recent months. Murdoch had chosen the group to distribute his newspapers *The Times, Sunday Times, Sun* and *News of the World*, from behind barbed wire in a modern printing plant in Wapping, in the heart of London's old docklands.

Murdoch's decision to fire almost 6,000 of his newspaper employees and go it alone with new technology had caused a political uproar. The unions were picketing in force outside Wapping; violence was rife, and even some of Mrs Thatcher's Ministers were expressing doubts about the sheer audacity of the Wapping move. .

One senior Westland source at least was not surprised by TNT's sudden interest in the helicopter company's affairs. 'Rupert undoubtedly knew what was going on,' he says, 'and he may have thought he could help out.' But there was an equally compelling stimulus to interest. Murdoch, who had just been granted American citizenship, was a non-executive director of United Technologies, Sikorsky's parent company.

The following Monday, January 27, yet another prospective buyer called Sterling Trust contacted Rowe & Pitman, this time from Geneva, Switzerland. Again the order was for a line of Westland shares, again amounting to just less than 5 per cent.

On this occasion there was less room for taking a relaxed attitude. Adrian Phillips in Rowe & Pitman's corporate finance department contacted Sitwell, who immediately ordered a check. It was only after a call to S. G. Warburg, the London merchant bank, that it was discovered that Sterling, though clearly a front for buyers who wished to remain secret, were indeed active property investors and share dealers in the London market. Several phone calls followed from Geneva, one from a Mr Hollander who informed a somewhat baffled Phillips that Sterling had used four different brokers over the past year and thirteen over the past ten years, not exactly the way to guarantee publicity.

When Phillips inquired about a reference, he was given the Royal Bank of Scotland branch in Lombard Street. Late on January 28, Rowe & Pitman dealt successfully on Sterling's behalf, snapping up just under the critical 5 per cent. At 9.15 the following morning the instruction came through to stop buying.

The philanthropic millionaire buying through the Swiss bank was later named as a Mr Mauricio de Castro of Los Angeles in the US. Mr de Castro, callers were later told, was out of town for an indefinite period. Slowly, a pattern was emerging, and one of which even Rowe & Pitman were not completely aware. While it was hesitating about the credentials of Sterling Trust, other mystery buyers were beginning to burrow into the stock market. Time was pressing; if Rowe & Pitman would not deal, then the mystery buyers would simply take their trade elsewhere.

That week, Scrimgeour Vickers, the broking house controlled by the big US bank Citicorp, bid for Westland stock at 135p. On whose behalf it was not clear, though it was later revealed in a confidential Stock Exchange report that they dealt for two buyers, both Swiss-based. The first was Rothschild Bank A.G. in Zurich, acting, it was later asserted, for another unknown millionaire called Marc A. Odermatt. His location was given as Spain: the resort of Palma,

Majorca. He bought 4.76 per cent. The second was called Banque les Fils Dreyfus et Cie. They eventually claimed to be acting for an unknown company registered in a fourth distant country which was even less accessible to inquirers: 'Lynx Marketing' of Panama.

Around the same time Banque les Fils Dreyfus also contacted Hoare Govett, a cheeky move because Hoare's were brokers to Bristow and the Consortium. Lynx Marketing acquired in total 4.83 per cent of Westland shares before they, too, withdrew. Horne, shooting for stock in the dark, was furious when he heard about Lynx. He was certain they were pro-Sikorsky but he could not prove it.

If there were ever any doubts that someone was orchestrating the buying, then they appeared to be dispelled on January 30, the day after Rowe & Pitman was instructed to withdraw by Sterling. This time it was a company, again Swiss-based, called Gulf & Occidental Investment Company. The call came at 10.30 and the voice at the end of the line informed Phillips that Gulf were in fact long-standing clients.

Phillips again contacted Sitwell, by this time extremely agitated about the number of mystery buyers placing buying orders through his firm as company brokers. He had been uneasy about dealing on Hanson's behalf; now everyone wanted to do business with him.

Sitwell had already been contacted by Sir Nicholas Goodison, chairman of the Stock Exchange, the previous week. Goodison was disturbed by the hectic Westland share dealing which he thought was giving the City a bad name. He wanted reassurances that no rules were being broken. Sitwell told Goodison that he was making every effort in difficult, if not extraordinary, circumstances, to comply with the rule-book.

The entry of Gulf & Occidental provoked Sitwell into even more thorough checks. He told Phillips that he was not to deal until he had references. Back came an immediate response from Gulf; call the National Bank of Abu Dhabi and the Qatar Investment Office for comfort. Gulf later said they were acting for yet another unknown millionaire in yet another exotic country. This time a Mr Guillermo Schiess of the Avenue Miraflores in Montevideo, Uruguay, was the man who developed a sudden interest in buying vastly overpriced Westland stock.

Rowe & Pitman never managed to push Gulf and Occidental's share stake beyond 1.53 per cent; but then this was not surprising since the mystery buyers, coupled with the continuing activities of Bristow and now Lloyds Merchant Bank (acting on behalf of the Consortium), had flushed out most of the major institutional shareholders and pension-fund sellers. By now the mystery buying had pushed the Westland share price to an unreal 141p, bearing no relation to the company's prospects. Something was very wrong.

Goodison decided it was time to launch an inquiry. The question was how to present this to the public. He took his cue from Whitehall and the Westland affair and went for the pre-emptive leak. The excuse was that the inquiry team, led by Peter Wills, a former deputy chairman of the Stock Exchange and a partner at Sheppards & Chase, had to be put under pressure to complete a swift inquiry. In fact, it was linked far more to the difficulties Goodison faced in fending off the proposed new supervisory authority for the City, the Securities and Investments Board, which threatened to encroach on the Exchange's own regulatory role.

Wills was furious: 'This is the first time I have read my own job description in the press,' he told friends. But as the inquiry unfolded, Wills was to be confronted with a host of other surprises.

Horne's reaction to the market's gyrations was a mixture of anger and resignation. He was the outsider. While Rowe & Pitman did a brilliant job in finding sellers to match the mystery buyers, Hoare Govett, when wearing their Consortium hat, were too often left on the sidelines. Faced with imminent defeat at the shareholders' meeting set for 12 February, Horne tried one last gamble with the Consortium's money.

On 29 January, he announced a tender offer for 12.63 million Westland shares, 21 per cent of the company. At 130p per share, the price was generous. (Though, interestingly, it was only made on behalf of the three European members, Aerospatiale, Agusta and MBB; GEC and British Aerospace clearly thought they had stumped up enough money and did not take part in the tender offer.) The aim was to attract the small shareholders who, Horne believed, had been ignored in the battle for institutional loyalty. By seeking to mop them up in the ten-day period for which the tender applied, Horne hoped to block Sikorsky/Fiat's chances of securing the simple majority vote for their rescue plan.

There is no doubt that Westland was alarmed by the tactic, even though it must have figured that the anonymous buyers passing through Rowe & Pitman were friendly. Sir John Treacher said, 'This latest manoeuvre has the potential to wreck the Sikorsky/Fiat deal.'

Sikorsky would have liked to buy more shares directly through Rowe & Pitman. But having moved up to 9.9 per cent, Sikorsky was in the Stock Exchange firing line, falling foul of what are known as the rules on Class Four transactions. In effect these say that no one who has a material interest in the outcome of an extraordinary general meeting can purchase more than 10 per cent of the company concerned. It was a rare public intervention by the authorities.

But still Sikorsky would not give up. One simple but highly effective tactic was to contact two institutions who had not sold – Norwich Union and Pearl Assurance – and offer them options to sell at a later date at a favourable price, between 135p and 151p. This meant that though Sikorsky did not actually buy the shares, it could more or less guarantee that neither of the two institutions would vote European. Though controversial, it was just about legitimate and again exposed the lack of unambiguous rules to deal with the City side of the Westland affair.

Mrs Thatcher had admitted that the Westland affair was stranger than fiction. But, for all the bizarre events within her Cabinet, she could hardly have suspected that 13,000 Westland shareholders would shrink to the point where, on the eve of the decisive shareholders' meeting on 12 February, the company would be controlled by a dozen people, several of whom preferred to hide behind the anonymity of Swiss banks.

Sir John Cuckney is adamant that he did not know the identity of the mystery buyers who moved into the market on behalf of Westland in the fortnight before the meeting. That is precisely what he said about Hanson Trust.

Privately, Cuckney is not averse to the idea that there was organised buying, though he has told close colleagues that he and his advisers, Rowe & Pitman and Lazard, remained scrupulously apart and distant from the meetings between Sikorsky, Fiat, Morgan Grenfell and Cazenove when they went into close session to discuss tactics. But proving a 'concert party' is a very different matter, since it presupposes the existence of legally binding agreements. He prefers to refer to the mystery buying as evidence of a Sikorsky 'Fan Club'.

The Stock Exchange inquiry's draft report, later toned down in its public version, was a little bolder:

> It is difficult to credit that overseas buyers should consider it worth their while to pay much more than the company's worth without some form of collaboration with one or other of the parties. It is not beyond the bounds of possibility that there are six ingenuous foreigners in the world, but the committee's credibility (*sic*) was sufficiently strained as to the absence of a concert party of some sort.

Discovering the identity of these foreigners was beyond the scope and ability of the inquiry team which was told to wrap up its investigation inside four weeks. But there is no doubt as to who benefited from their munificence; the answer, given the subsequent vote on 12 February, was Sikorsky and Fiat.

Fiat is the dark horse, appearing in November as Sikorsky's partner but never assuming a public profile. Unlike Sikorsky, it did not employ financial advisers in London, preferring to send over senior executives from Milan.

In Fiat's eyes, the Westland affair was as sensitive a political issue back in Italy as it was in Britain. The Italian government, led by the Socialist Prime Minister Craxi, was firmly behind the European cause. By joining Sikorsky, the hard-nosed capitalists from Milan were four-square against the Socialists in Rome. 'In domestic political terms, Fiat just could not afford to lose over Westland,' says one of Westland's advisers who dealt with the Italian auto and aviation giant.

Just how successful the 'fan club' had been in locking up blocks of shares became apparent on Monday 10 February when David Horne announced that the Consortium's tender offer had failed to attract enough support to take effect. He refused to say how successful he had been in picking up votes, but in fact the result was a devastating blow; a mere 4.8 per cent of shareholders had tendered their shares at 130p, despite the fact that the offer was some 10p to 20p above the prevailing market price over the previous two weeks.

Horne was left thinking that there had been double-dealing and subterfuge. The only alternative explanation was that Westland's small shareholders – representing what was generally assumed to be at least 40 per cent of the shares, individually or through fund managers – were either extraordinarily loyal to Cuckney or were convinced that there was more value in Black Hawks than cash.

From the moment Horne's tender offer failed, the question was merely the margin of victory for Sikorsky and Fiat at the shareholders' meeting, this time to be held in the less theatrical surroundings of the Connaught Rooms. But Wills and his committee of inquiry had uncovered material which appeared to undermine the very legitimacy of such a victory.

Around 5 pm on Tuesday, the day before the meeting, the Stock Exchange rushed out a press release (it was done so quickly there were at least two mistakes in it), offering what it described as the results of a preliminary inquiry into the dealing in Westland shares.

The astonishing news was that some 20.33 per cent of Westland was controlled by six mystery buyers, none of whom owned more than 5 per cent of the company. Underlining the frenetic activity in the shares, the Exchange noted that 60 per cent of its equity had changed hands in the previous month in 5,000 separate transactions, an extraordinarily high figure for a company supposed to be technically insolvent.

The motive behind the press announcement was to keep the Exchange's nose clean. They could not have expected to pressure Cuckney into adjourning the meeting. As was subsequently shown in the formal inquiry into the ownership of the shares and the related deals, there was nothing the Exchange could do to force the mystery buyers to come out into the open, nor were there any obvious rules which could be proved, beyond dispute, to have been broken.

The following day, in the Connaught Rooms, Cuckney gave a brief statement saying that he had discovered that six shareholders were listed on the company share register under the following names: R&P Nominees, Midland Overseas Nominees (referring to Midland Bank), Glyn's Nominees (referring to Williams & Glyn's Bank) and Vidacos Nominees (referring to Scrimgeour Vickers, the brokers). He repeated that he did not know the identity of the shareholders, but that the company was seeking to establish who they were. And with that the meeting began.

An attempt by Horne to call for an adjournment was outvoted and by 4.30 the result was known: 67.8 per cent in favour of the Sikorsky/Fiat rescue and 32.2 per cent for the Europeans. Bill Paul embraced his wife in the hall, and Sir John, restrained in his moment of victory, said, without a touch of irony, that 'a private-sector solution has prevailed'.

Cuckney was later to refine his remarks before friends, saying that Mrs Thatcher and her Ministers had made it clear on numerous occasions that they did not wish the Government to interfere in the affairs of Westland and preferred a private-sector solution. 'And when you have a private-sector solution,' said Cuckney, referring to the extraordinary share dealing in January and February, 'you play by private-sector rules.'

Chapter Fourteen

WHERE POWER LIES

*'There may be a scrap of paper in the hall or on
the stair.
But it's useless to investigate – Macavity's not
there!'*

– T. S. Eliot

There was little in the Westland affair that reflected well on Mrs
Thatcher's Government. It is hardly surprising, therefore, that the
dénouement should be a series of attempts to conceal the evidence
about it from Parliament and the public.

No fewer than three Parliamentary Committees had set themselves
the task of getting to the bottom of different aspects of the story. None
succeeded entirely in doing so, though each along the way threw up
some illuminating – and occasionally farcical – results.

One of the differences between the British and American political
systems is that the powers vested in US Senate and Congressional
committees make it possible to expose a political scandal if one is
there. This is not by any means so in Britain.

A US committee is independent of the executive. Its members have
their own power-bases, their own research staffs, and their own
powers to send for persons and papers. They are subject, of course, to
political influences, and they can have bruising clashes with the
administration over the release of information. But they do so from a
position of constitutional and political strength.

British Parliamentary Committees look similar on the surface; they
can choose what to investigate, say and do what they like under the
absolute protection of parliamentary privilege, and call for whatever
witnesses and documents they please. However, they may be no better
than Shakespeare's Glendower, who boasted, 'I can call spirits from
the vasty deep'; to which Hotspur responded, 'Why, so can I, or so can

196

any man; But will they come when you do call for them?'

The arguments for giving them greater powers grow ever stronger. Prime Ministers and Permanent Secretaries have accumulated more unchecked power in the twentieth century than is healthy for a sensible system of government – and unless internal struggles weaken them, Parliament generally looks on, powerless even to be told the facts.

The Select Committees of MPs, set up in the 1960s and strengthened in the 1970s, were severely flawed as independent bodies under Labour governments just as much as under Tory ones. Each Committee contains a majority of government MPs who can normally vote down any line of inquiry which threatens to embarrass the Prime Minister or her Cabinet colleagues. Successive Permanent Secretaries have also persuaded successive Prime Ministers to accept arcane codes of secrecy; names, documents, advice and decisions are all routinely concealed from the Committees under a code which includes anything 'in the field of political controversy'.

Michael Foot, no admirer of the Select Committees, refers to them contemptuously as 'sewing parties'.

Matters were not so easy for Mrs Thatcher over Westland, however. The Defence Committee, which took the lead, is one of the most solidly established of them all. Service on it is popular, perhaps because it gets the lion's share of the Commons budget for foreign trips; it tends to be packed with Privy Counsellors and ex-Ministers. The Labour vice-chairman, former Junior Minister and barrister John Gilbert, deliberately keeps Labour left-wingers off it to avoid internal dissension.

But the Westland affair was a row within the Conservative Party. The question therefore was, whose side were the Tory Committee members on? Few of them were automatic fans of Mrs Thatcher. The chairman, Humphrey Atkins, was a former Foreign Office minister, forced out after the Falklands débâcle. Winston Churchill and Keith Speed were sacked Junior Ministers. Michael Marshall had a business connection with British Aerospace, backers of the European Consortium. Michael Mates, a back-bencher, was a committed Heseltine supporter, long kept out of government for his insufficiently Thatcherite views. Only one of the Tories, Edward Leigh, was an ordinary back-bench loyalist. There was thus great scope for independence – or mischief.

There were two key pieces of paper which Heseltine claimed were proof that the Government had originally backed a European scheme, and that his role had therefore been justified. These were the report written by Leon Brittan in October, urging a European option; and the DTI minute of the 17 October meeting in which Brittan told Cuckney directly, 'A European solution is in the commercial and political interest of the Government.'

Downing Street refused to publish the documents. The Committee then demanded to see them, and called Sir Brian Hayes, head of the DTI, to testify. He refused to say what was in them. (He also refused to say who had attended the widely discussed Cabinet Committee meetings on Westland, on the grounds that the composition of such Committees was a state secret.) Atkins, egged on by Gilbert, pressed the demand for the documents with the Chief Whip, John Wakeham, who talked to Mrs Thatcher.

On 4 February Sir Brian Hayes was ordered to write, 'Ministers have now completed their consideration of this request. They do not think it appropriate or in accordance with the normal conventions to make available inter-departmental correspondence of this kind.'

Instead Hayes offered a 'summary', for confidential viewing by the Committee. This was the beginning of a period of what one Committee member calls 'infantile games'.

The summary did not contradict Heseltine on the key points (he, after all, as an ex-Minister, had access to his own copies). Instead there was a gentle process of Whitehall re-drafting, to change the tone of what Brittan had said. Where Brittan had written of the dangers of 'foreign ownership', the heading was changed to the blander phrase 'overseas shareholding'. Sikorsky's potential 'large shareholding' was changed to the neutral phrase, 'outside shareholding'.

Brittan had also said bluntly:

> Although Westland is the only UK helicopter manufacturer, it is not central to the UK aerospace industry... My department is not aware of any [company] which is financially dependent on Westland's continued existence... It is by no means certain that [letting the company go bankrupt] would be damaging to essential national interests, or more costly to the Government than participating in a reconstruction package... I believe it is a fairly fine judgment whether the risks involved in receivership are worth taking.

All these words were removed from the 'summary'. So were Brittan's warnings that bankruptcy might have a political consequence. He had said that Mrs Thatcher's government would 'get the blame'.

The overall effect of the deletions was to try and change a man who did not care very much about Westland and was disposed to dislike the Sikorsky deal into a man who was neutral about Sikorsky and much concerned with saving jobs.

The same civil servants' time was spent tinkering with the wording of the second document, recording Brittan's meeting with Cuckney. The result reveals an interesting archeological layer of Whitehall evasions.

At the original meeting, Brittan said, according to the memory of those present, 'For God's sake, give the Europeans a chance!'

But Cuckney replied, 'I don't want to go back to them. It would look like importuning.'

The faithful John Mogg smoothed out his Minister's remark for the departmental record, but left in Cuckney's. Now, when it came to the 'summary', the hand of another official hastily deleted Cuckney's response as well.

To the delight of the activists on the Committee, Michael Heseltine was prepared to continue causing trouble. He testified before them, and agreed with them that the summaries were not an adequate record. Atkins demanded the genuine texts once again.

Sir Brian Hayes was ordered to offer a compromise; Atkins, the Tory chairman, could personally inspect the documents, and reassure the rest of the Committee that they were more or less the same as the summaries. Gilbert, the Labour vice-chairman, protested vociferously; he too was a Privy Counsellor and thus entitled to see state secrets. Very well, they could both see them...

Gilbert continued to protest. 'It's a bloody charade!' he complained to Atkins. Veiled threats that he would publicly expose these antics were relayed back to Number Ten, which gave a little more ground. The Committee could secretly see 'extracts' from the authentic documents, if they promised to continue to call them 'summaries', for reasons of face.

Gilbert exploded. 'I'll call them what I fucking well like!' he roared.

The games ended with Atkins and Gilbert in Sir Brian Hayes's office, examining the sheets of paper spread out for them on his desk. They chose 'relevant' extracts, and agreed that Hayes could delete Foreign Office paragraphs and also 'two lines' detailing likely redundancies. Gilbert said, 'Thank you very much. We have no power to guarantee the Committee won't publish these papers – technically, the House could over-rule us on a vote anyway...'

Hayes became distressed: 'I hadn't appreciated that point...'

'It's a constitutional point.'

'Well, I won't release the documents on that basis.'

He tried to ring Sir Robert Armstrong, who eventually yielded. On 19 February, nearly three weeks after the original request, the Defence Committee published the documents 'with the exception of a small amount of classified material'. The unattributable voice of Bernard

Ingham could be heard in the background, insisting that the Government had still not lost face.

Leon Brittan, now a mere back-bencher, was called before the Committee. He exuded a nervous arrogance as he subjected each question to minute legal scrutiny and chastised the Committee by wagging a peremptory finger at them. The atmosphere became less like a parliamentary inquiry than that of a magistrate's court with a truculent witness in the box:

'Who selected the selective passages to leak?'

'I have no wish to add anything further.'

'I insist – did you say "leak the whole document" or "selectively"?'

'I am not in a position to answer.'

'You do not wish to answer?'

'That's not what I said.'

'Do you know the facts?'

'I share the Prime Minister's position on this...'

'Do you know the facts?'

'I repeat what I said before. The PM gave answers. There is nothing I wish to add.'

'Who did you talk to on the phone about the letter?'

'John Mogg.'

'Are you not prepared to answer about the nature of the clearance given?'

'There are an infinity of questions that can be devised... the answer will be the same.'

'You are not prepared to say whether there were any discussions with Number Ten about the Solicitor-General's letter?'

'No.'

The next task for Number Ten was to prevent Mrs Thatcher's officials, Bernard Ingham and Charles Powell, from testifying.

The two had been left as silent accomplices to Mrs Thatcher's tortuous and unlikely public explanations: that she had willed the ends but not the means; that her officials had heard the DTI application for consent to leak, but 'misunderstood' it; that she had 'given her consent' to publication, but disapproved of leaking; that her officials had acted wrongly without consulting her, but had not made her displeased; and that, while Ministers were always supposedly responsible for the misdeeds of their officials, in this case she appeared to be exempt.

The Committee asked to see all the five officials whom Armstrong had interviewed. There is no evidence that the three from the DTI were unwilling to testify. But they were ordered not to appear. Sir Brian Hayes wrote saying their evidence was 'not relevant' to inquiries about defence matters, and his minister would choose which officials to send.

He also introduced a new constitutional idea, namely that as the three had been questioned already by Armstrong it would be 'unfair' to make them answer questions twice. Gilbert, Michael Mates and Sir Humphrey Atkins got together to prepare a list of successive questions to ask Hayes in public session, which forced him to admit that he could not answer sensibly for Mogg, Michell or Bowe. It was ingenious because it stepped up the pressure on Mrs Thatcher to release Ingham and Powell.

Once again it was Armstrong who was produced by an increasingly frantic Downing Street. He was ordered by Mrs Thatcher to fly back post-haste from Honolulu, where he had been attending preparations for an economic summit, in order to send a letter:

> I understand you have invited Miss Colette Bowe, Mr M J Michell, Mr J F Mogg of DTI and Mr Bernard Ingham and Mr Charles Powell of the PM's office to attend and give evidence to the Committee.
>
> All five of these officials gave a full account of their role in these matters to me in the course of my recent inquiry, and cooperated fully in my investigation. The PM and the Secretary of State, DTI, believe that your Committee will recognise and share their view that it would be neither fair nor reasonable to expect these officials to submit to a second round of detailed questioning, of the kind that would be involved in giving evidence to your Committee.
>
> With the PM's agreement, I am writing to you to say that, if the Committee believed it would be helpful, I should be ready to accept an invitation... the basis of my evidence would, of course, be the comprehensive account which the PM gave the House of Commons... I would hope... to be able to deal as helpfully as possible with the Committee's questions, consistently with the normal conditions of confidence under which my inquiry was conducted.

The same morning the Defence Committee met for what were now becoming interminable private sessions. Tory sympathies, particularly those of its chairman, began to reassert themselves, under heavy pressure from the Chief Whip. Gilbert and Mates had dragged them into deep water. For the first time Gilbert lost a motion, to refuse the offer of Armstrong. Instead it was agreed that questions to him must be exhausted before the demand for officials was renewed. One of those involved said caustically, 'Halfway through the inquiry,

Atkins turned from being fairly unsound back into an ex-Government Chief Whip who seemed likely to get a peerage.'

They agreed to call Armstrong at 10.15 the following morning. The clerk's letter added stiffly, 'I am instructed that the Committee's request for named officials still stands.'

Armstrong turned in what some newspapers called next day a 'Rolls-Royce' performance. In fact he was uncharacteristically ill-at-ease. He refused to identify any of the officials by name – although their names were known to all – and said his inquiry backed Mrs Thatcher's story of a 'genuine misunderstanding' between Number Ten and the DTI. Nevertheless, having listened to him, the Committee Tories overbore Gilbert and said they would drop demands for all the officials except Ingham himself.

Wakeham, the Chief Whip, told Atkins, 'Ingham won't accept an invitation. However, you do have the power to make Ingham come, and we won't block you.'

He was referring to the arcane procedure by which the 'Sergeant-at-Arms' presents a witness with a summons. If he refuses, the Committee chairman might, according to the dusty textbooks, stride on to the floor of the House, halt all other business, and move that Bernard Ingham be sent for on pain of imprisonment in the Clock Tower. Wakeham undertook not to use his troops to vote such a proposition down – it would have been an embarrassing debate.

But he assured Sir Humphrey, 'When you bring Ingham he will simply refuse to speak.'

Atkins reported this impasse to the Committee.

'What are you after?' he said. 'Are you just trying to have somebody destroyed?' There was yet another compromise; Armstrong would come again. 'In private.' said Atkins. 'He's offered to tell us more that way. We don't want to have a public peepshow.' But the rest of the Committee decided that was exactly what they did want.

On 5 March Gilbert, with the thwarted air of a man whose fox has already been shot, lashed Armstrong in public. He accused him of using the mildest terms – 'regret' – about the scandalous goings-on surrounding the Mayhew leak:

> 'You use language which would be appropriate to a waiter spilling soup in a restaurant.... None of your officials appear to have paid any price at all... the first proposal for the commission of an improper act came from the head of Mogg... It was Bowe who committed the improper act. Ingham and Powell connived at the commission of an improper act. They didn't tell the PM what had happened; they didn't tell her who had authorised it... They were all in it up to their necks.'

'That's a grossly unfair description of the whole thing!'

'You can't challenge any of the facts... I have spoken to two former premiers, three former Permanent Secretaries and Cabinet ministers or former Cabinet ministers in all three political parties... I can tell you, you're surrounded by a sea of outrage!... Do you have responsibility for your officials when they've done something "regrettable"? I can take it *you* never considered resigning for what your officials did, which forced the Prime Minister to apologise?...'

'The Minister has accepted full responsibility... This is not a matter for disciplinary proceedings... The officials have paid a considerable price in terms of anxiety, public exposure, and the knowledge that this is with them...'

Armstrong seemed shaken. But the game was over. The Committee never did succeed in having the civil servants testify, and the inquiry petered out, as did a parallel inquiry in the Civil Service Committee.

Curiously, it was the more humdrum Trade and Industry Committee, chaired by Tory backbencher Kenneth Warren, which provoked the biggest Westland explosion. In April, Alan Bristow found himself under close questioning before these apparently innocuous inquisitors.

He was more than willing to give an account of the Westland affair to anybody who would listen. But before he appeared before the Committee he took legal advice on the precise amount of information he might have to disclose. He was left with the impression that there were some areas which the Committee could not delve into, either in public or private session. This turned out to be a grave misjudgment.

He appeared before the Committee, flanked by his lawyer and armed with a large brown suitcase full of relevant Westland documents. At first the questioning was fairly relaxed, covering the background to his failed bid. But then it turned to his dealings with the Westland Board at that time and certain critical financial information which he claimed had been deliberately withheld, forcing him to drop the bid. Bristow said he could only answer in private session.

Very soon he must have been regretting that he had ever decided to give evidence. The Committee began probing his claim that he had been offered a knighthood. Could he divulge the names of the two Conservative peers? The answer was a gruff 'No'. When pressed, Bristow retorted that he was not obliged to answer because the questions were outside the Committee's remit.

This was the equivalent of a Harvey Smith gesture to the cross-party

Committee. They rounded on him, with Warren issuing a warning that unless he answered he would find himself called before the House of Commons bar for contempt. Bristow refused to budge.

It was only later that Bristow was apprised of the gravity of his offence. According to one informed account, he was told that unless he complied he faced a fine and possibly a jail sentence. The warning was passed by John Wakeham, Chief Whip, through Sir Cranley Onslow, the Chairman of the 1922 Committee, who was also by coincidence a paid adviser to Bristow Helicopters, Bristow's old company.

A compromise was hatched. Bristow would reveal the names in confidence in an envelope to the Speaker of the House of Commons, Bernard Weatherill. The Speaker would then pass the names to Warren. Everyone's pride and honour would thus remain intact.

In fact, within a day or two of the names arriving, they were leaked to two diligent members of the Westminster lobby, and appeared in the *Daily Mirror*. Lord King had already been named in the *Observer* – and had denied it. He simply denied it again. Lord Forte disdained to comment. Bristow, who rang up both men to apologise, was mortified. He was shortly to be embarrassed even further.

In the Attorney-General's office, it was agreed that, if what Bristow was saying were true, then there might have been a contravention of the 1925 Honours (Prevention of Abuses Act), which had originally been passed following a scandal involving the sale of honours under the premiership of Lloyd George. It is a fair guess that Bristow had not heard of the Act when he passed on the names of his business friends and shooting colleagues.

Sir Tony Hetherington, the Director of Public Prosecutions, was told by Havers to call in the Serious Crimes Squad and – in effect – set them on to Bristow. Two officers flew to Aberdeen to interview him, then, on Friday 11 April, drove down to his estate in Cranleigh, Surrey, to take a witness statement.

They assured him, 'You don't need to say anything if you don't want to,' and indeed it was difficult to see the precise point of the police approach. Bristow lamented, 'It's just my word and all they have to do is deny it.'

The Bristow episode brought out into the open yet another aspect of the affair without satisfactorily disposing of it. Similarly, the Committees never discovered just how Sir John Cuckney and Bernard Ingham came to exert so much influence over events. Nor did they discover the real machinery of the manoeuvres against Michael Heseltine in the week before his resignation. Nor indeed did they discover anything of Heseltine's own frenetic activities behind the scenes.

Nevertheless, the image of Mrs Thatcher and her style of government had been deeply tarnished by the evidence that had emerged. Michael Heseltine pronounced his own verdict when he told friends, 'This is the end of Thatcherism.' Though it was a premature verdict, it was certainly fair to say that both the lady and her political philosophy would never be seen in quite the same light again. The public and humiliating collapse, shortly afterwards, of the Government's plans to sell off Austin-Rover to Ford, and the rest of British Leyland to General Motors – plans forged secretly in the days before Westland rated a headline – was a direct result of the damage she had suffered.

Heseltine himself emerged from the chrysalis of Cabinet conformity in political colours he had hitherto concealed. He embarked on a round of major speeches calling for an interventionist industrial policy and Europeanism on a model rather reminiscent of that laid down by Edward Heath – and signed up with a major publisher for a book containing his collected thoughts.

The Party kept a wary eye on him. Whether they would rally to his standard in the event of a disputed leadership election remained to be seen. His own verdict on the political wisdom of his resignation was a wry quotation of the old adage, 'He who wields the sword, never wears the crown.' But there was more than a suggestion that his fingers were firmly crossed.

His fallen colleague Leon Brittan adopted the path of loyalty. His reward was a good deal of 'informed speculation' that he would eventually be returned to a high post in a Thatcher government. He defined his view of the Heseltine approach to politics when he said, in the course of a speech:

> The key to sound government is not departmental reorganisation but sensible policies, coordinated across the board within government and then loyally and consistently followed by all Ministers... My own policies do not depend on the belief that our industrial future is best determined by a handful of Ministers frantically knocking heads together in a spurious spirit of dynamism...

As for Westland itself, the helicopter company survived, and the banks looked likely to get their money back, although the taxpayer did not. The European helicopter industry was undoubtedly weakened, as it dissolved again into its competing fragments.

But Heseltine's direst predictions were not borne out. Westland kept some of its European projects. As Admiral Dugage of Aerospatiale said afterwards, 'A business can't have moods.'

The giant US corporation, United Technologies, secured its European base, and the helicopter industry waited expectantly for it to twist the British Government's arm into buying with tax-payers' money the £500 million-worth of military Black Hawks which UT wanted to sell.

But the Westland affair was always about more than simply the helicopter industry, or even defence procurement. Like all political scandals, it revealed much about how power works, and by forcing into the open detailed evidence about the interplay between Whitehall and Westminster – civil servants and politicians – it shone unaccustomed light on our system of government, and the use and abuse of our institutions.

It showed, amongst other things, that the way issues are presented to the public rarely conforms to the reality of how they are handled behind the scenes. Throughout the affair, nothing was quite as it seemed at the time.

Behind the political savagery, for instance, was a genuine argument about Europeanism and its importance for Britain's future, which was never properly met. The idea has never held great appeal for Mrs Thatcher herself, and therefore was never permitted to flourish.

Whatever Heseltine's motives for taking the argument over the top of the parapet, it was undoubtedly one worth having.

It also raised the question of Cabinet government, and the collective responsibility of Ministers. Here Mrs Thatcher undoubtedly had grounds for complaint about Heseltine's interpretation of it, and few Prime Ministers would have been prepared to tolerate for so long the behaviour of a Minister so openly flouting a direct request to conform.

Yet, on the other hand, by downgrading the function of Cabinet government, keeping key decisions secret, and ensuring that few important policy changes were ever openly debated in full Cabinet, she was inevitably storing up potential for great resentment among any Ministers with strong views and no forum in which to present them. Heseltine's performance was, eventually, unacceptable. But so were the conditions that prompted it.

Westland was, too, an argument about the free market and the role of government towards it.

Here, as we have shown, there was hypocrisy of a high order. By paying lip-service to the concept of market forces and shareholder democracy, the Government was in effect offering to hand over to the banks decisions of enormous consequence for future employment and defence. At the same time, it was playing a strongly interventionist role to ensure that the 'right' decision, in the opinion of a small number of people, was eventually taken. The phrase 'even-handed' has never been so traduced.

This approach was supported by a strange and disturbing 'fan club' of business interests. At a critical point in the Westland saga, a handful of powerful City tycoons seem to have reached the same conclusion that the Sikorsky bid must not be allowed to fail. Who took those decisions, where they were taken, and why they were perceived to be so crucial, we can guess at, but we have not managed finally to determine. Once those decisions had been adopted, there was little that opponents could do to stop their relentless progress.

Commenting on this financial barony, one commentator adopted the phrase used to characterise the relationship between President Marcos of the Philippines and his network of business confederates. He called it 'crony capitalism'.

Finally, however, Westland is a story about political influence. It is worth making the point that although Mrs Thatcher and her Industry Secretary were to become implacable in their conviction that Sikorsky must be allowed a free run at a British helicopter firm, they were relatively indifferent on the subject until Sir John Cuckney began to persuade them otherwise.

It was his astute manipulation of the levers of power which succeeded in tilting the balance of the Government's opinion – which had potentially been against him – in favour of an American bid. More than that, he established lines of communication to the very top via a civil service that is supposed to be famous for its unyielding discretion and integrity. He won formidable support from the Prime Minister, her office and her closest Cabinet colleagues.

Those channels were never revealed or even remotely suspected during the period when the shareholders of Westland were allegedly determining the fate of their company.

The way these events have occurred is instructive and worrying. Whether they amount to a corruption of the British political system is a question that needs to be confronted. Certainly the pattern of private lobbying and influence revealed in the course of the Westland story is a disturbing one which has hitherto lain largely undiscovered. It represents an issue that must be recognised and dealt with.

INDEX

Aberconway, Lord, 30

Aerospatiale plane company, 25, 26, 27, 69, 70, 71, 76, 80, 85, 110, 134, 146

Agius, Marcus, 60, 97, 100, 115, 121, 188

Agnelli family, 77

Agusta helicopter company, 25, 28, 44, 59, 62, 69, 71, 75-6, 80, 84, 134

Air Hanson company, 41

Airspur Incorporated, 23, 24, 32

Aldington, Lord (Toby Low), 29, 32-3, 35, 37, 40, 42, 52: career, 29; concludes
    'corporatist' deal with Jack Jones, 30; pleads and demands cash to develop
    helicopters, 35; lack of interest shown in purchasing Black Hawk, 37;
    reports failure after talk with Michael Heseltine, 38; advised by Adam
    Butler to hire effective chief executive, 40; retirement, 44

Al-Fayed brothers, 61

Alison, Michael, 167

Annan, Lord, 67

Ansett airline, 189

Armstrong, Sir Robert, 5, 7, 58, 96, 101, 111, 128, 129-30, 137, 142, 152, 161:
    position regarding publicising of Sir Patrick Mayhew's letter, 137ff.;
    investigates leak of Sir Patrick Mayhew's letter, 152, 154, 161; delivers
    results of inquiry into Mayhew leak, 163; letter sent regarding roles of
    five officials in connection with Leon Brittan's letters, 201; refuses to
    identify officials by name, 202

Ashdown, Paddy, 38, 53

Atkins, Sir Humphrey, 197, 198, 199, 201, 202; demands genuine texts written
    by Leon Brittan, 199

Austin-Rover company, attempted sale of, 63

Ayios Nikolaos, leak of top secret information from, 17

Baker, Kenneth, 97, 98

Banque Les Fils Dreyfus, 191; purchaser of Westland shares, 191

Baughan, Michael, 93, 115, 188

Baynards Holdings AG, 39; share-buying for, 40, 43

Belgrano affair, 17

Bell helicopter company, 25

Berrington, Don, 116

Bevan, Timothy, 130, 131

Biffen, John, 92, 153

Blackwell, Sir Basil, 30, 31, 32-3, 34, 37, 44, 45, 47, 52, 179: lack of interest in
    purchase of Black Hawk, 37; refuses to drop Westland W30 in favour of
    Black Hawk, 40; opposes Bristow Rotorcraft's bid for Westland, 44;
    seeks help from Agusta company, 44; seeks assistance from GEC and
    British Aerospace companies, 45; approaches Lord Hanson regarding
    take-over of Westland, 45; recommends shareholders to accept Alan
    Bristow's take-over bid, 46; deposing of, 48

Bloomfield, Peter, 39, 115

Blue Ribbon club, 11

Blunt, Anthony, 154

Boardman, Lord, 130, 131

Boeing aircraft company, 25

Bourn, John, 118

Bowe, Colette, 136ff., 154: involved in Sir Patrick Mayhew's letter affair, 137; anger at pressure applied on, 152–3; offered immunity from prosecution, 154; interviewed by Sir Robert Armstrong regarding leak, 158; reaction regarding accusation of being 'leak', 158

Bramall, Sir Edwin, 9; objects to idea of appointment of Michael Heseltine as Defence Secretary, 9

Bristol company, 26

Bristow, Alan, 29, 32, 34, 40, 41, 44, 45, 53, 56, 161: his intention to take over Westland, 40; character, 40; as Westland chief test pilot, 40; his rudeness regarding Westland, 41; his public image as union-basher, 41; good contacts of, 41; his intention to make deal with Sikorsky, 44; proposes own deal to Sikorsky, 45; threats to withdraw bid for Westland made by, 46; demands Government bail him out, 46; refused Government help, 53; renews interest in Westland, 72; purchases Westland shares, 149, 176, 179; backs European Consortium, 169; receives impression offered high price to sell shares and knighthood offer, 183–4; meeting with Hubert Faure, 184; contacts Norman Tebbit regarding deals offered, 185; speech at shareholders' meeting, 186; under close questioning regarding Westland affair, 203; refuses to divulge names of two peers offering knighthood, 204; interviewed by Serious Crime Squad, 204

Bristow Helicopters, 40

Bristow Rotorcraft, 44; makes bid for Westland, 44

British Aerospace, 27, 33, 59: member of consortium bidding for Westland, 5; lack of interest expressed in take-over of Westland, 45; prepared to join consortium, 93; disturbed by public controversy, 187

Brittan, Leon, 4, 5, 6, 58: endorses PM's statement on future of Westland, 6; takes over Department of Trade and Industry, 59, 68; questioned as to whether letter received by PM from British Aerospace, 64; three qualities of, 65; career, 65; background, 65; marriage, 65; becomes Chief Secretary to Treasury, 65; as great favourite of PM, 66; promoted to Home Secretary, 66; errors of, 66–7; successes, 67; virtues and failings, 67; his contrast with Michael Heseltine, 67–8; considers encouragement by Westland to pursue possibility of European solution, 68–9; makes no mention to Sir John Cuckney of Michael Heseltine's proposal to form European Consortium, 73; impressed by 'European solution', 78; realises seriousness of situation, 91; irritated by Heseltine's meddling, 91; opposes NADs agreement, 91; argues choice to be left to Westland shareholders, 92; support received from Norman Tebbit and Sir Geoffrey Howe, 93; seeks to determine Michael Heseltine's intentions, 104; difficult position of, 108; passes views of Sir Patrick Mayhew to PM regarding Heseltine letter inaccuracy, 127; 'leak' by staff, 130; gives view regarding Sir Patrick Mayhew's letter, 135–6; campaigns to undermine Michael Heseltine, 143–4; delivers stern lecture to Admiral Sir Raymond Lygo, 145; misunderstanding over phrase 'to withdraw' to Sir Raymond Lygo, 147; informed by PM to make statement regarding Westland issue, 155–6; his replies to House regarding letter from British Aerospace, 157–9; apologies for misleading House over letter, 159; faces bitter opposition from House, 163; accusations made against Michael Heseltine, 163; attends meeting to hear results of inquiry into Mayhew leak, 163–4; readiness for PM to reveal his sanctioning of leak, 165; named as instigator of leak, 167; canvasses opinion regarding possible resignation, 168; tenders resignation, 170; removal of words from confidential summary of reports written by, 198; called before Defence Committee, 200; expresses his continued loyalty, 205

Butler, Adam, 21, 37, 40, 43, 44, 52

Cadbury, Peter, 115, 188
Cameron, Captain J., 32
Campbell-Savours, Dale, 164
Carey, Sir Peter, 115, 135
Carlton Club, 8: admits PM as first woman member, 8; meeting of British military establishment at, 8; theme of meeting, 9
Castle, Mrs. Barbara, 13
Cazenove, stockbrokers, 115, 178
Chemenko, Konstantin, 42
Cherniavsky, Andrew, 189; states bid made for holding in Westland shares, 189
Churchill, Winston, 109, 113, 197
Cierva, Juan de la, 25
City of London, considerable involvement of in Westland affair, 175, 177
Clark, Michael, 84
Clarke, Kenneth, 97, 98
Coleridge, Nicholas, 12
Cooper, Sir Frank, 30; chairman of United Scientific Holdings, 176
Craxi, Bettino, 89, 194; asked to desist sending messages of support to European consortium, 143
Critchley, Julian, 14, 111
Crosland, Susan, 12
Cuckney, Sir John, 5, 30, 48, 115–6, 161: his professional career, 49; as chairman of Westland, 49; referred to as 'company doctor', 49; shrewdness and skill of, 50; effectiveness at job, 50; given six months to devise reconstruction of Westland, 50; axing of Schroder Wagg, merchant bankers, 51; constructs draft deal with Sikorsky, 51ff.; visits Adam Butler and Department of Trade and Industry, 52; attempts to persuade British Aerospace to take over Westland, 53; his interview with Michael Heseltine regarding RAF order, and negative response from, 54; makes approaches to Agusta company, 59; dispenses with board members, 60; proposal made to Michael Heseltine regarding Sikorsky's stake in Westland, 62–3; seeks clarification of Government's position in Westland affair, 69; promises to pursue Agusta regarding bid for Westland, 74; informed opposition building up to Sikorsky, 76; states Michael Heseltine's involvement in European side a major obstacle, 80; seeks to secure backing of PM, 83; his absence from meeting on November 29th 1985, 83–4; anger at NADs agreement, 86; decides to see PM, 87; informs PM of proposed European intervention, 89; tells Leon Brittan of 'sabotaging' by Michael Heseltine through NADs agreement, 90; opines opposition from banks over NADs agreement, 90; lodges complaint with Department of Trade and Industry, 90; addresses Economic Affairs Committee, 97–8; his dislike of European offer, 105; announces Westland losses, 113; resents Michael Heseltine's intrusion, 119; states intention to recommend Sikorsky offer, 140; seeks clarification of MOD's Sea King order, 152; attempts made to seek help from institutional shareholders to back Sikorsky/Fiat, 176; does not name mystery buyer of Westland shares, 182; recounts situation at Westland, 185–6; attacks European Consortium, 186–7; decides to reformulate rescue plan, 186–7; unawareness of mystery buyer of Westland shares, 193
Curtis, Alan, 41

Dalyell, Tam, 17, 18, 156, 164; names Colette Bowe as person leaking Mayhew letter, 164
David, Pierre, 70, 76

Davies, Danzil, 18
Day, Sir Robin, 143
'Declaration of Principles' 1978, 28
Defence Committee: role of, 197; issues documents written by Leon Brittan, 198; asks to see five officials regarding document, 200
Defence Secretariat 19 (DS19), 10; disbanding of, 16

Economic Affairs Committee of British cabinet, 96; contents of secret documents of, 95–6; meeting of, 97–8
Eden, Anthony, 29
Eisenhower, President Dwight D., 24
Emley, John, 179
Eugster, Christopher, 179
European Consortium, threat of legal action by, 140
European Fighter Aircraft, 21; involvement by Michael Heseltine in, 21
Evergreen company, 24

Fahd, King of Saudi Arabia, 21
Fairey company, 26
Faure, Hubert, 60, 76, 77, 115, 161, 174, 184, 185
Fearn, John, 25
Fiat of Italy, 5, 76, 78, 114: its mercenary interest in Westland, 77; beneficiaries as result of huge buying of Westland shares, 194; regards Westland affair a sensitive political issue, 194
Fiechtmueller, Karl, 70, 76
Findlay, Jim, 188; instructs Peter Sitwell to put in highest bid for Westland shares, 188
Fletcher, Alexander, 167
Foot, Michael, 158; his criticism of parliamentary committee, 197
Forte, Lord, 41, 183, 204
Fowler, Norman, 5

Gallagher, John, 23
Gandhi, Mrs. Indira, 33, 42; aid by Foreign Office if agreeing to purchase 21 Westland helicopters, 34
Gandhi, Rajiv, 42, 60, 68, 69, 72: rejects PM's offers regarding purchase of Westland W30 helicopters, 42; states cancellation of W30 order, 45; uncertainty regarding purchase of W30 helicopters, 72
General Electric Company, 5, 26: member of consortium bidding for Westland and expresses no interest in take-over of Westland, 45
Gilbert, John, 138, 197, 198, 199, 201; accusation against Sir Robert Armstrong, 202
Giles, David, 7
Gilham, Malcolm, 27, 31
GJW company, 51, 62; hired by Captain Gueterbock, 40
Goodison, Sir Nicholas, 191: disturbed at hectic Westland dealing, 191; inquiry into leak by, 192; report on behalf of Stock Exchange, 192
Green, Colin, 76, 77; proposition made by, 76
Gregory, Bob, 115
Gueterbock, Captain Bill, 40, 62, 115; hired as lobbyist, 40, 62
Gulf & Occidental Investment Company, 191; as purchaser of Westland shares, 191

Hackett, General Sir John, 8
Hampson, Dr. Keith, 108
Hanson, Lord, 41, 45, 179: background, 180; wide and varied financial

interests, 181; states no interest in Westland, 179; indicates likely buyer of Robert Fleming's or Alan Bristow's share stake in Westland, 181; purchases of shares by, 181

Hanson Trust, 181

Harris, Lord, 88

Hart, David, 180

Havers, Sir Michael, 142, 164: letter to Sir Robert Armstrong, 142; seeks inquiry into leak of Solicitor-General's letter, 152–3

Hayes, Sir Brian, 56, 72, 103, 107, 129, 137, 148, 154: confirms waiving of launch-aid of £40 million to Sikorsky, 104; opposes Leon Brittan's proposed resignation, 168; refuses to divulge contents of documents, 198; offers 'summary' of contents for confidential viewing, 198; ordered to offer compromise, 199; introduces new constitutional proposal, 201

Heath, Edward, 14, 29, 66, 130, 131, 205

Helicopter projects mooted, 28–9

Heseltine, Anne, 3, 7, 12, 125; reaction at news of husband's resignation, 7

Heseltine, Michael, 3, 6, 8: protests at PM's proposal that future statements to be cleared by Cabinet Office, 6–7; unable to accept decision, 7; walks out of Cabinet meeting and resigns, 7, 149; confirms resignation, 8; favours strong European defence industry, 9; his powers of persuasion, 9; energy and flamboyance of, 9; a dynamic reputation as cost-cutter, 9; forms Defence Secretariat 19, 10; launches campaign against CND, 10, 16; description of style, 10; his character and personality, 10; attempts to quantify and reorganise local government spending, 11; few admissions of error; 11; his background, 11; education, 11; sufferer from dyslexia, 11; his career, 11ff.; clear ambitions of, 11; marriage, 12; wins first seat at Tavistock, 12; his wealth, 12; attention to sartorial detail, 12–13; acclaim at speeches made at Tory Conferences, 13; acquires nickname, 13; his determined attempt to tackle housing problems in Liverpool, 14; his reputation in Conservative Party, 14; promoted to Defence Secretary, 15; agreement with PM on secrecy issue, 15; views on handling Cruise missiles, 16; disagreement with PM over *Belgrano* affair, 17; persuades PM to release further information over *Belgrano* affair, 18; regards Clive Ponting's action in *Belgrano* affair as unforgiveable betrayal, 18; congratulated by PM on his reaction to Clive Ponting's revelations, 19; opposes proposed cuts in Defence Budget, 20; involved in commercial side of Defence, 20; sells arms to overseas countries, 20–1; cancels long-standing Westland helicopter maintenance contract, 34; approached by Lord Aldington and Sir Basil Blackwell to rescue Westland, 37; argument with PM over £140 million order for Cammell Laird, 37–8; objects to Lord Aldington's and Sir Basil Blackwell's lack of realism, 38; has conversation with Lord Hanson, 41; states 'Air Staff Target 404' officially withdrawn, 42; his positive proposal to save Westland, 47; increased activity in other big European deals, 55; secures European Fighter agreement, 55; vigorous denial of Sikorsky approach regarding stake in Westland, 62; commends argument for European strategy in arms procurement, 73; makes strong attack on Sikorsky bid, 73; suggests possible formation of European consortium to make offer for Westland partnership, 73; states Sir John Cuckney's lack of experience regarding European collaboration, 73; instructs Sir Clive Whitmore to hand over £6 million owed to Westland, 75; makes 'last-ditch' efforts to save Westland through European deal, 80; seeks further meeting with Sir John Cuckney, 81; discussion at conference, 81; proposes to West Germany support for European partnership with Westland, 82; conference on November 29th 1985 as critical turning-point in Westland affair, 82; realises extreme opposition to NADs agreement, 92; urges idea of European cooperation on Sir Austin Pearce, 94; public row with Leon Brittan, 94; claims clear majority for European proposal, 98;

extreme reactions regarding rejection of European offer, 101; considers resignation, 101; engages in delicate bribery, 104; dissension over Leon Brittan's statement, 107; invited to testify in secret session, 109; threats made by, 118; pressurises Sir John Cuckney, 119ff.; ordered to submit all documents in possession, 124; 'dirty trick' played by, 125; states Government's lack of intention of procuring Black Hawk, 126; replies to questions regarding proposed Westland deal with Sikorsky, 126; explains need for banks to favour Europeans, 131; hostility towards, 132; reasons given for resignation, 150–1; accuses PM of campaign of whispers, 153; accuses Leon Brittan of ordering British Aerospace to withdraw from European Consortium, 153; his unexpected support for PM, 173; reaction at hearing result of poll at Westland shareholders' meeting, 187; claims documents proving Government's support for European scheme, 197; makes major speeches, 205

Hetherington, Sir Tony, 204

Hoare Govett, stockbrokers, 39, 179, 192; orders given to purchase Westland shares, 39, 176

Horne, David, 76, 78, 87, 93, 102, 116, 125, 187: depressed at lack of information regarding Sikorsky bid for Westland, 78–9; proposes to put up £25 million, 93; faces problem regarding Consortium's proposals, 102–3; discovers substantial increase in Westland write-off figure, 103; states determination to fight against discarding of NADs agreement, 106; his negotiations with five different partners, 187; announces tender offer for 12.63 million Westland shares, 192; announces failure of Consortium's tender offer, 194

Howe, Sir Geoffrey, 16, 65, 92, 97, 143, 153; urges Leon Brittan not to resign, 168

Hurd, Douglas, 171

Independent European Programme Group, 38

Ingham, Bernard, 4, 15, 111ff.; 112, 113, 114, 135, 136, 142, 166, 200; warns civil service departments against 'leaks', 15–16; advises against sending Michael Heseltine ultimatum, 111–2

Iselin, Columbus, 36, 39, 42, 42, 45, 51, 55–6, 77, 105, 115; hired to find cooperative European firm to build Black Hawk, 36, 37; his admiration for Sir John Cuckney, 78

Jenkin, Patrick, 33, 143

Jones, Geoffrey, 39, 51

Jones, Jack, 30

Joseph, Sir Keith, 5, 16, 88

Kangol company, 52

Keays, Sara, 58

King, Lord, 41, 60, 61, 62, 204; appointed chairman of British Airways, 183

Kinnock, Neil, 158, 159; assault mounted on PM's integrity, 167; his speech in emergency debate, 172

Kirk, Shelby, 22–3

Kleinwort Benson, merchant bank, 179

Kohl, Helmut, 89

Lamont, Norman, 79, 163

Lawson, Nigel, 92

Lazards, bankers, 49, 76

Ledlie, John, 136
Leigh, Edward, 197
Levene, Peter, 20, 55ff.; 151; appointed head of Procurement Executive, 20, 151
Lloyds Merchant Bank, 76; meeting presenting Westland position held at, 77
Lopex PR company, 115
Lowe, Air Chief Marshal Sir Douglas, 8
Lygo, Admiral Sir Raymond, 8, 26-7, 59, 94, 122, 140, 161: views on dealing with French, 27; meeting with Sikorsky company, 59-60; chosen to present case for Europe involvement to Press, 94; pays tribute to Michael Heseltine's 'expertise', 113; his dispute with Admiral Treacher, 122; conclusions on rejection of European offers for Westland, 141; draws up new scheme for Westland, 144; denunciation of Sir John Cuckney, 144; reaction to Leon Brittan's lecture, 146-7; angered by Leon Brittan's threats, 147-8; seeks confirmation from Sir Clive Whitmore of ratification of NADs agreement, 148; notes of meeting published, 161; accepts Leon Brittan's assurance not saying British Aerospace campaign 'against national interest', 162; sudden climb-down over Leon Brittan meeting, 187
Lynx Marketing, 191; purchase of Westland shares, 191

MacDonald, Alistair, 82, 90, 145
Mace, episode of, 13
Macmillan, Harold, 29
Malone, Gerald, 156, 157, 162; reports prejudice against Leon Brittan, 168
Marcos, ex-President Ferdinand, 207
Marmon Corporation of Chicago, 52
Marshall, Michael, 109, 161, 197; backs European Consortium, 169
Martre, Jean, 85
Mason, Roy, 29
Mates, Michael, 108ff., 197, 201
Mayhew, Sir Patrick, 124, 127ff., 133; his manipulation regarding 'material inaccuracy' in Michael Heseltine letter, 127; contacts Michael Heseltine regarding letter inaccuracy, 128; his classified and confidential letter, 133ff.; 'leak' of letter, 135ff.
McDonald, Lord, 41
McDonnell Douglas (Hughes Aircraft) company, 25
McGregor, John, 46, 73, 92, 97, 126
McGuinness, Martin, 67
Melville, Sir Ronald, 30
Messerchmitt-Bolkow-Blohm (MBB) company, 25, 69, 70, 76, 134, 147
Michell, John, 113, 123, 135, 145, 155; his brief favouring Westland, 123
Miller, Bob, 39, 51
MINIS (Management Information Service), 9, 20
Ministry of Defence Procurement Executive Department, 20
Mitterand, President François, 36
Mogg, John, 73, 104, 106, 136ff., 145, 152, 155; compiles minute of meeting between Admiral Sir Raymond Lygo and Leon Brittan, 152
Moncrieff, Chris, 7, 137-8
Morgan Grenfell, bankers, 115, 135, 178
Mortimer, David, 189; seeks purchase of Westland shares, 189
Mottram, Richard, 38, 62, 101, 134, 148; demands text of PM's note, 123
Mulley, Fred, 28
Murdoch, Rupert, 180, 189; involvement in opposition to newspaper move to Wapping, 189-90

Narges, Karl-Heinz, 144; as backer of European Consortium, 144
'National Armaments Directors', 82, 83; agreement, 84–5, 88, 89, 90; terms of agreement, 89
Norton, Rose, Botterell & Roche, solicitors, 115
Nott, Sir John, 15, 17, 51, 60, 62, 66, 83, 115, 161

Onassis, Aristotle, 40
Onslow, Sir Cranley, 28, 167, 204; views on proposed resignation of Leon Brittan, 168–9
Overseas Development Agency, 46, 68
Owen, Dr. David, 165

Parkinson, Cecil, 58
Parliamentary Committees, status and role of, 196ff.
Pattie, Geoffrey, 39, 40, 47–8, 53, 56, 107, 145: statement on Westland manoeuvres, 47–8 approached by Sikorsky, 56
Paul, Bill, 40, 51–2, 59, 60, 62, 71, 77, 115, 187: shock at terms of NADs agreement, 87; problem of purchasing shares on Sikorsky's behalf, 178
Pearce, Sir Austin, 45, 54, 94, 106, 144, 157: seeks help from British Aerospace, 54; publication of and contents of letter, 158
Perry, Sir David, 82
Phillips, Adrian, 190
Ponting, Clive, 17, 18–19, 128, 137, 154: instructed to prepare exhaustive report on background to *Belgrano* affair, 18; leaks minute to Tam Dalyell, 18
Powell, Charles, 121, 123, 127, 128, 135, 155
Price, George, 36
Price Waterhouse, accountants, 51, 53; report made by, 56, 76, 79
Prior, James, 45, 120, 130, 131, 143, 163
Prolific Unit Trusts, 189
Pym, Francis, 5

Quiles, Paul, 80

Raison, Timothy, 43, 73; threatens Rajiv Gandhi regarding purchase of W30 helicopters, 43
Reagan, President Ronald, 89
Reece, Sir Gordon, 83, 116, 120, 121, 140, 141: a hired propagandist, 60–2; honoured by knighthood, 83; informs PM of Heseltine's conduct, 121
Reed, Tony, 51, 60
Riddell, Peter, 130
Ridley, Nicholas, 100, 153; mounts rescue operation, 163
Rogers, Air Chief Marshal Sir John, 43
Rolls Royce company, 33, 57
Ross, Michael, 115
Roulleaux-Dugage, Henri-Jean, 71, 110, 146; states Leon Brittan used pressure, 146
Rowe & Pitman, stockbrokers, 175, 176, 189, 190, 191, 192; buying and selling of Westland shares by, 176, 190
Royle, Anthony, *later* Lord Fanshawe, 60, 81, 83, 115, 127, 141

Saunders, Ernest, 61
Saunders-Roe company, 26
Schroder Wagg, bankers, 45
Scrimgeour Vickers, stockbrokers, 190; bid for Westland stock by, 190
Sedgemore, Brian, 164

Shandwick, Richard, 115
Shaw, Jackson, 22
Shelbourne, Sir Philip, 41
Sheppards & Chase, stockbrokers, 192
Short Brothers, approach made by Sikorsky to persuade MOD to offer Black Hawk under licence, 37; given contract to construct RAF trainers, 39–40
Sikorsky company, 5, 24, 25: bid for control of Westland by, 5; high standard of performance of Black Hawk, 36; number of sales of Black Hawk, 36; attempts to sell Black Hawk to Europe, 37; awareness of financial plight of Westland, 37; refuses Sir Basil Blackwell's take-over bid, 45; lobbying of Ministry of Defence, 55; considers deal with Westland, 56; murky dealings with Fiat company, 77; submission of proposals to Lazards, 105; plan for company to buy Alan Bristow's stake or Robert Fleming's block of shares, 178; prepares to buy on own behalf, 188; attempts to buy Westland shares, 197
Sikorsky, Igor, 24; pioneer of Sikorsky helicopter, 24
Sitwell, Peter Wilmot, stockbrokers, 115, 176, 179, 188: reports Robert Fleming Investments Management intention to vote for European consortium, 176; phones Lord Hanson regarding possible investment in Westland, 179
Skinner, Dennis, 157
Slaughter & May, solicitors, 115, 182
Smith, John, 156, 157
Spaddini, Giovanni, 79
Speed, Keith, 197
Spicer, Michael, 97, 98
Stanley, John, 18
Steel, David, 153
Steel, Henry, 128
Sterling Trust, 190; seeks purchase of Westland shares, 190
Stevas, Norman St. John, 167; his call for unity, 167
Steward, Hugh, 186

Tebbit, Norman, 6, 16, 37, 46, 47, 55, 73, 92, 97, 98, 107, 185
Teti, Raffaello, 44, 59, 70, 71, 94, 95, 103, 110, 125, 141: accuses Sir John Cuckney of double-dealing, 59; frustration at lack of communication from Westland, 70; unaware of American bid for Westland, 71; meet Sikorsky team, 75; urges founding of British 'front' for Consortium, under impression European offer supported by British government, warns American offer could create trading problems for Westland Europe, 103; reaction to rejection of European offers, 141
Thatcher, Mrs. Margaret, 3ff.: decides ultimatum to be given to Michael Heseltine, 3, 111; states failure of Westland matter for board, 6; proposes future statements to be cleared by Cabinet and Office, 6–7; her attention to sartorial detail, 13; incompatibility with Michael Heseltine, 14; her disapproval of 'leaks', 15; lectures Rajiv Gandhi regarding proposed purchase of W30 helicopters, 43; states Britain's cancellation of 'aid' for India, 45; puts forward Government's position regarding Westland crisis, 47; views that Sikorsky bid be 'openly considered', 47; reshuffles government, 58; only cursory intervention in Westland affair by, 88; her concern regarding government spending, 88; her affinity with Sir John Cuckney, 89; not pro-Europe, 89; warmth of feeling for America, 89; determined to thwart opposition to American bid for Westland, 90; line of argument at Economic Affairs Committee meeting, 97; states firm proposal to be put to Westland board, 99; irritated by Michael Heseltine's intransigence, 110; reaffirms government policy, 112; makes significant move to support Sir John

Cuckney, 121; acceptance of Sir Patrick Mayhew's ruling regarding Westland's future, 125; outraged at publication of Michael Heseltine's letter, 126; requests Sir Patrick Mayhew to write critical letter to Michael Heseltine, 127; states final ultimatum be presented to Michael Heseltine, 132; speaks privately to Leon Brittan regarding 'leak', 142; adverse criticism of, 154; announces setting up of confidential enquiry into 'leak', 158; gives first full detailed account of Westland affair, 159; the Sir Patrick Mayhew intervention proposed in first place by, 164; gives statement to House regarding leaking of Mayhew letter, 166-7; decision of 1922 Committee conveyed to, 168; states Leon Brittan not resigning, 169; attempts to persuade Leon Brittan not to resign, 170; reaction to Leon Brittan's resignation, 170; blames Michael Heseltine for Westland debacle, 171; explanation of 'leak' given in emergency debate, 172ff.; success of speech, 174; states future of Westland to be determined by shareholders, 175; her high opinion of Lord Hanson, 180; tarnishing of image and government, 205; damage suffered through Westland affair, 205; indifference of M.T. and Leon Brittan on proposed take-over by Sikorsky of Westland, 207

Thatcher, Mark, 17-18
Thomas, Sir John Maldwyn, 60, 115
Thomas Nationwide Transport, 189
Thompson, Peter, 76
Tisdall, Sarah, 16
Treacher, Admiral Sir John, 23, 27, 30, 35, 40, 42, 43, 48, 51, 52, 59, 80, 115, 122, 127, 140, 182, 186: his seething criticism of European companies, 71
Treasury: insistence on fall in Defence Budget, 19; rejection of Government rescue bid for Westland, 47; initial approval to Sir John Cuckney of £25 million order, 107
Turbomeca company, 57
Turner, Philip, 41
Tuzo, General Sir Harry, 8

United Scientific Instruments, 151, 176
United Technologies, 24, 36, 56; secures European base, 206

Verrall, Charles, 60

Wakeham, John, 3, 97, 98, 105, 111, 131, 148, 160, 167, 202, 204: urges pro-Leon Brittan lobby, 111; advises resignation of Leon Brittan, 167
Walker, Bill, 39, 59, 62
Walker, David, 47
Walker, Peter, 97
Warren, Kenneth, 203, 204
Weekes, Wilf, 110, 115
Weinstock, Lord, 45, 131, 144
Westland company, 4, 6, 21: experiencing considerable financial difficulties, 21; redesigns tail rotor of W30 helicopter, 23; opening of factory, 25; their 'Wapiti' planes, 25; concludes deal with Sikorsky, 25; develops Sea King Helicopter, 26; decides to design and build brand new machine, 29, 31; lent £40 million by Government to improve W30, 33; attempts to sell W30 helicopters to India, 32, 33-4; number of unsold W30s, 34; attempts to sell helicopters to Armed Forces, 35; plot to take over company, 41; declining fortunes of, 42; falling price of shares, 43; crisis regarding company 49ff.; uncertainty overshadowing workers at, 58; real possibility of going into receivership, 68; failure in effort to secure new government subsidy, 70; publicising of plight, 72; makes full presentation of position to Sikorsky, 77;

unimpressed by European Consortium, 80; rejection of European offer, 106; circularising of shareholders regarding Sikorsky plan, 117; annoyance with Government, 127; makes improved offer to meet Consortium bid, 130; views on Michael Heseltine's resignation, 151–2; result of meeting of shareholders, 163; unveils revised £80 million package, 174; its financial problem, 176–7; plan for banks to hold *preference* shares, 177; calls shareholders' meeting, 185; results of poll, 186; controlled by six mystery buyers, 192; survival of, 205

Westmacott, Richard, 179

White, Sir Gordon, 161, 180–1, 184; chairman of Hanson Industries, 180; keenness in aiding Sikorsky, 180

Whitelaw, Lord, 3, 5, 9, 14, 66, 92, 105, 111, 131, 165; incensed at Michael Heseltine's public letter, 131; urges Leon Brittan not to resign, 168

Wicks, Nigel, 83, 135, 138, 142

Whitmore, Sir Clive, 20, 37, 44, 56, 62, 72, 75, 83, 85, 93, 114, 148

Wilkinson, John, 37

Wills, Peter, 192, 194

Woerner, Manfred, 81–2, 119: enthusiastic response to Michael Heseltine's proposal, 82

Young, David, 100

Young, Lord, 97

Younger, George, 7, 132, 152; is offered and accepts post of Secretary of State for Defence, 7